The Chinese Digital Economy

Ma Huateng · Meng Zhaoli · Yan Deli ·
Wang Hualei

The Chinese Digital Economy

palgrave
macmillan

Ma Huateng
Tencent Research Institute
Shenzhen, China

Meng Zhaoli
Tencent Research Institute
Shenzhen, China

Yan Deli
Tencent Research Institute
Shenzhen, China

Wang Hualei
Tencent Research Institute
Shenzhen, China

Editor-in-Chief
Guo Kaitian
Shenzhen, China

Si Xiao
Shenzhen, China

ISBN 978-981-33-6007-5 ISBN 978-981-33-6005-1 (eBook)
https://doi.org/10.1007/978-981-33-6005-1

Jointly published with CITIC Press Corporation
The print edition is not for sale in China Mainland. Customers from China Mainland please order the print book from: CITIC Press Corporation.
ISBN of the Mainland edition: 978-750-86-7423-0

Translated from the Chinese language edition: *数字经济: 中国创新增长新动能*, © CITIC Press Corporation 2016. Published by CITIC Press Corporation. All Rights Reserved.

This Palgrave Macmillan imprint is published by the registered company Springer Nature Singapore Pte Ltd.
The registered company address is: 152 Beach Road, #21-01/04 Gateway East, Singapore 189721, Singapore

Foreword by Guo Kaitian: Technology Neutrality and Social Welfare

The digital economy, one of the key drivers for global economic growth, results from the deep impact of a new generation of general technologies on various economic and social aspects. Such technologies include mobile internet, cloud computing, big data, and the like. For the last two years, China's digital economy has seen unprecedented rapid development, which is mainly attributable to the innovative fusion of digital technologies and traditional industries as driven by the "Internet Plus" action plan. According to Tencent Research Institute, China's digital economy in 2016 was RMB 22.77 trillion in scale, registering a year-on-year growth rate of 62%. It became a highlight during the difficult overall transition and upgrading period of China's economy.

From the perspective of development, it is easy to understand why all sectors of society have great expectations of technological advancement. People tend to believe that technology would automatically penetrate production and living, realizing the great integration and great unity of the whole society by lowering costs and creating value. However, nearly half a century of practice in the human world has proven that reality is often the contrary. The popularization of technology does have incurred costs, while the profound influences of technology on society are far more complex than just an increase in productivity envisioned by people. These influences are bound to have a spillover effect on the division of labor and income distribution structure of the society. British poet Clive Staples Lewis writes, "What we call Man's power over Nature turns out to be a power exercised by some men over other men with Nature as their instrument." While celebrating the huge economic success achieved with technological advancement, any serious researcher should not abandon his or her rational thinking on the interactions between technology and society from the perspective of humanity and social sciences.

There is no doubt that digital technologies, or technological advancements in general, have huge effects on social welfare as a whole. In particular, such general technologies as mobile internet, cloud computing, and big data often bring forth "sweet troubles" beyond economics as they push forward the entire human civilization. Such sweet troubles could be illustrated with three paradoxes.

The first paradox is about the visibility of technological advancement, which stems from Robert Solow's 1987 quip, "You can see the computer age everywhere but in the productivity statistics." Jokes aside, the findings of extensive macroeconomic studies have shown that labor productivity in the USA did not grow in leaps and bounds due to the use of computers but rather declined slightly in certain years. Though everyone has had a taste of the considerable progress in technology, those technological products that people frequently use on a daily basis turn invisible if one tries to look for them in statistics. The extension of the life expectancy of humans, the enhancement of the quality of education, and the improvement of the home environment are all not reflected in gross domestic product (GDP) figures. This has become a running joke between economists. The paradox about the visibility of technological advancements, which could be seen, touched but not measured, has been puzzling the academic community.

The second paradox questions the equality of technological advancements by viewing micro-level technological advancements from the perspective of the macro-level income distribution of the society, thus having drawn an even more confusing conclusion. In the bestselling book *Capital in the Twenty-First Century*,[1] Thomas Piketty associates the widening of the gap between the rich and the poor with technological advancements. Over the 30 years after the Solow computer paradox was put forward, technology has been advancing at a remarkable speed but all people have not benefited from it equally. Just on the contrary, most people have been left behind by the rapid development of technology.

[1] Editor's note: The Chinese version of *Capital in the Twenty-First Century* was published by China CITIC Press in September 2014.

While the overall welfare of the society has improved, the quality of life of middle-class and lower-class groups has declined and the proportion of the top one percent in wealth distribution has been getting larger and larger. This makes us ponder: What is the ultimate impact of technological advancement on social welfare? Is the unequal distribution of income the result of technological advancement, or is it distorted by the existing social system? This sums up the equality paradox of technological advancement.

The third paradox highlights the relevance of technological advancement to social progress. Robert J. Gordon, professor of economics at Northwestern University, mentions the history of the development of lighting in his 2016 book titled *The Rise and Fall of American Growth*. From the candles in the middle age to the kerosene lamps and electric lights in the nineteenth century, then to the light-emitting diodes (LEDs) of modern times, lighting tools have achieved several rounds of increase in efficiency, falls in prices, and extensions of service life at exponential rates close to Moore's law. Kerosene lamps used to be a pillar industry to maintain the economic development in the nineteenth century, but now the lighting industry has been gradually marginalized in the overall economic development with its minimal effect on employment, investment, and consumption. The lighting industry hence becomes a favorite example quoted by some economists: When the direction of technological advancement deviates from that of increased social demands, technological advancement will cease to create value and thus become irrelevant to the society. This is how the relevance paradox comes into being—technological advancement is clearly visible, but its effect on social welfare is almost negligible.

Could the digital economy evade the traps of visibility, equality, and relevance to bring a balanced, stable, and predictable future for the Chinese society? Perhaps the answer does not lie in the development of the digital economy itself but in a thorough plan taking into consideration the realities of China, the development stage of its society, and the coordination of policies. We are at a time where the trend of development of technologies, such as virtual reality and artificial intelligence, is becoming increasingly apparent, and the new round of technological advancement and integrated innovation is inevitable. Generally, we should be cautiously optimistic that we could properly handle the relationship between technology and society.

Such optimism first comes from technological advancement itself. From mobile internet and big data to virtual reality and artificial intelligence, this round of technological advancement is naturally suited to human society. The first application scenarios of new technologies are not factory workshops on the production side. Instead, those new technologies have emerged from social networking, finance, education, healthcare, and the like, the fields that are closely related to daily life. This round of technological advancement fundamentally differs from previous ones, as it may bridge the equality trap at a relatively low cost thanks to its intrinsic social nature and close relations with human beings.

Second, with a view on China's present stage of development, the primitive accumulation of capital in society has been completed. The Chinese society is undergoing a long process of consumption upgrading as the needs of affluent citizens shift from basic ones, such as clothing, food, shelter, and transportation, to higher ones. The new generation of technological advancements would greatly smooth over contradictions in this process, which is in line with the changes in aggregate demand of the society. Therefore, the relevance trap is not an issue.

The difficult part is problems with measurement faced by the new generation of technologies and previous ones alike. Regarding this, the only thing we could do is to thoroughly understand the technologies, which requires us to get down to carefully observe and faithfully record every bit of effect of technological advancement on all walks of life. This book could be viewed as an attempt at such observation, in the hope of inspiring an understanding of the digital economy among the people. It also aims to ensure that those achievements of the human civilization could integrate into and serve the society in acceptable ways.

The modernization of society requires the modernization of control measures and ideas. Technology empowers people; with greater power and more diverse ideas in individuals, the society as an aggregate of all individuals would certainly be more developed, more mature, and more controllable. After all, technological advancement is but one of the ultimate driving forces for the progress of human society—the other being the consciousness to reflect upon ourselves.

Guo Kaitian
Senior Vice President of Tencent
Chairman of Tencent Research Institute
Shenzhen, China

Foreword by Yin Libo: Digital Economy Leads China's Economic Transition

At the G20 Summit 2016, China facilitated the signing of the *G20 Digital Economy Development and Cooperation Initiative*, in which the expression "digital economy" first appeared in an official document of China. Later, the *Report on the Work of the Government* (2017) stated, "We will push forward with the Internet Plus action plan and speed up the development of the digital economy… benefit both businesses and our people." Following that, "digital economy" has become a buzz expression in China. But what is the digital economy on earth? This remains a mystery to many. In order to illustrate the concept and meaning of the digital economy, the overall development of the digital economy globally, how to speed up the development of the digital economy, and other fundamental issues systematically, Tencent has sponsored to compile this book titled *Digital Economy*. China Industrial Control Systems Cyber Emergency Response Team has been invited to participate in the compilation and provide strategic support.

This book introduces the overall development of the digital economy overseas to provide readers with a global perspective on the digital economy. The concept "digital economy" has been in use for two or three decades abroad. In the 1990s, the digital economy emerged in developed countries in the west, such as the USA, along with the development of the Internet and its widespread application in the economy and daily life. It has become a key driving force for economic growth and is gradually made a global consensus. International organizations, including the World Bank, the World Economic Forum, and the Organization for Economic Co-operation and Development, have been making great efforts to promote the development of digital economy with various measures. Countries and regions, including the USA, the European Union, and the UK, have also been releasing strategies related to the digital economy and promoting the digital transformation of the economy and the society continuously.

This book is a clarion call for the vigorous development of digital economy about to unfold in China. In recent years, China's digital economy has been developing on the right track though we have long been using the term "information economy" instead of "digital economy." "Information economy" is a concept with a broader meaning than "digital economy." Different people may interpret information economy differently: some believe that it is about analyzing the economic impact of imperfect information on the processes of searching information and making decisions; some take it as "knowledge economy" with an emphasis on the impact of information on the economy; some others view it as a synonym for "digital economy," which has been the meaning carried by the term information economy used by China. Considering the potential ambiguity of the concept "information economy" and the fact that "digital economy" is in common use in most countries, China first put forward the concept "digital economy" in 2016. Its proposal is conducive for China to better benchmark against international standards, promote the development of its digital economy, and engage in cross-border cooperation in the field of digital economy.

This book introduces the meaning, characteristics, functions, foundation, and developments in major fields of the digital economy, so that readers could get to know the general picture, direction of development, and focus of attention of digital economy around the globe. It is a useful popular read for the public to gain a comprehensive understanding of "digital economy." It is worthy of recommendation as it has a chapter dedicated to countermeasures with reference to digital transformation, a key topic concerning the development of the global digital economy in recent years. In that chapter, potential problems that may arise in the digital transformation process of the economy and the society are introduced, with countermeasures and viable paths to proper digital transformation by enterprises and governments put forward. To promote economic and social transformation with digital technologies is certainly consistent with the "Internet Plus," "replacing old growth drivers with new ones and speeding up structural improvement and upgrading," and other efforts going on in China, and it is conducive to realizing the goals of supply-side structural reform. Decision-makers in government agencies, enterprises, and other organizations could draw valuable lessons from this book and use it for reference.

Yin Libo
Director (of Electronic Technology Information Research Institute, i.e., First Electronics Research Institute, Ministry of Industry and Information Technology)
China Industrial Control Systems
Cyber Emergency Response Team
Beijing, China

Preface

The digital economy currently takes up 30.6% of China's GDP, adding 2.8 million new jobs, or 21% of the total in China. There is no doubt that the digital economy is the sector in which the most robust development in China's economy has been witnessed. In 2017, the expression "digital economy" made its first appearance in the *Report on the Work of the Government*. It is viewed as a new impetus for the rapid economic growth of China.

The preliminary achievements of the development of China's digital economy show the world the huge potential and appeal of growth in leaps and bounds driven by technology. It only took China a few years to popularize mobile payment and overturn the age of credit cards established for decades or even nearly a century. It is now possible to use a mobile phone to cater to most of the daily transactions in first- and second-tier cities, without the need to rely on point-of-sale (POS) terminals.

With the digital economy put into application in public service, concrete and remarkable results have been achieved in global economic growth at the "China speed." People are using their mobile phones to make appointments to see the doctor, pay utility bills, and pay traffic tickets. During extreme weather conditions, such as typhoons and rainstorms, all people participate in reporting dangers and sending alarms via their mobile phones. With digital information from the people and for the people, there has formed a virtuous cycle.

"Internet Plus" is the means for the development of the "digital economy." For the last two years, "Internet Plus" has taken root in China. It has become a tool in consumer-oriented segments in such fields as finance, healthcare, education, transportation, and online to offline (O2O). It changes the way to interact with users, breeds new business models, or brings about improvements in efficiency through information exchange in those segments. Undoubtedly, the changes brought forth in various industries by "Internet Plus" are just at the beginning. For example, "Internet Plus Healthcare" is definitely more than simply using mobile phones to make appointments and pay with medical insurance. In the future, the development of the digital economy will reshape the core competencies of various industries.

The development of the digital economy is changing people's outlook on life and their way of thinking. The digital economy has promoted the integration of the sharing economy in more sectors. The right to use an item is separated from its ownership through digital interactions—with shared bicycles, shared cars, and even shared housing, ownership is no longer a necessity. The convenience brought about by rental facilitates the optimal use and maximum saving of all resources in the society as a whole.

The digital economy is also building trust, a basic element of a cohesive society, with technology. The digital era establishes a digital credit profile for every participant with unprecedented advantages, including low costs, ease of keeping records, and real-time query. Thanks to digital credit, we could purchase goods thousands of miles away, feel safe hitching a stranger's ride, and conveniently gain access to financial lending services.

The digital economy ushers in the best era for the development of China's internet companies. Those companies, born in the wild and raised in the jungle, form an ecosystem that differs from that in those developed economies in the west. Decentralized development has made digital connection a form of infrastructure in the lower tier, thus enabling spontaneous rapid growth of all players in the ecosystem. Just take the content industry as an example. China sets the new trend in the commercialization of digital content globally. Its content industry used to have inadequate protection of copyright, but now boasts the highest commercial value for user-generated content in the world. With multiple types of content, including audio, streaming, We Media, and literature, and diversified means of commercialization, such as Q&A and tipping, the industry has entered an era featured with the rapid growth of both content creation and revenue. China's content industry has found its own way out of the jungle of barbaric growth to see greater potentials for development ahead.

The most expectable future development of the digital economy lies in its integration with manufacturing. The manufacturing industry is the foundation of China's economic development and also the backbone of economic growth. In those user-oriented segments, the digital economy adopts a development model featured with agility, small steps with a quick pace, and rapid upgrades. However, when it comes to the integration of the digital economy with manufacturing, there should be more systemic planning. Changes should start from the top-level design, and supply should be triggered by demands. Means of production should be allocated most efficiently through cloud computing, big data, and flexible manufacturing, so as to truly unleash the power of data and improve the efficiency.

The digital economy is the way to achieve the sustainable development of the global economy. It not only increases the economic output of underdeveloped areas but, more importantly, also gives those people living there the potential for all sorts of changes. By virtue of digital connectivity, people living in the even most remote areas could also get the same high-quality contents as those living in first-tier cities do with no distinction or discrimination. People living in underdeveloped areas could obtain the most needed information about education, healthcare, trade, and the like with the lowest digital costs and sell their agricultural produce at more reasonable prices. The digital economy provides those living in absolute poverty desperately in need of help with the means to reach out, which contributes to achieving targeted poverty alleviation. This offers valuable inspiration to less developed countries globally.

We are lucky to live in this era and witness how technology changes our life. To date, there are still 3.9 billion people, or more than half of the world's population, without access to the Internet, around the world. For those not yet connected to the Internet, the construction of infrastructure for such technologies as the fourth-generation mobile communication (4G) and the provision of supporting mobile internet services are undoubtedly the most cost-effective investment made to improve their living conditions. The development of the digital economy worldwide is a future that we all look forward to.

The latest technologies, such as artificial intelligence, virtual reality, and machine learning, have already been penetrating every facet of production and living. The boundary between the digital economy and the real economy will gradually fade away and eventually disappear. There would no longer be pure internet companies as the Internet would be an infrastructure covering the whole society, nor would there be pure traditional industries as all traditional industries would be embedded with the genes of the Internet. We often say if nobody speaks of the Internet as an independent concept, it would be the time that the "Internet Plus" process is to be truly completed. Great integration is the true theme of technological advancement.

Shenzhen, China

Ma Huateng
Chairman and Chief Executive
Officer of Tencent

Contents

List of Figures

PART I

Theories: Digital Economy, a New Form of Economy and a New Driver for Growth

CHAPTER 1

Connotation and Characteristics of the Digital Economy

The *Report on the Work of the Government (2017)* restated that we will push forward the in-depth development of "Internet Plus" and explicitly stated the requirement of accelerating the growth of the digital economy for the first time. The development from the Internet to "Internet Plus" and then to the digital economy is a continuous process that advances with the times. The Internet represents emerging technologies and advanced productive forces. "Internet Plus," a burst of value as the result of the Internet upgrading, invigorating, innovating, and empowering other industries, highlights connectivity. However, the digital economy presents the outputs and benefits generated after achieving universal connection. That is, "Internet Plus" is the means while the digital economy is the outcome. The traditional industries and the Internet industry realize a cross-sector integration through "Internet Plus," bringing about major developments in the digital economy: on the one hand, such developments smooth over the process of replacing old growth drivers with new ones and facilitate the supply-side structural reform; on the other hand, they help to give impetus to achieving the goal of building China's strength in cyberspace.

What Is the Digital Economy

The digital economy is a new form of economic and social development after the agricultural economy and the industrial economy. People's

M. Huateng et al., *The Chinese Digital Economy*, https://doi.org/10.1007/978-981-33-6005-1_1

understanding of the digital economy is a process that has been deepened progressively. Among those numerous definitions of the digital economy, the one put forward in the *G20 Digital Economy Development and Cooperation Initiative* released during the 2016 G20 Hangzhou Summit is the most representative. The initiative holds that the digital economy refers to a series of economic activities with digitalized knowledge and information as key factors of production, the modern information network as their primary carrier, and the effective use of information and communications technology (ICT) as a major driving force for increasing efficiency and optimizing the economic structure.

With the in-depth development of the digital economy, both its connotation and denotation are constantly evolving. It is difficult to accurately draw a line between the digital economy and other economic forms based on the current classification of industries in the national economy and the existing statistical system. The infrastructure industries of the digital economy, including computer manufacturing, communication equipment manufacturing, electronic device manufacturing, telecommunications, radio and television, and satellite communication services, and software and information technology services, and industries, and such sectors as Internet retailing, Internet, and internet-related services are almost all completely built upon digitalization and thus could be regarded as falling into the category of digital economy. Another obstacle to accurately defining the digital economy is that a digital economy is an economy characterized by integration. The increase in output and improvement in efficiency arising from the application of information and communications technology and the transformation towards digitalization in other industries form the main part of the digital economy. With its proportion in the digital economy increasing, it is getting more and more difficult to measure such a part accurately.

In fact, the concept of digital economy is transitional. The Internet is bound to be an ecological element penetrating all industries and all segments of economic and social activities, just like water and electricity, continuously providing impetus to the national economy. By then, no one would mention the digital economy just as no one would say he or she owns a company that uses electricity today.

The History of the Digital Economy

In the 1990s, the global economy was sluggish but the United States managed to maintain its sustained rapid development. As of the end of the year 2000, the United States had registered 118 consecutive months of growth, thus recording the longest growth. That period was characterized by the coexistence of "two 'high's and two 'low's," namely, a high economic growth rate, a high production growth rate, low unemployment, and low inflation. Such high-quality growth had been rarely seen in the history of capitalism, with a lot of emerging new features that differ from those of the previous development models. The most prominent feature was that the modern information and communications technology had appeared among factors driving growth for the first time—the 1990s also the era witnessed revolutions driven by the information and communications technology in full swing and the commercialization process of the Internet at the beginning. Former US Labor Secretary Robert Reich once commented that 70% of such a round of growth in the US economy should be attributed to computers and the Internet. The bitstream composed of 0's and 1's on the internet has changed the way information is transmitted and exchanged, and the way commodities are circulated and traded. Once the Internet was commercialized, it demonstrated its strong vitality. Under such a background, the concept of the digital economy was proposed, attracting widespread attention.

Canadian business strategy guru Don Tapscott is arguably one of the first to put forward the concept of "digital economy." In his 1995 book titled *The Digital Economy*, he discusses the impact of the Internet on the economy and the society in detail. Following that, with the publication of a series of works, including *The Information Age: Economy, Society and Culture* by Manuel Castells and *Being Digital* by Nicholas Negroponte, the digital economy quickly became a popular idea. Governments in various countries also began to take the development of the digital economy as an important measure for promoting economic growth. The Ministry of Economy, Trade and Industry of Japan started to use the term "digital economy" in 1997. The US Department of Commerce released a report entitled *The Emerging Digital Economy* in 1998. After that, the department kept its focus on such a "new economy" phenomenon closely related to the Internet technology, and released multiple annual research reports centering on the theme of "digital economy." Upon moving on into the twenty-first century, particularly since the outbreak of the 2008 global financial crisis, various countries in the world have started to formulate their respective strategies on the digital economy with the hope of stimulating their economic recovery through developing the digital economy.

China also attaches great importance to the role of information and communications technology in promoting economic and social development; but in specific progress of efforts, it mainly used such expressions as "Golden Projects," "information industry," "informatization," and "integration of informatization and industrialization," among others. The *Report on the Work of the Government (2015)* proposed the "Internet Plus" for the first time to accelerate the pace of economic transformation and upgrading by giving full play to the role of the Internet in integrated innovation. At present, China is vigorously developing the new economy and fostering new drivers of growth while starting to consider the issue of digitalization more from economic perspectives. The digital economy has been the highlight at such major events as the 2016 World Internet Conference, the G20 Hangzhou Summit, the group study session of the Political Bureau of the CPC Central Committee on the strategy of building China's strength in cyberspace, and the Symposium on Cybersecurity and IT Application. In 2017, the expression "digital economy" made its first appearance in the *Report on the Work of the Government*, which opened a new chapter for its development.

Characteristics of the Digital Economy

As a new economic form, the digital economy presents its unique characteristics setting it apart from the traditional industrial economy, which are mainly manifested in the few aspects below.

Data Has Become a Key Factor of Production Driving the Economic Growth

With the booming mobile Internet and Internet of Things (IoT), the interconnection between people and people, that between people and things, as well as that between things and things have come true; thus, data see an explosive growth in amount. The growth rate of global data accords with the Moore's Law of Big Data, which means that the data tend to get roughly doubled every two years. The sheer amount of data, coupled with the demands for processing and applying the data, has bred the concept of big data. Data has increasingly become an asset of strategic importance. Data resources will be the core strength of an enterprise—whoever has data in hand will win an advantage. The same goes for a country. The US government believes that big data is "the new oil of the future," the "currency" in the digital economy, and "another core national asset other than land, sea, and air."

Just like land and labor in the agricultural era or technology and capital in the industrial era, data has become not only a factor of production but also the most important one in the era of the digital economy. Innovation driven by data is expanding to various fields, such as technological research and development, economy, and society, and has become a key form of and the important direction for the innovation and development of a country.

Digital Infrastructure Has Become a New Type of Infrastructure

In the era of industrial economy, economic activities were based on physical infrastructure represented by railways, highways, and airports. After the emergence of digital technologies, the Internet and cloud computing have become vital information infrastructure. With the development of the digital economy, the concept of digital infrastructure has been expanded to cover both information infrastructure, such as broadband connection and wireless networks, and the digital transformation of traditional physical infrastructures, such as water mains installed with sensors, digital parking systems, and digital transportation systems. The infrastructure of those two types has provided a necessary basic condition for the development of the digital economy and boosted the transformation of infrastructure from being represented by "brick and mortar" in the industrial era towards being represented by "optical fiber and chips" in the digital era.

Digital Literacy Has Become a New Requirement for Workers and Consumers

In the eras of the agricultural economy and the industrial economy, there was basically no requirement on the literacy of most consumers; though there were some requirements on the literacy of workers, such requirements were often limited to certain occupations and positions. However, digital literacy has become an important capability that both workers and consumers must possess in the context of the digital economy.

As digital technologies penetrate various fields, it is increasingly necessary for workers to get provided with dual skills—digital skills and professional skills. However, there is a general shortage of talents adept at digital technologies in various countries and 40% of companies find it difficult for them to get data talents they need.[1] Therefore, whether a worker has relatively high digital literacy has become an important factor for a worker to excel out in the job market. If a consumer does not have basic digital literacy, he or she would be an "illiterate" in the digital era incapable of using digital products and services correctly.

Therefore, digital literacy is one of the basic human rights in the digital era and a basic competency equally important as listening, speaking, reading, and writing. As improving digital literacy is conducive to both digital consumption and digital production, it has become a key factor for the development of the digital economy that will play its important role in laying the foundation.

The Boundary Between Supply and Demand Has Become Less and Less Clear

In traditional economic activities, the supply side was strictly divided from the demand side with a very clear boundary between the supply side and the demand side of an economic activity. However, the boundary between the supply side and the demand side will become less and less clear as the digital economy develops and suppliers and the demand side are gradually integrating into "prosumers."

On the supply side, new technologies have emerged in many industries. The users' needs are fully taken into consideration in the process of providing products and services, thus not only having created new ways to meet existing needs but also having changed the value chain in the industries. For example, many companies are using the big data technology to find out the users' needs and have the products designed and works of film, television, and literature developed accordingly. Some even make use of the 3D printing technology to achieve fully personalized design and production. The same goes for the provision of public services. The governments are collecting opinions from the people to gain knowledge of economic and social data in a timely manner, so as to make sound decisions and implement them precisely. Correspondingly, there have also occurred major changes in demands. With increased transparency, consumer participation, and the emergence of new consumption

[1] Quoted from the e-Skill Manifesto 2015 of the European Commission. Please refer to http://eskills4jobs.ec.europa.ea/manifesto.

models, companies have no choice but to change the original means of design, promotion, and delivery.

Increasing Fusion of the Human Society, the Cyberspace, and the Physical World

With the development of digital technologies, cyberspace is no longer just a virtual image of the physical world. It has truly evolved into a new world for human society, becoming a new space for human beings to live in. At the same time, the fusion of digital technologies and the physical world has also enabled the real physical world to develop at a speed comparable to that of cyberspace, bringing an exponential increase in the growth rate of human society. The fusion of the cyberspace and the physical world is mainly achieved based on the cyber physical system (CPS) as a unity of the information system and the physical system. The CPS, which is made up of ubiquitous systems engineering, such as environmental perception, embedded systems, network communication, and network control, is an integrated control system that combines computing with sensors and actuators. It enables various objects around us to get provided with such functions as computing, communication, precise control, telecollaboration, and self-organization so that the computing power is closely combined and coordinated with physical systems.

On such a foundation, with the development of technologies including artificial intelligence, virtual reality (VR), and augmented reality (AR), there occurs a cyber-physical-human system (hereinafter abbreviated as "CPHS") featured with the fusion of man, machine and material. This system has changed the way human beings interact with the physical world, and a greater emphasis has been laid on the man-machine interaction and the seamless collaboration between machines and human beings. CPHS promotes the gradual disappearance of the boundaries between the physical world, cyberspace, and human society, forming a new, interconnected world.

Advancements in Information Technologies Constantly Drive the Development of the Digital Economy

Technological advancement spurs industrial revolution. The steam engine powered the Industrial Revolution while the information and communications technology triggered the information revolution, which in turn has boosted the continuous growth of the digital economy. In recent years, the breakthroughs made in and integrated development of such information technologies as mobile Internet, cloud computing, big data, artificial intelligence, IoT, and blockchain have facilitated the rapid development of the digital economy.

The development of the mobile Internet has fundamentally broken away from the restrictions and constraints of the wired Internet, expanded application scenarios of the Internet, and promoted extensive innovations concerning mobile applications. The mobile Internet itself has also evolved from the third-generation mobile communication technology 3G to 4G and then 5G. 5G focuses on expanding from the mobile Internet to IoT applications, so as to meet the future needs for the thousand-fold growth in traffic and the need of billions of devices for access to the Internet.

The popularized application of cloud computing technology has changed the ways in which investment is made in information technology (IT) facilities and the ways in which such facilities are constructed and operated, reduced the construction, operation and maintenance costs of IT facilities, shortened the construction cycle of IT facilities, improved the bearing capacity of IT facilities, and accelerated the access of devices and the deployment of systems. The development of the mobile Internet and cloud computing, together with the reduction in costs of sensors, has promoted the development of IoT. It has been estimated that 50 billion devices will be connected to the IoT in 2020 and the number is bound to increase ten times to a hundred times in the future. The data capacity of IoT will also increase exponentially, and it will get doubled every two years.

To process data collected from the IoT, the big data technology will be inevitably required. The development of the big data technology has been driven by the increasing computing power, the continuous fall in computing costs, and the lowering costs of data transmission, storage, and analysis. The big data technology has, in turn, promoted the sound development of the IoT, making it the important platform for data collection and data sharing and promoting improvements in business applications and the capability for business insight.

The development of technologies in the field of artificial intelligence has significantly improved the capabilities for the automatic analysis of big data. Without such intelligent technologies, big data could not possibly be collected, processed, and analyzed even if there is the huge amount of data required nor could new meanings be thus discovered and new values created. Artificial intelligence technologies can be used to understand videos, audios, and even natural languages of human beings. In turn, hidden patterns could be summarized from the massive fragmented, unstructured data in the IoT, so as to support intelligent decision-making. In addition, the development of artificial intelligence helps to address the incompatibility of various communication protocols between IoT devices. Therefore, with the big data and artificial intelligence technologies put into effective application, the development of the IoT will be boosted and breakthroughs will be made from quantitative changes to a qualitative change in the IoT.

The development of the IoT will accelerate the fading out of boundaries between the physical world, the digital world, and human society. As the computing technology enters a phase featured with the integrated development of man, machine, and material, VR has become an important support for such integration. VR, a profound revolution in the display technology, is seen as another common technology platform after computers and smartphones. TV screens, computer screens, and mobile phone screens are all two-dimensional displays, but VR provides us with a display for three-dimensional graphics. This has brought about a tremendous change in the way human beings understand and transform the world. The development of VR technology is also in no way independent from others. To achieve the effective interaction between virtual reality and actual reality, there must require an effective combination of other technologies, including high-speed data transmission, recognition, and computing.

Relying on the encryption technology, the blockchain could establish a decentralized distributed database that is reliable, transparent, secure, and traceable. It has transformed how data on the Internet is recorded, transmitted, stored, and managed, greatly reduced the cost of credit, streamlined the business processes, and made transactions more efficient.

As a result, it has restructured the existing industrial organization models and social governance models, improved the standard of public services, and realized the transformation of the Internet from a means of information transmission to a means of value transfer. Therefore, the blockchain technology is also known as a "trust machine" or a new type of business infrastructure. In the past two years, the blockchain technology has been sought after in the capital market and quickly put into application in multiple fields. Many countries have put forth corresponding blockchain-specific policies. The blockchain technology is essentially a distributed database—a new way to record, transmit, and store data on the Internet. The analysis into and interpretation to relevant data are also much dependent on big data and artificial intelligence technologies. The interconnection of relevant objects requires the technical support from the IoT as well.

In addition, such technologies as advanced robotics, autonomous driving, 3D printing, digital identification, biometrics, quantum computing, and renewable energy may also become key technologies in future. These technologies are experiencing exponential growth driven by continuous innovation and integration with those technologies discussed above. The holistic evolution of multiple technologies and their breakthrough in groups are empowering the sustained innovation and development of the digital economy.

CHAPTER 2

Digital Economy as a New Driver for Growth

The *G20 Digital Economy Development and Cooperation Initiative* points out that the digital economy, an ever-increasingly important driver for global economic growth, is experiencing its rapid growth and fast innovation. The digital economy is playing a vital role in accelerating economic development, increasing the labor productivity in the existing industries, cultivating new markets and new growth drivers in industries, and achieving inclusive growth and sustainable development.

The Digital Economy as a Major Source of Power for Economic Growth Boosts the Quality of Economic Growth

The digital economy, which plays a significant role in boosting economic growth, is becoming a new driver for global economic development day by day. Oxford Economics and Accenture have proposed the digital density index to quantify the penetration of digital technologies in enterprises and economies of various countries. Studies have shown that increasing the digital density could considerably boost economic growth. Calculated based on the 2014 price level, for every 10-point increase in digital density (on a scale of 100 points), the average GDP growth rate of developed economies over the next five years would increase by 0.25 percentage points while that of emerging economies would increase by

M. Huateng et al., *The Chinese Digital Economy*,
https://doi.org/10.1007/978-981-33-6005-1_2

0.5 percentage points. That means that by 2020, the USA and China would add USD 365 billion and USD 418 billion to their value of output respectively (as shown in Fig. 2.1). The analysis in the *Global Information*

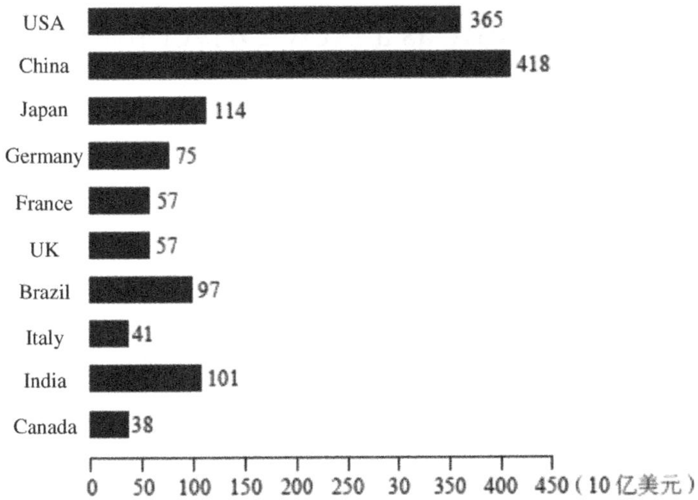

Fig. 2.1 Increase in GDP of various countries for every 10-point increase in digital density (*Sources* Accenture and Oxford Economics, March 2015)

Technology Report 2012 released by the World Economic Forum also indicates that if the degree of digitalization was improved by 10%, the GDP per capita would increase by 0.5–0.62%.

Increase in 2020 GDP Figures of the World's Top 10 Economies for Every 10-Point Increase in Digital Density (Calculated Based on the 2014 Price Level).

China's Digital Economy Catches Up from Behind

China's digital economy started late, and lagged behind developed countries in Europe and the USA for a rather long period of time. According to data from China Info 100, the digital economy in China amounted to USD 43 billion in scale in 1996, which was only a sixty-third of that in the USA, a twenty-third of that in Japan, and a sixth of that in the UK. At the beginning of the twenty-first century, especially the past ten years, China's digital economy accelerated its development with an evident trend of "catching up from behind."

The *China "Internet Plus" & Digital Economy Index 2017* report released by Tencent Research Institute shows that the overall scale of China's digital economy was around RMB 22.77 trillion (converted into about USD 3.9 trillion) in 2016, making China the second-largest digital economy in the world after the USA (as shown in Fig. 2.2). China has long been the number one in the world in terms of personal computer shipment, smartphone shipment, number of Internet users, and online sales. So far as the development of the mobile Internet is concerned, China takes the lead in the world while the world's top 10 Internet companies are either from China or from the USA.

The status of the digital economy in China's national economy is continuously improving, with its proportion in GDP rising quickly to reach 30.61% in 2016, up by 25.61 percentage points as compared to that in 1996. However, compared with that in the USA, the UK, Japan, and other developed countries, China still lags behind in terms of such a proportion, with much room for its future development (as shown in Fig. 2.3).

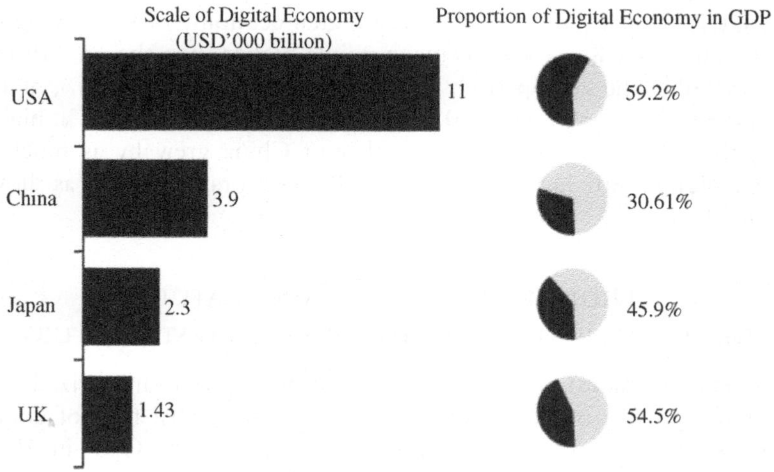

Fig. 2.2 Scale of the digital economy in major countries in the world and the corresponding proportions in the GDP in 2016 (*Sources* Tencent Research Institute and China Info 100)

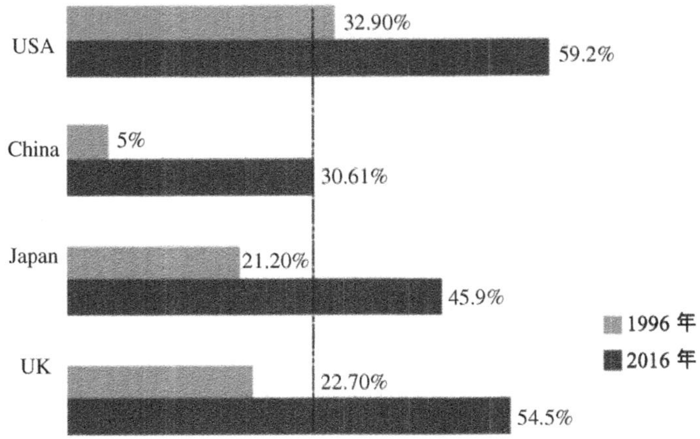

Fig. 2.3 Proportion of the digital economy in the GDP in major countries (Figures in 1996 and 2016 used for an example) (*Sources* Tencent Research Institute and China Info 100)

According to data from China Info 100, the digital economy in all major economies is growing at a rate significantly higher than their respective GDP growth rates. In 2016, the digital economy of the USA grew by as much as 6.8%, 1.6 percentage points higher than the growth rate of its GDP in the same period; that of Japan grew by about 5.5%, higher than the GDP growth rate of 0.9%; that of the UK grew by 5.4%, higher than the GDP growth rate of 2%; that of China grew by as much as 16.6%, significantly higher than the GDP growth rate of 6.7% (as shown in Fig. 2.4).

Digital Flow as a Main Feature of Globalization in the Twenty-First Century

Economic globalization in the twentieth century was characterized with the rapid growth of trade and capital flows. The global flow of goods, services, and money accounted for 53% of the world's GDP in 2007. After reaching such a record high, such rapid expansion has since entered a period of stasis—the growth of global trade in goods has been flat, the flow of capital has plunged, and trade in services has been growing slowly. However, that does not necessarily mean that the globalization process has come to a stop. In fact, with the rapid development of the digital economy, globalization has been witnessing tremendous changes

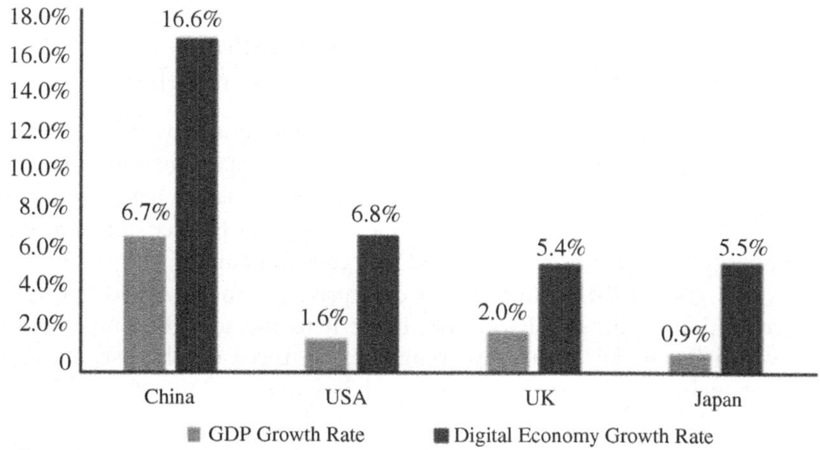

Fig. 2.4 Comparison between China, the USA, the UK, and Japan in terms of digital economy growth rate and GDP growth rate (*Source* China Info 100)

in terms of content and form—the flow of data has become a new feature of globalization in the twenty-first century.

In recent years, digital flows involving business, information, searching, images, and communications have been surging with their more and more extensive participation in the global economy. According to data from McKinsey & Company, cross-border broadband traffic increased by 45 times over the ten-year period from 2005 to 2014 and it is expected to further increase by 9 times in the next five years. During those ten years, the global flows of goods and data, as well as foreign direct investment, had contributed to a 10% increase in the world's GDP. In 2014 alone, the contribution was equivalent to USD 7.8 trillion, of which USD 2.8 trillion was generated by the flow of data, accounting for 36% of the total. It is evident that when it comes to driving economic growth, the flow of data has a more significant effect than the flow of traditional goods.

The twenty-first century is being increasingly defined as a new era for globalization characterized by the flow of data and information. A more efficient and more transparent global market has been formed thanks to the digital platforms. The near-zero marginal costs of digital communications and transactions have opened up new possibilities for large-scale transnational business.

Digital Enterprises Typified by Internet Companies Are on the Rise

With the accelerated development of the digital economy, digital enterprises are building up their strength day by day and playing an increasingly important role in the national economy. Those companies have started to take the place of traditional giants in such sectors as finance, automobile, and energy to rank among the world's largest companies.

By the end of 2016, five digital enterprises, namely, Apple, Google, Microsoft, Amazon, and Facebook, made it to the top 10 companies in the world by market value, sweeping the top three on the list; another four, namely, American Telephone and Telegraph Company (AT&T), Tencent, BT Group PLC, and Alibaba, made it to the top 20, taking up 9 out of the Top 20. Digital enterprises account for about half of the world's largest companies, and the proportion is still growing (as shown in Table 2.1).

Moreover, traditional enterprises are also engaged in digital transformation with digital technologies put into application. As the number one Fortune 500 company, Walmart started to use computers for inventory management early as in the 1970s, successfully applying management software systems and satellite communication systems to its business. It dominates the global retailing industry thanks to the support offered through putting the computer technology into application in its global expansion. Walmart also actively embraced the Internet. It launched Walmart.com, its e-commerce website, early as in 2000, with its online retail business covering 11 countries as of now. In 2016, Walmart acquired Jet.com, an e-commerce startup, with USD 3.3 billion. In the same year, it spun off YHD.com in exchange for shares in JD.com and Dada Group, thus securing its position in the Chinese market. To further accelerate the development of its e-commerce business, Walmart took the lead to cancel the annual fees for two-day shipping in the USA in early 2017. According to data from The Internet Retailer, an online retailing business, Walmart has become the fourth largest online retailer in the world, thus having achieved a remarkable outcome of its digital transformation.

Table 2.1 The world's top 20 companies by market value (by the end of 2016)

Ranking	*Company*	*Market value (USD 'billion)*	*Country*
1	Apple	621.7	USA
2	Google	550.4	USA
3	Microsoft	488.9	USA
4	Berkshire Hathaway	404.8	USA
5	ExxonMobil	375.0	USA
6	Amazon	360.2	USA
7	Facebook	332.7	USA
8	Johnson & Johnson	314.6	USA
9	JPMorgan Chase & Co.	306.5	USA
10	GE	280.9	USA
11	Wells Fargo	275.0	USA
12	AT&T	262.5	USA
13	Diageo	259.6	UK
14	Barclays Bank	258.5	UK
15	Royal Dutch Shell	232.1	The Netherlands
16	Tencent	231.6	China
17	BT Group PLC	229.3	UK
18	ICBC	229.2	China
19	Procter & Gamble	226.1	USA
20	Alibaba	222.9	China

Source Tencent Research Institute, January 2017

The Digital Economy Boosts the Quality of Economic Growth

The digital economy not only powers rapid economic growth and promotes global trade, but also improves the quality of economic growth and accelerates the transformation and upgrading of the real economy, which are conducive to entrepreneurship, innovation, energy conservation, and emission reduction.

Facilitating the Transformation and Upgrading of the Real Economy

The digital economy is an economy characterized by integration, with a significant empowering effect. It has not only achieved rapid development on its own but also helped to optimize resource allocation, adjust the industrial structure, and achieve transformation and upgrading in traditional industries. At the Symposium on Cybersecurity and IT Application held on April 19, 2016, General Secretary Xi Jinping emphasized that rigorous efforts should be made to integrate the Internet more deeply into the real economy, using information flows to facilitate the flow of technologies, capital, talents, and materials and the optimization of resource allocation.

The manufacturing industry as the main part of the national economy is the major battlefield for implementing the "Internet Plus" action plan and developing the digital economy. The new generation of information technology is accelerating its in-depth integration with the traditional manufacturing industry in all aspects, and is becoming a source of power leading the digital transformation of the traditional manufacturing industry.

In recent years, developed countries in the West led by the USA and Germany have formulated national strategies one after another to accelerate the deep integration of the manufacturing industry and the internet. Such integrated development is regarded as a key focus in a number of advanced manufacturing partnership plans announced by the USA, the Industry 4.0 strategy of Germany, the high value manufacturing of the UK, the New Industrial France program of France, the New Robot Strategy of Japan, and the integrated IT development strategy of South Korea.

Leading companies in the manufacturing industry worldwide are all actively embracing the digital revolution, and more and more small and medium-sized enterprises (SMEs) have achieved their innovative transformation by virtue of integrated technologies. For example, in 2012, General Electric (GE) invested in a highly digital and flexible "multimodal factory" in Pune, India, integrating design, product engineering, manufacturing, supply chain, and distribution into a cohesive smart digital link. It analyzes the huge amount of data flowing between machines and products to achieve optimization. With a smart design, it can simultaneously produce aircraft engines, power generation equipment, oil and gas production equipment, and their components, significantly improving the production efficiency of customized products. The Amberg Electronics Plant built by German company Siemens using digital factory solutions could perform changes to products and processes within a minute, a feat achieved with digital means running through the entire process of product design, production planning, process planning, production execution, and service. The defect rate of products has dropped from 600 parts per million 20 years ago to 12 parts per million at present. Production efficiency has been increased by eight times without increasing the area of the production site.

The transformation of China's manufacturing industry has achieved remarkable results, with significant improvement made in digital, networking, and intelligent capabilities of the industry. The innovative integration of the digital economy and the traditional manufacturing industry has been generating new business formats and models that meet market demands, such as networked collaborative manufacturing, large-scale customization, and smart remote services. Weichai Power Co., Ltd. has established a global collaborative R&D platform for engines, which has shortened the R&D cycle of engines from 24 months in the past to 18 months and R&D time by 1/3. With a model characterized by customization, the sales and profits from customization of Qingdao Redcollar Clothing Co., Ltd. doubled year-on-year in 2016. Sany Heavy Industry Co. Ltd. added over RMB 2 billion to its profits in the past three years by providing real-time monitoring and operation and maintenance services for more than 200,000 devices worldwide through its smart service platform. CASICloud provides such services as industrial software and solutions to more than 440,000 registered corporate users on the platform, with a total turnover of RMB 19.3 billion in 2016.

Promoting Entrepreneurship and Innovation

Due to the effect of multiple factors, such as dramatic fluctuations of the global economy, shifts in the demographic structure, and accelerated changes in new technologies, governments of all countries are paying increasingly more attention to entrepreneurship. In order to enhance the national competitiveness and create more jobs, various countries have actively introduced policies aimed at encouraging entrepreneurship and helping startups strengthen industrial competitiveness. Many countries have stepped up their efforts to train the digital skills and entrepreneurial competencies of students. For example, EU member countries have introduced the cultivation of entrepreneurial spirit into both elementary education to higher education. In order to improve the digital skills of young people and remove technical barriers to entrepreneurial ventures, 17 countries have introduced information and communications technology (ICT) into the core curricula at schools; 16 have proposed to introduce entrepreneurial skills into the core curricula or require students to pass examinations on their entrepreneurial skills.

Driven by a new round of technological revolution and industrial transformation, especially with the strong advocation by the government, China is breeding a new wave of entrepreneurship and innovation in the field of digital economy. Entrepreneurship and innovation have become a trend in the whole society with the explosive growth of startups, venture capital, and entrepreneurial platforms and the rapid increase in the number of entrepreneurs. The development of the digital economy has nurtured a number of internet companies with great potential for development, becoming a driver for stimulating innovation and entrepreneurship and creating jobs.

The innovation capabilities of Chinese enterprises are being constantly improved thanks to China's huge, vibrant market and large manufacturing system. China's mobile Internet has already surpassed that of the USA in certain respects, attracting the attention of the Silicon Valley in search of innovative ideas from China's WeChat, Alipay, and DiDi among many applications.

Promoting Green Development

The Information and communications technology (ICT) is conducive to energy conservation and emission reduction, hence promoting green development. On the one hand, the development of ICT itself helps to reduce some materials consumed in social and economic activities, thereby reducing the energy consumption of producing these materials. On the other hand, applying ICT to other industries can bring about greater energy-saving effects.

The International Telecommunication Union (ITU) estimates that ICT could help reduce global carbon emissions by 15–40%. By applying ICT to other industries, energy equal to five times the consumption of the ICT industry itself could be saved. The US Department of Energy has listed industrial wireless technology in its future industrial planning with the goal of saving energy and reducing consumption. The President's

Council of Advisors on Science and Technology of the USA pointed out in its "Federal Energy Research and Development Plan for the 21st Century" that the application of industrial wireless technology is going to increase the efficiency of industrial production by 10% and reduce emissions and pollution by 25%. The European Commission has suggested that the research into and application of innovative performance information communication solutions will enable the whole of the European economy to achieve low carbon emissions. For example, the use of ICT could increase the power generation efficiency by 40% and power transmission efficiency by 10%; its use in optimizing logistics arrangements and intelligent traffic management could also help improve the efficiency of transportation by 17%.

The Digital Economy as Vital Support for Promoting Supply-Side Structural Reform

Currently, China must simultaneously deal with the slowdown in economic growth, make difficult structural adjustments, and absorb the effects of previous economic stimulus policies. Under such a backdrop, the outstanding problems hindering economic growth are partly problems with aggregate supply and demand, but structural problems are more acute. Advancing the supply-side structural reform is a major innovative measure to adapt to and guide the new normal in economic development. To address the deep-seated problems that hinder development, it has become an inevitable choice to give full play to the comparative advantages of the Internet, develop the digital economy, facilitate the supply-demand matchmaking, gather innovative factors, and optimize resource allocation.

First, the Internet significantly increases the capacity for effective supply. It is the main direction for the supply-side structural reform, which aims to cut down ineffective and lower-end supplies while increasing effective and medium- and high-end supplies through fulfilling the five major tasks of "tackling overcapacity, de-stocking, de-leveraging, lowering corporate costs, and improving weak growth areas." The in-depth integration of the Internet into such traditional industries as manufacturing, logistics, and agriculture promotes innovation in industrial organization, business model, and supply chain management greatly improves the operating and organizational efficiency of production, and promotes the upgrading of traditional industries. At the same time, new technologies, products, models, and business formats based on the Internet are flourishing. As a basic platform for public participation in entrepreneurship and innovation, the Internet is unleashing the infinite wisdom and creativity that people did not know they had.

Second, the Internet expands aggregate demand appropriately. It is an indispensable part of the supply-side structural reform. As China has moved on to the middle-income stage with the consumption of citizens upgrading, customized production and sales could better meet the diverse needs of the people. The Internet further expands the long-tail markets and consumption potentials in various fields integrated with it. It provides better products, more convenient services, and more diverse business formats; it enhances user experiences; it optimizes the consumption environment; it also actively cultivates new types of consumption and taps into traditional types, so as to develop new consumption patterns and unlock effective consumer demands. At the same time, progress made in the implementation of the "Internet Plus" action plan and the "Made in China 2025" strategy will effectively drive the investment into and the construction of a new generation of information infrastructure, accelerate the implementation of a number of major "Internet Plus" projects, such as smart manufacturing and smart product innovation, and expand effective investment.

Third, the Internet promotes the upgrading from a low-level equilibrium of supplies and demands to a high-level one. The fundamental purpose of the supply-side structural reform is to improve the quality of supplies to meet the demands so that the supply capacity could better meet the ever-growing, constantly upgrading and personalized material, cultural and environmental needs of the people. The rapid development of the Internet as a driver for the development of the structure of supply from the lower-end supply to a higher-end one, and changes the structure of demands from existential demands to quality-based demands. It increases the total factor productivity through releasing and developing social productive forces, promoting structural adjustments by means of reform, and enhancing the adaptability and flexibility of the structure of supply to changes in the demands.

The Digital Economy Creates Jobs and Improves People's Well-Being

Creating Jobs

The digital economy triggers a shift in the industrial structure by facilitating a substantial leap in the production capacity through stimulating human intelligence and improving people's cognitive abilities. It plays a significant role in creating jobs. The *China "Internet Plus" & Digital Economy Index 2017* report released by Tencent Research Institute shows that China's digital economy brought about some 2.8 million new jobs in 2016, or 21% of the total of the newly-employed in 2016. Many countries view the development of the digital economy as an important means of creating jobs. The European Union released the *i2010—A European Information Society for Growth and Employment* in 2005 in the hope of using ICT as a powerful driving force to promote economic growth and create more jobs. The *2015 White Paper on Information and Communications in Japan* states that if local enterprises make full use of ICT, such as smartphones and cloud services like their counterparts in large cities, there would create about 200,000 new jobs created.

The Internet lowers the costs of transactions, bringing more opportunities for those who have difficulty finding a job or inputs for production, with benefits to women, the physically challenged, and people living in remote areas. In terms of modes of employment, employees have greater freedom with the constraints of time and space removed for them. The workplace may no longer be a factory but a virtual organization online; the organizational structure of jobs may no longer be project-based teams or partnerships but freelancing, in which the value of individuals is more freely created, channeled, and shared.

For the economy as a whole, the most profound impact of the Internet on individuals lies in improving the productivity of workers. After routine and repetitive work is taken over by technology, workers can focus on activities with higher value. They can make use of technology to obtain information about prices, inputs, or new technologies more quickly, which not only lowers costs but also reduces conflicts and uncertainty.

Improving People's Well-Being

Increasing the degree of digitization helps to improve people's happiness and social welfare. The higher the digital density, the faster the improvement of happiness. A survey conducted by the World Economic Forum on 34 OECD member states shows that for every increase in digitalization by 10 percentage points, the happiness index would increase by about 1.3 percentage points. More importantly, the digital economy helps to bridge the digital divide between regions and brings welfare to more people living in remote areas. The *China "Internet Plus" & Digital Economy Index 2017* report released by Tencent Research Institute shows that smart livelihood is accelerating its spread to the fourth- and fifth-tier cities. In those cities, the availability of public services, such as public security and healthcare on mobile platforms, has been increased to 50%, with little difference in user satisfaction as compared to public services in developed cities. The digital divide of people's well-being between regions tends to narrow.

The improvement of people's well-being as a result of digital technologies is reflected in all aspects of daily life, including shopping, banking, entertainment, and interactions between friends and family members. For example, the payment system for registration fees in Côte d'Ivoire used to be troubled by many problems, including wasting parents' time in long queues and the risk of robbery. In 2011, the Ministry of National Education of Côte d'Ivoire began working with mobile money service providers to digitize the payment of annual registration fees of nearly 1.5 million middle school students. In the 2014–2015 school year, more than 99% of students paid their registration fees via digital means, of which 94% of the fees were paid through the three local mobile money service providers in the country. In China, Shenzhen has been conducting a pilot for mobile payment with medical insurance, enabling users to make mobile payments for appointments and outpatient services using medical insurance directly through WeChat. Thus, a total of 80,600 h have been saved for 900,000 Shenzhen residents in half a year.

PART II

Basics: Improving Digital Infrastructure to Facilitate Economic Prosperity

CHAPTER 3

Accelerate the Construction of Digitalized Infrastructure

The construction of digitalized infrastructure is vital to the development of the digital economy. The infrastructure here covers not only traditional information infrastructure, such as high-speed broadband Internet, Internet Protocol (IP) addresses, and domain names, but also the digitalization of traditional infrastructure, such as railways, highways, water transportation, and electric power.

Continuously Improving Information Infrastructure

Strengthening the Construction of Broadband Infrastructure

Currently, 146 countries worldwide have implemented broadband strategies or action plans. These strategies have one goal in common: giving full play to the key role of information infrastructure in building a digital society, increasing internet user penetration by expanding the popularity of broadband internet, hence accelerating the digitization process of society.

Currently, the overall coverage of 4G is relatively high in developed countries such as South Korea, Japan, the UK, France, and Germany. According to data provided by OpenSignal, as of Q3 2015, South Korea's 4G coverage reached 99.6%, and the speed of its mobile Internet neared 41 Mbps (megabits per second), making it the country with the fastest

M. Huateng et al., *The Chinese Digital Economy*,
https://doi.org/10.1007/978-981-33-6005-1_3

mobile Internet speed in the world. Japan's 4G coverage rate is also above 90%, ranking second in the world.

China attaches great importance to the construction of high-speed broadband internet. It has made remarkable achievements by actively facilitating faster and more affordable internet connections and building "Broadband China." By the end of 2016, the number of broadband internet access ports in China had reached 690 million, and more than 95% of China's netizens were able to gain access to the internet on their mobile phones, amounting to 695 million mobile internet users.

At the "Two Sessions" in 2017, Premier Li Keqiang stated in the Report on the Work of the Government, "In the age of the Internet, faster, safer, and more cost-effective information networks are crucial to the development of every sector. This year, we will do more to increase broadband speed and lower rates for Internet services. Mobile rates for domestic roaming and long-distance calls will be cancelled; rates for broadband services for small and medium enterprises will be slashed; and rates for international calls will be lowered."[1] His words were acclaimed with the excitement of the people.

Accelerating the Development of the 5G Network

Compared with 4G, 5G has a higher speed and a wider bandwidth, which could satisfy the consumers' demand for better network experience, such as virtual reality and ultra-high definition video. It is also more reliable with lower latency, enabling it to meet the needs of industrial applications, such as autonomous driving and smart manufacturing, in a better manner. Realizing the "Internet of Everything" could offer stronger support for the innovation and development of the economy and society.

China, a latecomer in the field of mobile communications, is among global leaders in the research and development of 5G standards. China officially launched technical research and test for 5G in early 2016; at the end of the same year, Huawei's polar code proposal was accepted as an international standard for 5G. China has set the goal of commercializing 5G in 2020.

[1] Refer to http://lianghui.people.com.cn/n1/0316/c410899-29150065.html.

Bridging the Digital Divide

With the gradual unfolding of broadband strategies of various countries, the coverage and speed of broadband Internet have been effectively increased. However, the broadband Internet in remote areas still lags behind that in the cities by a large margin due to the relatively low population density and high construction costs in the local areas.

The USA has taken a series of measures to address such problems. In October 2011, the Federal Communications Commission passed a plan for reforming the Universal Service Fund (USF) and intercarrier compensation (ICC) system, and established the "Connect America Fund" with an annual budget of as much as USD 4.5 billion. The fund is used to offset the high costs of constructing and operating high-speed internet connection in sparsely populated areas, and encourage enterprises to invest in construction projects in these areas. The USA also extends loans to broadband internet service providers in rural areas. The US Department of Agriculture has special programs in place to provide financing for eligible network operators in rural areas, so as to help these operators invest in the construction of high-speed broadband internet infrastructure in rural areas not yet covered.

In 2010, the British government allocated 530 million pounds for the deployment of high-speed broadband in rural areas through its "Building Digital UK" (BDUK) project. In 2017, the British government announced an additional 440 million pounds of investment in the construction of internet connection. The UK has proposed to build a digital entrance to rural areas, and has launched a financing program named as "Rural Gigabit Connectivity" to make up for the shortage of funding in the construction of internet connection in rural areas. At present, the superfast broadband coverage project launched by the government has extended its coverage to more than 3 million households and businesses. The second phase of the project is bound to be completed by the end of 2017, which means that the coverage of superfast broadband internet to premises would increase from 90 to 95%.

China is also accelerating the pilot for universal telecommunication service and promoting the development of broadband in rural and remote areas. It has set the goal of "extending broadband internet coverage to more than 90% poor villages by 2020." Such efforts as increasing broadband speed and lowering rates for internet services as well as poverty alleviation by means of the Internet would narrow the digital divide between urban and rural areas, fully facilitate the development of the internet in rural areas, and play a significant role in lifting farmers out of poverty and increasing their income.

Digitalizing Traditional Infrastructure Brings Huge Value

The development of the digital economy has brought about new economic opportunities in the transformation of the traditional "brick and mortar" infrastructure to the mixed digitalized infrastructure, creating jobs and improving the quality of economic growth.

Improving the Quality and Efficiency of Infrastructure as a Service

Service data that could not get quantified easily in the past could be obtained by applying the Internet of Things (IoT) technology on traditional infrastructure and adding a digital layer—an embedded IoT-enabled sensor layer—so that relevant departments could provide better infrastructure as a service for the public. For instance, through sensors embedded in the transportation system, city administrators and planners could see whether the system meets the needs of commuters and thus make infrastructure planning more efficient. The digital parking system helps city managers to know whether there are enough parking lots and whether there are parking lots not fully utilized. The new-generation air transportation system provides more routes for aircraft, enabling aircraft to fly in straight lines between airports, and reducing the distance traveled between takeoff and landing. This way, flight distance and time could be much shortened, with reductions in corresponding oil costs.

Monitoring the Condition of Infrastructure in Real Time to Enhance Safety

It is difficult to know the real-time condition of traditional infrastructure in operation. Digitalized infrastructure, on the other hand, could significantly improve economic benefits and public safety through data collection and early warning. For instance, the collapse of a bridge is likely the result of the continuous weakening of its structure due to multiple factors, but these changes are not clearly visible to the naked eye. If IoT-enabled sensors are installed, such changes could be detected. Protective maintenance measures could then be promptly implemented at reduced costs to prevent heavy loss of life and property, or at least minimize the loss through early warning from the digital system. Another example would be sensors installed in water bodies, which could send timely warning signals when the nitrogen and phosphorus content in the water approaches the limit.

Giving Full Play to the Market Mechanism to Balance Supply and Demand

Through real-time monitoring, digitalized infrastructure makes prices of services more readily available, enabling the closer, more dynamic matching of supply to demand. For instance, an analog electricity meter could not read electricity usage in real time, but a smart meter can. The latter enables electricity suppliers to implement differential pricing for usage in peak hours and other periods of time, and detect electrical leakage from electricity usage data. Smart transportation charges commuters differently in different areas and different periods of time, which has the potential to make the efficiency of the transportation network much more efficient. It is also a common practice of internet service providers to offer different packages according to the bandwidth and usage of users.

Significant Comprehensive Economic and Social Benefits

The application of digitalized infrastructure in one field often brings comprehensive benefits beyond the particular field, and there are some impacts that are not currently calculable or foreseeable, as more advanced analytical techniques emerge with the development of the Internet of Things technology.

For example, smart transportation systems have brought many changes to the field of transportation: means of road tolling and payment have been revolutionized; traditional traffic signals have been replaced with smart ones, which have significantly improved the flow of traffic by reducing the number of stops by 40%, fuel consumption by 10% and exhaust emissions by 22%; there are better ways to maintain and repair infrastructure now. The benefits associated with them are significant. Overall, the traditional approach of merely expanding highway capacity has an input-output ratio of 1:2.7 while that of improving operating practices of the transportation system is around 1:9 or even higher.

Similarly, the application of smart meters, advanced control systems, and communication networks for the real-time collection, transmission, and response of electricity usage information in a smart grid could improve the efficiency of electricity usage and enhance the safety of the grid. It could also promote the development of new energy, particularly energy storage technology and plug-in hybrid electric vehicles. It is estimated that in the next 20 years, smart grid and differential pricing will be capable of generating USD 31 billion to 50 billion of benefits annually.

Digitalization of Railway Infrastructure

In recent years, the railways in China have developed rapidly with the continued expansion of the network. As of the end of 2016, China's railways in operation were as long as 124 thousand kilometers, among which high-speed railways were 22 thousand kilometers long, or accounted for 60% of the total in the world. There has been increasing digitalization of railway infrastructure. By the end of 2015, there had been over 1,600 mainframes, mid-range computers, and minicomputers, as well as some 100 thousand microcomputers in the railway communication network connecting China State Railway Group Co., Ltd., National Railway Administration, and major railway sections. The railway communication network is composed of the transmission network and the data network.

Railway Transmission Network

The railway transmission network is a combination of the backbone layer, the distribution layer, and the access layer. The backbone layer, which adopts a blend of SDH and DWDM transmission technologies, mainly undertakes the transmission from China State Railway Group Co., Ltd. to the National Railway Administration and various railway bureaus, and provides a protected detour channel for the network of National Railway Administration. The distribution layer is responsible for transmitting the service information accessed along the railways managed by the National

Railway Administration to the dispatching station links of the administration and the core network links, and providing a protected detour channel for the adjacent network of National Railway Administration. This layer also adopts a blend of SDH and DWDM transmission technologies to realize the transmission of service information between railway sections themselves as well as between railway sections and dispatching stations of the administration. The access layer transmission network adopts the MSTP transmission technology to undertake the information access and transmission of stations and sections along the railways, choosing stations or sections as its links.

Railway Data Network

The data network is a dedicated broadband data communication network based on IP technology established for the railway system, covering all station grounds of the entire railway. It undertakes such services as dispatch management information system (DMIS), transportation management information system (TMIS), and ticket system by means of MPLS VPN. The existing railway data network has established independent IP data transmitting networks separately for DMIS, TMIS, ticket system, and other systems, with relatively low-bandwidth networks formed for each type of service information—most of them are 2M or n × 2M connections.

In addition, China has successively developed a variety of applied information systems such as train dispatching command system, railway transportation management information system, and ticket sales and reservation systems.[2]

Digitalization of Highway Infrastructure

Currently, China has basically achieved the interconnection of its comprehensive highway transportation channels featuring "five vertical and five horizontal arteries," with its highway network continuously expanding. By the end of 2015, the total mileage of highways nationwide was 4.57 million km, among which expressways accounted for more than 120,000 km. The total length of the highway optical fiber network

[2] Refer to http://bbs.railcn.net/thread-1540178-1-1.html for the status quo and future plans for the China Railway Information Construction.

reached 120,000 km, among which 19,000 km fall into the category of backbone optical fiber networks, covering 28 provinces (as well as autonomous regions and municipalities directly under the central government) of the country.

National Expressway Information Communication System Networking Project

The construction of China's expressways has had a long period of rapid growth, but the communication and transmission resources, network structures, equipment configurations, and protective measures of various sections suffer from a lack of overall consideration for a unified network. This is due to such problems as inconsistent subjects of investment and construction in early expressways and incompatible technical standards. As a result, the scattered optical fiber transmission facilities fail to provide adequate conditions for networking.

In December 2011, the Ministry of Transport issued the *Overall Construction Plan for the National Expressway Information Communication System Networking Project*, which specified detailed technical plans and standards of the project. At the National Transportation Conference in early 2013, the Ministry of Transport also explicitly proposed plans to further promote the construction of the national expressway information communication system networking project. The overall objective of the project is to build a nationwide highway communication network. It means forming a large-capacity, high-bit-rate digital optical fiber communication network covering the whole of China, so as to promote the IT-based development of transportation, improve industry management and public service standards, strengthen emergency response capabilities, and enhance the combat readiness of the country.

After a few years of construction led by local administrations, as of September 30, 2014, the optical fiber network has completed the joint commissioning of arterial transmission equipment at all 259 stations of the system, with verification tests conducted on it. The five ring networks of Central China, Southeast China, Northwest China, Central West China, and Southwest China, as well as the Northeast China chain, have been fully connected. The networks cover 28 provinces (as well as autonomous regions and municipalities directly under the central government), namely, Beijing, Liaoning, Jilin, Heilongjiang, Hebei, Tianjin, Shandong, Anhui, Jiangsu, Shanghai, Zhejiang, Fujian, Jiangxi, Hunan,

Hubei, Henan, Shanxi, Inner Mongolia, Ningxia, Gansu, Qinghai, Shaanxi, Sichuan, Chongqing, Yunnan, Guizhou, Guangxi, and Guangdong. The full interconnection between networks has been achieved in those areas, with five ring networks and one linear chain about 19,000 km in length constructed using a combination of optical transmission network and synchronous digital hierarchy.

IT-Based Basic Information Communication Network for Transportation

During the "13th Five-Year Plan," China proposed to build a unified backbone information communication network for transportation in each province by making full use of such resources as egovernment.gov.cn, ChinaNet, or industrial networks, and connect it to the arterial transmission network for national expressway information communication. It aims to further improve the stability and reliability of the arterial transmission system for national expressway information communication, and conduct research to establish a sound market-based operation and maintenance support mechanism. It will implement the "Broadband China" strategy, support the construction of broadband networks by telecommunications companies making full use of communication pipeline resources of expressways, and facilitate the internet coverage of multiple broadband operators at bus passenger stations and other transportation stations, so as to make sure users have a fair choice. It shall build maritime satellite and search and rescue satellite systems in conjunction with the other countries in the world to strengthen its control over certain international resources, basically forming an integrated aerial and ground IT-based basic information communication network for transportation with global coverage.[3] Relevant administrations have digitalized more than 3,000 km along the Qinghai-Tibet and Sichuan-Tibet highways using high-resolution remote sensing satellites, providing basic data to support disaster monitoring, management, and maintenance for the roads.

[3] *IT-based Development Plan for Transportation in the 13th Five-Year Plan* by the Ministry of Transport. Please refer to http://www.moc.gov.cn/sj/zongheghs/guihuagl_ghs/201605/t20160503_2021656.html.

Digitalization of Water Transportation Infrastructure

The distribution of China's network of water transportation infrastructure is becoming more and more streamlined. By the end of 2015, there were more than 2,100 berths capable of accommodating ships above 10,000 tons in coastal ports, with 500 new ones built within the last five years. The total throughput reached 7.9 billion tons, among which containers accounted for 188 million transmission extension units (TEUs). The scaling-up, specialization and modernization standards of ports have been further improved. The construction along "two horizontals, one vertical, two networks and eighteen lanes" of inland waterways has made substantial progress, and 13,600 km of inland river courses have qualified for high-grade waterways. With the rapid advancement of construction work in the industry, the infrastructure of the water transportation industry is also accelerating its digitalization process, with continuously enhancing broadband access capabilities.

Data Center for the Water Transportation Industry

In 2013, the plan for establishing a national data center for the water transportation industry was formulated, which clearly defined efforts to further promote the aggregation, integration, and extensive application of industry data resources under the framework of ministry-level data centers. There have been significant breakthroughs in the construction of the maritime cloud data center, which has basically realized the gathering and cleansing of the basic data for China's maritime system. Ports and shipping enterprises have taken the initiative to build an information hub platform with data resources as the core, strengthening the accumulation and consolidation of data while ensuring data support and services are provided properly. It is particularly worth mentioning that the volume of data in the "China Shipping Database" initiated by the Shanghai International Shipping Institute has exceeded 800,000 entries, a good start for big data mining applications that follow.

Public Information Service Platform for the Water Transportation Industry

In May 2015, the *National Development Plan for Water Transportation in the 13th Five-Year Plan* was released, which proposes to "focus on supporting the integration of port logistics information resources by ports and shipping companies, and establish a one-stop external service platform integrating such functions as online preparation, application acceptance, electronic booking, and electronic payment." The plan would further promote the integration and construction of a cross-industry, cross-region, and cross-department public information platform for logistics. Agencies led by Shanghai Shipping Exchange, Dalian Branch Center of China E-Port, Shanghai International Shipping Institute and others have been actively establishing regional information hub platforms and expanding the scope of extended services while providing high-quality public information services for the industry.

Smart Water Transportation

Since the idea of "smart water transportation" was first proposed in 2010, the water transportation industry has been actively exploring and promoting developments in this field. Various relevant basic research activities, demonstrations and pilot projects have been carried out successively, penetrating industry supervision, production operations and transportation services in all respects. There has been initial progress with projects such as "smart port and shipping," "smart maritime affairs," "smart port city," "smart navigation," and "smart channel," providing strong support for the modernization process of water transport.[4]

Digitalization of Electric Power Infrastructure

Electric power has become the core of the energy sector, hence innovation in the electric power industry is of great importance to the energy system. According to the statistics in the Report on China's Electric Power Information Industry issued by Forward Industry Research Institute, China's

[4] *IT-based Development Plan for Transportation in the 13th Five-Year Plan* by the Ministry of Transport. Please refer to http://www.moc.gov.cn/sj/zongheghs/guihuagl_ghs/201605/t20160503_2021656.html.

investment in the field has been gradually increasing in recent years, amounting to more than RMB 50 billion as of now. After over a decade of continuous development, the IT-based application and construction process of the electric power industry has made significant achievements. The total length of optical fiber cables used in State Grid's electric power communication network has exceeded 1 million km, covering almost all urban and rural areas. Information technology is showing increasing importance in the electric power industry, especially in production, operation, and management processes. A solid foundation has been laid for the construction of smart grids in China.

After decades of construction efforts, the national electric power communication network of China has begun to take shape. An interconnected communication network covering 36 provincial grid companies across the country with Beijing at its center has been established with various means of communication such as satellite, microwave, carrier wave, and optical fiber cables. The first-class backbone transmission network is composed of optical fiber, digital microwave, and satellite communications, with all its dispatch centers, monitoring centers, and satellite center main stations set up in the headquarters of the communication center of State Grid. The tandem centers of the switched communication network for electric power, the network management centers of the digital data network (DDN), and the control centers of the teleconference system and the video and telephone conference system are also set up in the headquarters of the center.

With the increasing importance of the communications industry in the development of society, services based on the electric power communication network have evolved from mere narrowband services in its nascent stage, such as program-controlled voice networking and transmission of dispatch real-time control information, to simultaneous delivery of multiple data services, including customer service centers, marketing systems, geographic information systems (GIS), human resource management systems, office automation (OA) systems, video conferencing, and IP telephony. Electric power communication has duly performed its duties in coordinating the joint operation of generation, transmission, transformation, distribution, consumption and others in the electric power system and ensuring the safe, economic, stable, and reliable operation of the power grids. It has also done well in supporting communication needs in such fields as electric power generation, capital construction, administration, flood control, power dispatch, reservoir dispatch, fuel dispatch, relaying, automatic safety devices, computer communication, and automation of power grid dispatch. Though the economic benefits of electric power communication are not expressed directly, such benefits underlying in electric power generation and management are enormous. In the meantime, electric power communication has been increasingly valued by society thanks to its unique advantages in development.

CHAPTER 4

Make Efforts to Improve the Digital Literacy

The concept of "digital literacy" was first proposed in 1997 by Paul Gilster, a famous scholar. He believes that digital literacy mainly encompasses the ability to acquire, understand and integrate digital information—specifically, skills such as searching the internet, navigating hypertext, and evaluating and assembling digital information. This effectively distinguishes digital literacy from the ability to read and write traditional print media.

Digital literacy is constantly picking up more content in practice to better adapt to the characteristics of a new era. The "digital literacy" today can be seen as the ability of a person to use digital resources throughout the entire process of acquiring, understanding, integrating, evaluating and communicating information in the new technological environment, and effectively participate in social processes. It covers both the ability to take in digital resources and the ability to give them out.

Digital Literacy Is a Primary Skill in the Twenty-First Century

Improving digital literacy is of great importance to both individuals and countries. For an individual, digital literacy determines one's adaptability to the times, and decides whether one could effectively acquire information, pass on information, and enjoy the convenience brought about

M. Huateng et al., *The Chinese Digital Economy*, https://doi.org/10.1007/978-981-33-6005-1_4

by a society characterized by digital media in the face of today's huge amount of digital information. For a country, the digital literacy of its people is increasingly becoming an important part in improving national literacy, influencing the comprehensive qualities of the country's citizens, and even deciding whether the country could gain a head start in the era of digital economy.

More and more countries and organizations are beginning to recognize the functions and significance of digital literacy. The "21st century skills" proposed by the Partnership for twenty-first Century Skills put "digital literacy" as the primary type of literacy to emphasize its importance. Developed countries are also actively introducing measures to improve digital literacy.

The USA has formed a diversified, comprehensive training system supported by multiple entities. The government, as the leader and service provider, enacts preferential policies to guide the cultivation of digital literacy in the society and provides extensive funding for the construction of infrastructure, hence laying a solid foundation for the cultivation of digital literacy. Educators, as the principal trainers, formulate a set of reasonable, feasible standards through scientific, and systemic research and implement them through diversified curricula. Non-governmental organizations also play a vital role in this process: on the one hand, they offer advice to policymakers; on the other hand, they are independent educators who provide useful supplements to those out of the reach of the government and the education system.

Similar to the USA, Europe has also established a system with joint efforts from the government, educational institutions and non-governmental sectors. However, the government chiefly plays a role in guiding and setting the framework of digital literacy education. Educational institutions offer training not by directly establishing a digital literacy curriculum, but by integrating it into the teaching of various courses. The non-governmental sectors undertaking the responsibility of education are not represented by research institutions, such as think tanks, as in the US model but by libraries and library associations, thus forming a unique yet effective European model.

The "Japanese model" is a digital media literacy training model built upon the individual practice of citizens rather than receiving education passively. The foundation for such a model to function well is laid through the relatively advanced media literacy education in Japan, where citizens could improve their digital media literacy through continuous practice and extend their media literacy to the interaction with digital resources in the contemporary digital era.

Focuses of Cultivating Digital Literacy

Improving the Quality of the Labor Force

With the continuous advancement of technologies in the digital era, all sorts of jobs have set higher standards for the digital literacy of the labor force. Forms of work are also increasingly shifting to online forms involving the use of computers or mobile devices. There is no doubt that these jobs would require job seekers to have basic digital literacy for them to be hired or promoted. In jobs with a wider job scope, employers require workers to have basic knowledge of computers and the internet to meet the demands of the jobs and increase productivity.

This applies to "blue-collar jobs" in the traditional sense as well. Even employers such as manufacturers and retailers of daily necessities would collect and analyze necessary sales data to keep up with the trends in the market and stay relevant. In such a context, employees of these manufacturers and retailers are also expected to have certain digital literacy, so that they could collect and sort out these digital resources to provide useful information and feedback to employers. Therefore, in the new era, digital literacy is in no way negligible for improving the quality of the "white collar workers" and even the traditional "blue collar workers" in the labor force.

Bridging the Digital Divide Between Users

The digital divide includes two major aspects: one is the disparity in terms of digital devices and infrastructure, and the other is the gap in digital literacy. Conversely, the key to bridging the digital divide lies in strengthening the construction of digital infrastructure and improving digital literacy. Both digital natives and digital immigrants must cultivate digital literacy to improve their ability to make use of digital media and digital resources in the digital era comprehensively. This is of utmost significance for turning the digital divide into digital opportunities.

Cleansing the Cyberspace

In the age of information explosion, digital literacy has evident value in the application field of social media. The ability to express freely on social media and verify massive amounts of information is determined by the user's digital literacy. Digital literacy has a profound influence on the words and deeds of Internet users on social media. It determines their identities and whether they could cope with social media communication, which is an unavoidable part of this era.

Cultivating the digital creativity of people on digital media is a good way to cultivate digital literacy. Such a creativity helps people communicate with others through social media and catch up with the trends of the times, deliver correct and useful information, discern false information on the internet, and keep the Internet clean. Social media, such as Facebook and Google, have also adopted proactive measures to crack down on fake news. Facebook is going to set up a new report button and address the spread of false information through changes in functional design and algorithms. Apart from the efforts of the government and enterprises, improvements in the digital literacy of the people will also play a significant role in reducing the spread of false information.

Reforming the Education System to Improve Digital Literacy

Digital literacy is getting integrated into the national education curriculum in more and more countries, while more and more schools are taking the cultivation of digital literacy as an important goal of their teaching, hoping to keep up with the pace of accelerated changes in technology. Through the cultivation of digital literacy among students, their academic literacy and academic abilities could be significantly improved. In addition, digital literacy itself is an important part of teaching students how to adapt to the times. As a result, the role of digital literacy in the field of education is also reflected in the fact that the education system itself requires teachers to have adequate digital literacy, so that they are capable of teaching students how to obtain resources and pass on digital resources to students.

In addition to schools, social organizations are also responsible for education. In the digital era, libraries, as important information hubs of the society, have been gradually developing more and more conducive digital library environments and playing their part in digital literacy education.

CHAPTER 5

Boost the Internet and Information Technology Industry to Develop Vigorously

As the foundation for the development of the digital economy, the Internet and information technology industry is a relatively broad concept. At present, it provides the technical conditions and industrial foundation for the development of the digital economy, with technologies including the Internet, big data, cloud computing, artificial intelligence, and blockchain being hot spots of its development.

A General Picture of the Current Development of the Internet

Netizens: Penetrating Nearly Half of the Global Population

According to data from the International Telecommunication Union (ITU), the number of Internet users in the world reached 3.488 billion in 2016, accounting for 47.1% or nearly half of the world's population. According to data from Internet World Stats, an Internet data statistic agency, the penetration rate of the Internet in such countries as Iceland, Denmark, the Netherlands, Norway, and Cyprus has exceeded 95%. The state of affairs that "all citizens are netizens" is coming faster than expected. In terms of sheer size, the netizen numbers in seven countries, including China, India, the USA, Brazil, Indonesia, Japan, and Russia, rank among the top, with more than 100 million each. The numbers in

M. Huateng et al., *The Chinese Digital Economy*,
https://doi.org/10.1007/978-981-33-6005-1_5

India and Indonesia, two populous countries, has grown rapidly in recent years.

After more than ten years of rapid growth in China's Internet users, the growth rate has stabilized as it gradually ceases to enjoy a demographic dividend. According to data from China Internet Network Information Center (CNNIC), as of December 2016, the number of Internet users in China reached 731 million, with a total of 42.99 million new users added throughout the year; the penetration rate of the Internet was 53.2%, an increase of 2.9% points as compared to the end of 2015.

Terminals: The Internet Has Moved on to the Post-mobile Era

Since January 2007, when Apple launched the epoch-making iPhone, the mobile Internet has been developing for ten years. In the past ten years, it has made great strides, which has overturned the traditional Internet business models to breed many new business formats such as the sharing economy and online-to-offline (O2O). The mobile Internet has become the main infrastructure for the development of the Internet industry.

According to data from StatCounter, a market research agency, smartphones and tablets accounted for 51.3% of global Internet usage in October 2016, while PC accounted for 48.7%. For the first time in history, mobile Internet usage exceeded PC Internet on a global scale (as shown in Fig. 5.1). Mobile Internet has already achieved an absolute advantage in such countries as China, Japan, South Korea, and the UK. For example, according to data from iResearch, in 2016, shopping on mobile platforms accounted for 70.7% of all online shopping transactions in China. This marks that the world has entered the height of the mobile Internet era, and the development of the Internet has moved on to the post-mobile era.

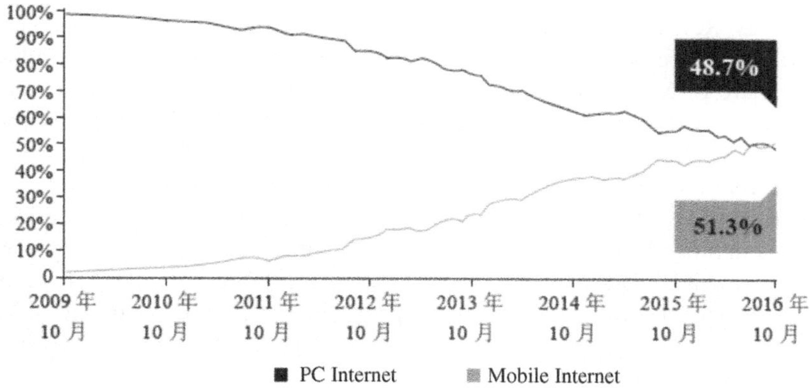

Fig. 5.1 Comparison of internet usage worldwide (October 2009–October 2016) (*Source* StatCounter, November 2016)

The Market Is Reaping Benefits at the 10th Anniversary of Cloud Computing

Google was the first in the industry to propose the concept of "cloud computing" in August 2006; in the same year, Amazon launched such cloud services as Simple Storage Service (S3) and Elastic Compute Cloud (EC2). The two industrial giants have jointly unleashed the rapid development of cloud computing. In the past ten years, various types of enterprises have been embracing this concept. It has almost changed the landscape of the entire IT industry, and the market has started to reap benefits.

Industrial Giants Such as Amazon and Google Are Leading the Development of Cloud Computing in the World

Amazon, Microsoft, IBM, and Google dominate the global cloud computing market. According to data from Gartner, an information technology research and analysis company, those four companies occupy more than half of the global market for cloud computing basic services.

AWS, Amazon's cloud computing business, is an unexpected success. Today, it has become the world's largest cloud computing service provider that could be said to be dominating the market. According to data from

Synergy Research Group, in Q3 2016, AWS's share in the global IaaS (Infrastructure as a Service) open market was 45%, more than double the share of Microsoft, Google, and IBM combined. In the global PaaS (platform-as-a-service) open market, AWS's share almost surpasses the sum of Salesforce's, Microsoft's, and IBM's (as shown in Fig. 5.2).

Revenue from Cloud Infrastructure Service in Q3 2016

In 2016, AWS's revenue reached USD 12.2 billion, with 42 availability zones deployed in 16 regions around the world. It keeps launching new products and reducing the prices of existing products. In the ten years since its establishment, AWS has cut prices 52 times. Thanks to the huge success of the cloud computing business, Amazon became the world's fifth-largest listed company in 2016.

Microsoft is the paradigm of a traditional IT vendor successfully transformed into a cloud service provider. In 2014, Microsoft established the new "mobile-first, cloud-first" strategy. With the dual engines of Office 365 and Azure, Microsoft has secured the second position in the industry. The growth of Azure is particularly robust: as of the end of 2016, the revenue from Azure Premium had achieved triple-digit growth for ten consecutive quarters. Fueled by the development of cloud computing and artificial intelligence, in January 2017, Microsoft's market value reclaimed the record high of USD 500 billion it had achieved 17 years ago.

The transformation of IBM, another traditional IT giant, has been relatively difficult. It first transformed into a software and consulting service provider before moving on to cloud computing. Though IBM

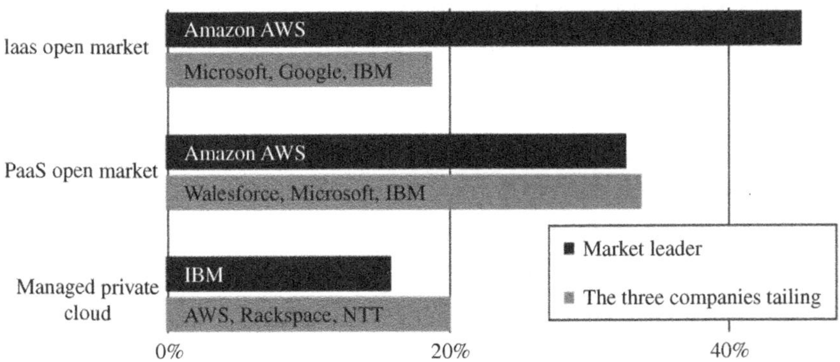

Fig. 5.2 Structure of the world's cloud computing basic service industry (*Source* Synergy Research Group, October 2016)

has become a leader in private cloud, it has yet to reverse the declining trend of the company's performance.

In order to quicken the pace of catching up with Amazon and Microsoft, Google has made adjustments to increase its input in cloud computing. In November 2015, Google spent as much as USD 380 million to headhunt VMware co-founder Diane Greene, who would take charge of its newly established cloud computing application and infrastructure department. In October 2016, Google put many of its software and hardware departments, including business communication service Google for Work, Google Docs, Cloud Platform, and even Android phones, tablets, and Chromebooks for computers, in the charge of Greene. It was the most significant adjustment to Google's organizational structure by then.

Companies in the Second Echelon Are Stepping Up Investment and Acquisition Efforts

The dominance of the four major manufacturers, namely, Amazon, Microsoft, IBM, and Google, has been well-established, which is unlikely to change in the short term. However, cloud computing is a huge market covering a wide range. There are still numerous successful enterprises in its many sub-sectors, especially those powerful cloud service providers in the second echelon. In 2016, enterprises in the second echelon represented by Oracle and Salesforce had outstanding performance. They mainly resort to stepping up investment and M&A efforts to consolidate their advantages and make up for their shortcomings.

Oracle, the world's second-largest software company, is well-known for the sheer number of its acquisitions. According to data from CrunchBase, a database for startups, the total number of Oracle's acquisitions has reached 115. There are many famous deals in its history, for example, the acquisition of PeopleSoft for USD 10.3 billion, while the deals for another four companies, namely, BEA Systems, SUN, Siebel Systems, and Micros Systems, are all above USD 5 billion.

Oracle is now actively transforming to cloud computing. Since 2010, the focus of its acquisitions has shifted to cloud computing, particularly SaaS vendors, to fill the gaps in specific vertical markets. In 2016, Oracle actively engaged in mergers and acquisitions, spending a total of USD 12 billion to successfully acquire nine companies. Among them, the biggest deal is the acquisition of cloud solution provider NetSuite for USD 9.3 billion, which is also the second-largest acquisition in the history of Oracle. The acquisition costs for another four companies, namely, cloud software startup Ravello Systems, architectural engineering cloud service provider Textura, energy-saving data cloud service company Opower, and cloud-based Internet performance and domain name system (DNS) provider Dyn, are all above USD 500 million. Oracle's transformation has made some progress: in Q2 fiscal 2017, its total revenue from cloud services surpassed the USD 1 billion mark for the first time to reach USD 1.05 billion, with a growth rate of 62%.

Salesforce is a leader in enterprise SaaS as well as online customer relationship management (CRM). In 2016, Salesforce engaged in a slew of acquisitions, spending USD 13 billion to buy 13 companies. The biggest of the deals is the acquisition of online retail solution provider Demandware for USD 2.8 billion. The acquisition of team collaboration application Quip and that of marketing data startup Krux cost more than USD 700 million each.

Alibaba and Tencent Are Leaders in China

The size of China's cloud computing market is relatively small, but it is experiencing rapid development. In the market, Alibaba Cloud and Tencent Cloud are in leading positions. Cloud computing is now the highlight of Alibaba's development. As of the end of 2016, the number of paying users on Alibaba Cloud increased to 765 thousand, which doubled year-on-year; since Q2 2015, Alibaba Cloud's revenue has achieved triple-digit growth for seven consecutive quarters. Tencent's revenue from cloud service has also exploded, with a more than double growth in 2016.

In December 2016, Tencent Cloud opened 11 overseas service branches. So far, the number of Tencent Cloud's overseas service branches has increased to 14, amounting to a total of 19 branches globally, taking into account the 5 domestic ones. As a result, Tencent Cloud has become the Chinese Internet cloud service provider with the most well-established cloud computing infrastructure (Fig. 5.3).

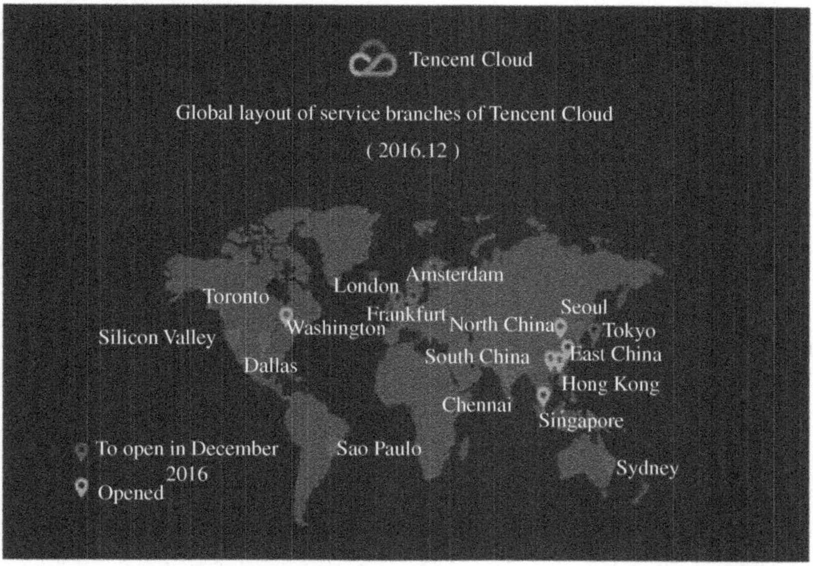

Fig. 5.3 Global layout of service branches of Tencent Cloud (*Source* Tencent)

Technology Companies Are Embracing Cloud Computing

The rapid development of cloud computing has revolutionized the traditional IT infrastructure with a huge impact on IT vendors. IT giants are actively adjusting their business architecture. For example, Symantec and Hewlett-Packard have each been split into two, IBM has sold its x series server business, and Dell has acquired EMC. Most importantly, established vendors such as Microsoft, IBM, Oracle, SAP, Cisco, Lenovo, and Intel have gradually shifted their strategic focuses to cloud computing.

In China, more and more players are entering the cloud computing market. In December 2014, Kingsoft announced a three-year strategy called "All-in Cloud," and pioneered a differentiated strategy focusing on industry cloud. Since 2015, NetEase has successively launched cloud services such as NetEase Yunxin and NetEase Qiyu. In 2016, it officially announced a cloud strategy featuring scenario-based service and knowledge system output. JD.com has also been vigorously developing its cloud computing business, taking 2016 as its first year of cloud computing. Baidu Cloud and Meituan Cloud are also growing rapidly.

Summary

After ten years, cloud computing has changed the traditional business models and the mode of operation of the entire market. With growing market acceptance, cloud computing has entered a stage whereby the market is reaping benefits, becoming a strategic focus and a growth driver for technology companies. Looking to the future, cloud computing is anticipating new opportunities brought about by the vigorous development of deep learning and artificial intelligence technologies, with much more to expect of it.

Artificial Intelligence Ushers in a Golden Age at Its 60th Anniversary

In 1956, artificial intelligence (AI) was proposed for the first time in history by ten young scholars, including John McCarthy and Claude Shannon, at the Dartmouth Artificial Intelligence Conference. Over the past 60 years, the development of artificial intelligence has been through ups and downs. The last of the ten scientists, Marvin Minsky, also passed away in early 2016.

2016 is the end of an era and the beginning of a new one. In March, Google's AlphaGo defeated Lee Sedol 9P, a South Korean Go player, shocking the world and quickly drawing people's attention to artificial intelligence. The deep-seated reason behind the widespread enthusiasm is that a new round of technological innovation has brought the development of artificial intelligence to a fast lane. Due to the ubiquitous Internet, big data and sensors, large-scale computing capabilities based on cloud platforms, and major breakthroughs in algorithms, computers are already able to complete more complex tasks independently with deep learning. Artificial intelligence is everywhere.

Various Countries in the World Are Announcing Artificial Intelligence Strategies One After Another

The USA, the cradle of information technology, leads the development of artificial intelligence. Since 2013, the USA has issued a number of artificial intelligence plans, and stepped up its layout in artificial intelligence in 2016. The Ministry of National Defense attaches great importance to artificial intelligence technology, and believes that human-machine collaboration is the "high-tech holy grail" in the third offset strategy. In 2015, a new DIUx external office was established in Silicon Valley to strengthen cooperation with emerging innovative enterprises. As the inventor of the Internet, the Defense Advanced Research Projects Agency (DARPA) is accelerating the research on artificial intelligence technology, releasing a wide-ranging institutional announcement of the "Explainable Artificial Intelligence" (XAI) project in August 2016. In addition to national defense, the White House issued two important documents, namely, *Preparing for the Future of Artificial Intelligence* and *National Artificial Intelligence Research and Development Strategic Plan*, in October 2016, and followed them up in December by releasing *Artificial Intelligence, Automation, and the Economy*. The report raised artificial intelligence to a national strategic level, formulating a grand plan and blueprint for the development of artificial intelligence in the USA.

In addition to the USA, many governments also released relevant development strategies and plans in 2016. For example, the UK government released a report titled *Artificial Intelligence: Opportunities and Implications for the Future of Decision Making*; the Ministry of Education, Culture, Sports, Science and Technology of Japan determined the 2016 strategic goals of "Advanced Integrated Intelligence Platform Project (AIP) – Artificial Intelligence / Big Data / Internet of Things / Cybersecurity" (AIP Project) while its "Revitalization Strategy 2016" lists the development of artificial intelligence as the first and foremost of its ten revival strategies; China released the *Robotics Industry Development Plan (2016–2020)* and *Three-Year Guidance for Internet Plus Artificial Intelligence Plan (2016–2018)*. Before 2016, the European Union has also launched the *Human Brain Project*.

Artificial Intelligence Is Becoming a Strategic Pivot for Technology Giants

At present, the bonus for mobile Internet development is gradually disappearing, and the post-mobile era has arrived. Technology giants have taken artificial intelligence as a strategic pivot in the post-mobile era, striving to build an ecosystem of artificial intelligence services on the cloud.

In 2016, as if by prior agreement, Facebook, Amazon, Google, and Baidu announced that artificial intelligence is the core of their future business. Mark Zuckerberg released Facebook's plan for the next ten years at the F8 Developer Conference in April, in which artificial intelligence has become one of the three pillars of its vision. Amazon founder Jeff Bezos said in June that Alexa voice assistant is expected to become the company's fourth pillar of its business after e-commerce, Amazon Prime (Amazon's premium membership service), and Amazon Web Services (AWS). Google announced in October that its development strategy had shifted from "Mobile First" to "AI First."

Faced with the opportunities and challenges of artificial intelligence, five American technology giants, namely, Alphabet, IBM, Facebook, Amazon, and Microsoft, announced the formation of Partnership on AI in September 2016; four months later, Apple joined the partnership. The Partnership on AI is committed to promoting the public's understanding of artificial intelligence technology. It will also establish a code of conduct for future researchers in the field of artificial intelligence to follow, and provide useful and effective practices for the challenges and opportunities in the field.

In China, Baidu ventured to artificial intelligence early, with its Institute of Deep Learning and Silicon Valley Artificial Intelligence Laboratory established in 2013. Baidu Brain was announced in September 2016. At the press conference, Robin Li emphasized that artificial intelligence will be the core of Baidu's cores. Tencent also established an artificial intelligence laboratory, focusing on the four major development directions of natural language processing, speech recognition, machine learning, and computer vision.

Fierce Competitions for Top Talents

The development of artificial intelligence could go nowhere without top scientists. The world's top artificial intelligence talents are very scarce, with only a few dozen people mainly distributed in colleges and universities represented by Carnegie Mellon University and Stanford University. In 2016, the competition for artificial intelligence talents by technology companies became increasingly fierce. They do not hesitate to spend a lot of money, and the salaries offered are comparable to the signing fees of National Football League (NFL) stars.

Among them, Google's grab for artificial intelligence talents is the most eye-catching. In March 2013, Google signed Geoffrey Hinton, a professor of the Department of Computer Science at the University of Toronto and the founder of deep learning. In November 2016, Google attracted two leaders in the field of computer vision—Fei-Fei Li, a tenured professor of the Computer Science Department at Stanford University and the director of the Stanford Artificial Intelligence Laboratory and the Stanford Vision and Learning Lab, and Jia Li, head of research at Snapchat, who will together manage and lead Google's newly established Machine Learning Department.

In addition to Google, other competitors are also vigorously recruiting experts in artificial intelligence. As early as 2013, Facebook hired Yann LeCun, a computer scientist at New York University and a famous professor in the field of artificial intelligence, to serve as the director of the newly established Artificial Intelligence Lab. Uber hired 40 of the 140 staff members at Carnegie Mellon University's National Robotics Engineering Center in 2015 and dedicated a team to explore autonomous vehicles. In October 2016, Apple invited Russ Salakhutdinov, a machine learning professor at Carnegie Mellon University, to serve as the company's head of artificial intelligence research. Microsoft has the richest talent pool in the field of artificial intelligence. In 2016, the new Microsoft AI and Research Group was established. In early 2017, through the acquisition of Canadian deep learning startup Maluuba, it hired Yoshua Bengio, Maluuba's consultant and an outstanding figure in the field of deep learning, as a special consultant for Microsoft.

In China, Baidu hired Andrew Ng as chief scientist in 2014 to take charge of Baidu Research Institute. In early 2017, Lu Qi, Microsoft's global executive vice president and technical authority in the field of artificial intelligence, joined Baidu. Robotics startup UBTECH headhunted Howard Michel, the former chairman of the Institute of Electrical and Electronics Engineers (IEEE), in late 2016.

Rapid Growth of Investment in Entrepreneurship and Innovation

Since 2012, investment in artificial intelligence startups has grown rapidly, especially in 2016. According to the statistics on the CB Insight website, there were 658 investment transactions in the field of artificial intelligence in 2016, with an amount of USD 5 billion financed, an increase of 64% over that in 2015 (as shown in Fig. 5.4).

The situation in China is equally optimistic. *Wuzhen Index: Global Artificial Intelligence Development Report 2016* shows that Chinese investment in artificial intelligence reached a scale of about USD 600 million in the first half of 2016, of which the second quarter reached a record high of USD 470 million, showing that investment in the field of artificial intelligence has accelerated significantly to closely follow developed countries such as the USA and Western European countries.

In 2016, three new unicorn companies emerged in the field of artificial intelligence, namely the self-driving car startup Zoox, China's health care

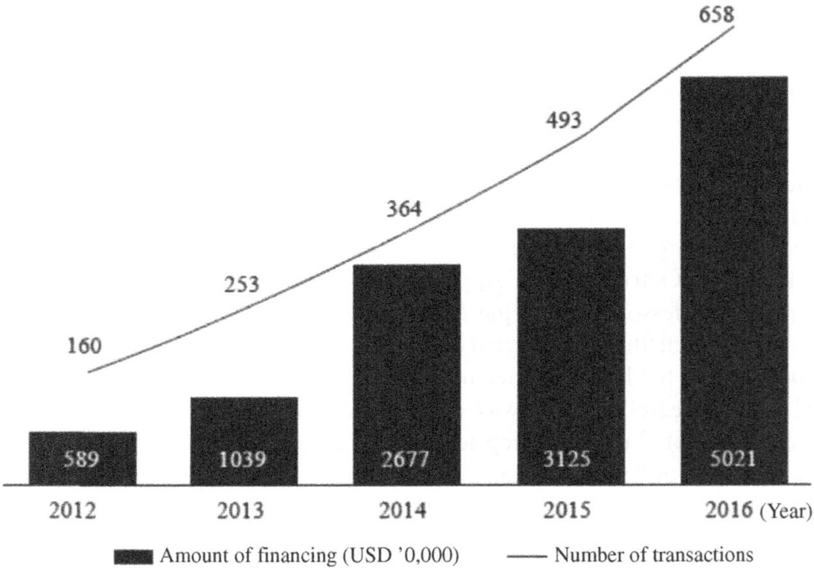

Fig. 5.4 Global investment and financing for artificial intelligence in recent years (2012–2016) (*Source* CB Insights, January 2017)

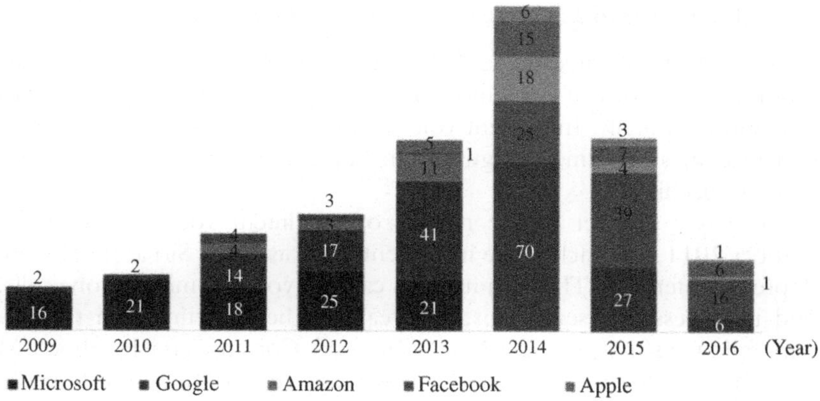

Fig. 5.5 Number of patent applications for artificial intelligence by five major technology companies in the USA (*Source* CB Insights, January 2017)

artificial intelligence startup CarbonX, and the US artificial intelligence network security startup Cylance.

Technology companies have also intensified competition in patents. According to data from CB Insights, Microsoft and Google are leading in the number of artificial intelligence patent applications among the top five technology giants in the USA (as shown in Fig. 5.5). Since 2009, Microsoft has applied for more than 200 patents related to artificial intelligence, while Google has applied for more than 150. In 2013, Google applied for far more artificial intelligence technology patents than Microsoft, while Apple's patents were relatively fewer in numbers.

Emergence of Typical Industry Applications

Artificial intelligence has a wide range of applications in many fields. The applications that are currently deployed extensively include speech recognition, natural language processing, image recognition, computer vision, autonomous driving, drones, and intelligent robots, with relatively successful applications in home furnishing, media, medical, financial, and other industries. The following highlights the progress of artificial intelligence in the fields of voice, media, and autonomous driving.

Voice Assistants: Amazon's Alexa Has Become a Superstar

In recent years, scientists have dedicated efforts to improve the communication capabilities of machines so that they could communicate with users more naturally. Intelligent voice assistants could then communicate with machines in human language, and even communicate with nature through machines.

Apple is a pioneer in the market of intelligent voice assistants. In October 2011, it launched the intelligent voice assistant Siri at the iPhone 4S press conference. Through it, users can use voice to make phone calls, send text messages, set alarms, and realize other functions. In the few years following that, Google Now, Microsoft Cortana, and Facebook M were born. In 2016, the market for voice assistants continued to flourish. Samsung acquired such companies as Harman and Viv Labs, and launched Bixby, a voice assistant based on Vix, at the end of the year; Nokia is also stepping up efforts in the development of its own voice assistant Viki.

Unlike most manufacturers that start with smartphones, Amazon has taken another path, which is to develop voice assistants from smart homes, and achieved great success. In November 2014, Amazon released the Echo smart speaker with Alexa voice assistant built-in. Alexa is an artificial intelligence voice assistant software that is completely controlled by voice commands without the need for a screen. Users can wake it up by saying "Alexa" and use it to realize the functions of playing music, getting weather forecasts, setting alarms, taxiing, reading recipes, shopping, and so on. In August 2015, Alexa was officially opened to third parties. At present, there are more than 10,000 hardware categories installed with Alexa. The product categories include electrical appliances, mobile phones, robots, and in-vehicle infotainment systems. The brands include LG, Huawei, GE, Ford, Volkswagen, Lenovo, and UBTECH.

The success of Amazon Alexa has attracted the entry of other manufacturers. In May 2016, Google launched Google Assistant, a new generation of intelligent assistant that is an upgraded version of Google Now, and Google Assistant-based smart home product Google Home. Microsoft cooperates with Harman Kardon to integrate the Cortana smart assistant into smart speakers, which are expected to be available in 2017. In China, JD.com and HKUST Xunfei has jointly released Dingdong Smart Speaker, while Baidu has released Duer.

Media: Personalized Recommendations and Writing Bots Are the Highlights

Personalized recommendations, with rapid development in recent years, have changed the traditional reading modes. Products such as Toutiao, Tiantian Express, Yidian Zixun, and SmartNews have been on the rise. Among them, the valuation of Toutiao in 2016 rose to 10 billion US dollars.

Robots are more and more widely used in news reporting. It is especially suitable for rapid news writing in programmatic and templated fields, such as finance and sports reports. Wordsmith is a very popular automatic writing software. It is good at analyzing and processing massive amounts of data, and it writes very fast. In the next second of the release of a company's financial report, it can automatically generate a news article with 300–500 words. The Associated Press adopted the Wordsmith robot for financial reporting as early as 2014. Before using, the Associated Press would publish about 300 such news articles every quarter, and now it produces up to 4,300 articles. Organizations such as Yahoo, *Forbes*, and *The New York Times* are also scrambling to apply Wordsmith, and even extending its scope of application to education, public safety, and other fields. In addition to Wordsmith, Quill developed by Narrative Science is also a competitive language processing platform.

The application of robots by Chinese news media is also in full swing. In September 2015, Tencent launched Dreamwriter, a writing robot that would write more than 3,000 news reports on events at the 2016 Rio Olympics. Xinhua News Agency also launched a robot writing system named "Fast Pen Xiaoxin" in November 2015, serving in the Department of Sports, the Department of Economic Information, and the *China Securities Journal*.

Autonomous Driving: Technology Companies and Automobile Manufacturers Are Jumping on the Bandwagon

Autonomous driving is one of the areas with the largest market potential in the artificial intelligence industry. Google started early: in 2009, an autonomous driving project was secretly launched in the Google X laboratory. In the past eight years, Google has tested more than 2 million miles on public roads with driverless cars. According to data from the California Department of Motor Vehicles, Google drove a total of 636,000 miles in its self-driving car trials in 2016, an increase of 50% from that in

2015. The number of emergency disengagements of the driverless mode per 1,000 miles has been reduced from 0.8 in 2015 to 0.2 at present. In short, Google's autonomous driving technology is becoming more mature and more reliable. In all road tests conducted in 2016, Google registered a total of 124 emergency disengagements. Most of them were due to failures of the driving software, while other problems included abnormal behavior of persons on the road, unnecessary manipulative actions of self-driving cars, deviations in the recognition of surrounding environment and objects, and the like.

In order to accelerate the pace of commercialization, Google spun off its self-driving car business from Google X laboratory in December 2016 to establish Waymo, an independent entity, as Alphabet's 12th business unit. Waymo will become a technology solution provider, no longer developing self-driving car hardware. It mainly focuses on autonomous driving systems, and will license the technology to traditional auto manufacturers in the future. At the beginning of 2017, Waymo announced that it had achieved significant progress in the field of cutting-edge technologies in radar sensors, which is bound to reduce production costs by 90%. This translates into a 45% reduction in the costs of vehicles.

Apart from Google, technology companies such as Apple, Tesla, Baidu, and Uber are also developing autonomous driving technologies. Similar to Google, Apple made adjustments to its autonomous driving project in 2016 to focus on research and development of autonomous driving systems. Tesla released the Autopilot 2.0 system enabling fully automated driving in October 2016. At the beginning of 2017, Baidu released Baidu iV and RoadHackers open platforms for autonomous driving. Uber plans to apply self-driving technology to the taxi industry. In September 2016, it launched a small fleet of self-driving cars in Pittsburgh, and then launched a self-driving car service in San Francisco (which has been moved to Arizona). In 2016, Uber also secured a partnership with Volvo to acquire Otto, a self-driving truck startup, for USD 680 million.

Traditional car manufacturers such as Ford, BMW, Toyota, Audi, Volvo, and Daimler and chip manufacturers such as Nvidia and Intel have entered the autonomous driving industry one after another, pushing autonomous vehicles to hit the road officially by 2021. As of February 2017, the California Department of Motor Vehicles had issued 22 test permits for autonomous driving. Automakers have stepped up investment into and acquisition of artificial intelligence companies. In October

2016, General Motors spent USD 1 billion to acquire Cruise Automation, a startup with autonomous driving technology. In February 2017, Ford injected USD 1 billion into artificial intelligence technology startup Argo AI to help it develop artificial intelligence software for autonomous driving. This has been the largest single investment in the field of autonomous driving by the Detroit-based traditional auto industry.

The development of autonomous driving technology is in full swing, but at the same time faces many regulatory and legal obstacles. In May 2016, a Tesla owner died in a traffic accident while the intelligent driving system Autopilot was turned on, resulting in many controversies over the question of who should be responsible. This requires government departments to introduce relevant policies to safeguard the long-term development of autonomous driving quickly.

Artificial Intelligence Would Have a Structural Impact on Employment

The development and progress of technology will inevitably improve social efficiency and liberate manpower. The first industrial revolution caused a "machine problem" as a large number of workers were replaced by machines. The development of artificial intelligence will also result in huge changes in the employment structure. Those repetitive jobs involving a single specific field and those with thinking patterns that can be reasonably calculated will be largely replaced. Such professionals as translators, journalists, assistants, security guards, drivers, sales representatives, customer service representatives, dealers, accountants, and nannies will be greatly cut back in the next ten years. At the same time, the development of artificial intelligence will create many new jobs, such as data scientists, automation experts, and robot monitoring professionals, and high-end demand will increase significantly. Changes in the employment structure require that education, social security, and other fields accelerate reforms and respond beforehand.

Is Artificial Intelligence Going to Pose a Threat to the Existence of Human Beings?

Many people worry that artificial intelligence will outrun humans and threaten our survival. Even physicist Stephen Hawking, Microsoft co-founder Bill Gates, Tesla CEO Elon Musk and others have expressed similar concerns.

While it is true that the development of artificial intelligence has made tremendous progress enabling computers to fulfill some specific tasks smoothly, we are still at the initial stage of weak artificial intelligence, and relevant business models are still undergoing early-stage practice and exploration. The common sense in the eyes of ordinary human beings remains an extremely difficult task for computers lacking general intelligence. For a long time to come, artificial intelligence is nothing more than a tool for humans, playing the roles of collaborators, boosters, and accelerators in social and economic life.

Of course, changes in employment structure, ethics, and applicability of the legal system arising from the development of artificial intelligence would require active responses from us.

The Blockchain: Building Trust to Facilitate the Global Flow of Value

The blockchain technology originated from the foundational paper "Bitcoin: A Peer-to-Peer Electronic Cash System" published in 2008 by a scholar who calls himself Satoshi Nakamoto. Blockchain endows traditional distributed systems with a new, more extensive collaboration model, and solves the problem of data consistency in peer-to-peer networks. Unlike traditional trust mechanisms based on a single credit endorsement entity, blockchain technology creates a new type of trust mechanism with consensus-based algorithms. Due to the objectivity of the algorithm, even if there are malicious nodes in the network, it can still guarantee that a consensus is reached, achieving the correct processing of the business. This is the significant value brought about by the blockchain technology, which could benefit multiple sectors.

Various Countries in the World Are Putting a Strong Emphasis on the Development of Blockchain

As the basic technology of Bitcoin, the road traveled by blockchain is full of twists and turns. Initially, the regulatory bodies of various countries had varying opinions on the supervision and efficiency of Bitcoin. It was not until the last two years that a universal understanding of the huge application potential of blockchain technology in the future provision of public services, reform of the economic system, and optimization of social life mechanisms. With the continuous improvement of the recognition of blockchain by various governments, relevant government departments in various countries have been paying close attention to and promoting the development of blockchain from the perspective of national strategies, and striving to take up a leading position in the future development of blockchain technology.

With a view on international organizations, the United Nations Research Institute for Social Development (UNRISD) released a report titled *How Can Cryptocurrency and Blockchain Technology Play a Role in Building Social and Solidarity Finance?* in early 2016, which proposed the idea of using the blockchain technology to build a more stable financial system, and believed that the blockchain technology would have great potentials for application and development in the fields of improving international exchange, international settlement, and international economic cooperation; the International Monetary Fund has also issued a report titled *Discussion on Cryptocurrencies* in response to the digital currency issues that various countries are concerned about. The report provides a detailed analysis and elaboration of the future development of cryptocurrency based on blockchain technology.

With a view on the Americas, multiple regulatory agencies have indicated their support for the development of blockchain technology in their respective regulatory fields. For example, the US Department of Justice held a digital currency summit on November 10, 2015, calling on the government and the industry to strengthen communication between them. The US Stock Exchange has approved the trading of stocks of listed companies on the blockchain. The US Commodity Futures Trading Commission is further strengthening supervision while paying attention to the development of blockchain technology. At present, the Commission has been supervising Bitcoin as a commodity. The US Department of Homeland Security has also begun to dedicate efforts to study the application of blockchain in homeland security analysis and identity management.

So far as Europe is concerned, the British government released a study report on distributed ledger technology in early 2016. It was the first country to conduct a comprehensive analysis of the future development and application of blockchain technology and offer suggestions. The report is by far the most thorough study report from the highest perspective, providing a useful reference for the formulation of policies and the research in the field of blockchain in other countries. At the end of 2015, the Russian Institute of Internet Development submitted a report to President Putin containing a roadmap for the development of blockchain technology, which plans the future legal framework for the development of the technology. At the end of December 2015, Tunisia announced that it had begun to explore the issuance of its currency with encryption technology to enhance its financial services capabilities. Lithuania hosted the largest blockchain conference in the Baltic region in April 2016, which focused on digital currency solutions and distributed ledger agreements, striving to build Lithuania into a global FinTech center. Recently, the European Central Bank has also been exploring how to apply blockchain technology to securities and payment settlement systems in the region.

In the Asia-Pacific region, the Central Bank of Australia has expressed its support for banks to explore the distributed ledger technology actively. It has also proposed to issue the Australian dollar as a fully digital currency to tap into the advantages of blockchain technology in reforming traditional financial services. On October 16, 2015, the Ministry of Economy, Trade and Industry of Japan held a financial technology conference, which specifically studied and discussed the future development and impact of blockchain technology. On November 13, 2015, the Prime Minister of Singapore called on banks and regulators of the country to pay close attention to the development of the latest technologies such as blockchain, and continuously update their own technologies, create new business models, and improve service standards. On February 3, 2016, the Bank of Korea released a study report titled "Status and Implications of the Distributed Ledger Technology and Digital Currency" to actively study and discuss these technologies.

In China, the People's Bank of China and the Ministry of Industry and Information Technology are also actively discussing the promotion of the development of blockchain technology and its applications to facilitate the realization of its value and prevent risks beforehand.

Emergence of Typical Industry Applications

Blockchain has a wide range of applications in a variety of fields. The focuses of current applications include digital currency, cross-border payment, issuance of securities, digital assets, supply chain finance, mutual insurance, billing services, copyright protection, and logistics tracking. The following content highlights the progress in cross-border payment, issuance of securities, and logistics tracking.

Cross-Border Payment: Ripple

Ripple, founded in the USA, is a fintech company that uses its blockchain-like technology to develop cross-border settlement. It has built a distributed payment network without a central node, with a view to offering a cross-border remittance platform that could replace the Society for Worldwide Interbank Financial Telecommunications (SWIFT) network, creating a globally unified network financial transmission protocol.

Traditional cross-border payments had to go through a number of institutions, including the bank of deposit, the central bank, the overseas bank, the agency bank, and the clearing bank. Each institution has its own accounting system; hence, the processing is slow and the efficiency of execution is low. With the blockchain technology put into application, those operating costs and expenses incurred in intermediate processes could be cut down while lengthy, complicated procedures and errors in manual reviews could be minimized.

Ripple's interledger protocol allows participants to see the same ledger. Through the company's network, banker customers could realize real-time peer-to-peer cross-border remittance without the need for management by a central organization, which supports the different currencies of various countries. At present, banks in 17 countries have joined the cooperation and participated in solutions that Ripple has created for financial institutions.

Issuance of Securities: Nasdaq Linq

In October 2015, the Nasdaq Stock Exchange of the USA launched a new blockchain platform named Nasdaq Linq, giving those who issue shares through this platform digital ownership. On December 31, 2015, Linq issued its first private equity. Nasdaq said that Chain was the first company to use Linq to complete and record private equity transactions.

In traditional securities trading, after the owner of securities sends a trading instruction, the owner needs to coordinate with the securities broker, the asset custodian, the central bank, and the central registration agency to complete the transaction. Generally speaking, it takes "T+3" days (three days between buying and selling) from the time when the security owner issues a trading order to when the transaction is eventually confirmed at the registration authority. Using the blockchain technology, buyers and sellers could achieve automatic matching, automatic clearing, and automatic settlement directly through smart contracts, which is bound to save a lot on transaction fees and make the transaction process more transparent and more efficient.

Logistics Tracking: Everledger

In December 2015, Everledger became the first blockchain startup to receive the "Meffy Award" for fintech by the Mobile Ecosystem Forum (MEF). Everledger's main business involves the uploading of the characteristics, history, and owner identity information of important assets, such as diamonds, to the blockchain, forming a permanent blockchain record to guarantee the source and authenticity of goods. Everledger's blockchain-based diamond information ledger uses the BigchainDB blockchain database of Ascribe as the extensive data technology support for it. To date, Everledger has recorded more than 1 million diamonds on the blockchain to prevent the appearance of counterfeit diamonds.

Security Hazards of Blockchain

Certain people regard security as the most prominent advantage of blockchain. Bitcoin is recognized as the most successful global application based on blockchain, but security incidents involving Bitcoin occur from time to time. Such events as the theft of Mt. Gox, the world's largest Bitcoin exchange in June 2011 and the hacking of the Bitfinex Exchange in August 2016 reveal that Bitcoin, though safer and more reliable than existing systems, is far from ideal. In addition, the world's largest crowd-funding project "The DAO" based on Ethereum was hacked in July 2016, resulting in the theft of USD 60 million worth of ETH, which could only be solved by a hard fork. On February 25, 2017, the SHA-1 cryptographic computer security algorithm was cracked as Google released a practical case of breaking it. How far is blockchain using the SHA-2 cryptographic algorithm from becoming "insecure?"

PART III

Industries: Unleashing Digital Dividends to Promote Transformation and Upgrading

CHAPTER 6

Vigorously Promoting Digital Transformation in Manufacturing

The manufacturing industry is the framework and pillar of the real economy. It is also the main battlefield for revitalizing the real economy. With the advancement of "Internet Plus," the in-depth integration of digital technologies into manufacturing has become an unstoppable trend. Vigorously promoting the digital transformation of the manufacturing industry is helpful to economic transformation and upgrading, and helps to foster new drivers for economic growth.

The Manufacturing Industry Is the Main Battlefield of the Digital Economy

The manufacturing industry as the mainstay of the national economy is the main battlefield for the implementation of the "Internet Plus" action plan and the development of the digital economy. Its status as the main battlefield is determined by its strategic role in the national economy, the new round of competition for dominance in manufacturing, the characteristics and trends of the integration of the Internet into manufacturing, and the development strategy of the state.

M. Huateng et al., *The Chinese Digital Economy*,
https://doi.org/10.1007/978-981-33-6005-1_6

The Manufacturing Industry Is the Mainstay of China's National Economy

The manufacturing industry as the mainstay of the national economy is the basis upon which a country is established, the tool for national rejuvenation, and the foundation for a powerful nation. It is also a key high ground for empowering innovation and seizing the future, and it decides the quality and efficiency of the real economy. Only by making "made in China" a stronger brand could we revitalize the real economy.

China Has a Big Manufacturing Industry Which Ranks the First in the World

With 40 years of accumulation and development since the reform and opening-up, the comprehensive strength and international competitiveness of China's manufacturing industry have increased significantly. The added value of China's manufacturing industry amounted to RMB 24.8 trillion in 2016, accounting for 33.3% of the GDP.[1] In an international context, China's manufacturing output accounts for more than 20% of that of the whole world, and China has maintained its status as the country with the largest manufacturing industry in the world for seven consecutive years. China ranks the first in the world in seven out of the all 22 major categories of manufacturing based on standard international classification. China ranks the first in the world in more than 220 out of more than 500 kinds of industrial products. With its exported finished industrial products accounting for about 1/7 of the total in the world, China is the world's largest exporter of such products.[2]

The Manufacturing Industry Has Created More Jobs Than Any Other Industry

The rapid development of the manufacturing industry has created a lot of jobs, making it the industry with the largest number of people employed in China. At the end of 2015, the manufacturing industry employed

[1] National Bureau of Statistics, *Statistical Communiqué of the People's Republic of China on the 2016 National Economic and Social Development*.

[2] Miao Wei, "Fully Implementing *Made in China 2025* and Focusing on Revitalizing the Real Economy", *Study Times*, March 2017.

50.687 million workers in China's urban areas, which accounted for 28% of the total number employed in urban areas, ranking first among all industries.[3] The industry has a strong impact on promoting employment as its development could serve as a strong driver for employment in various industries, such as transportation, wholesale, retail, accommodation, and catering.

The Manufacturing Industry Is the Principal Source of Wealth Creation in Society

Manufacturing has become an important support for national security and national defense capabilities, and the base for people's wellbeing and harmony and stability in the society. It is also a major driver for achieving the simultaneous development of industrialization, informatization, urbanization, and agricultural modernization of China, with its significant contributions to China's economic and social development.

Developed Countries Are Actively Seizing High Grounds in a New Round of Competition in Manufacturing

After the global financial crisis, the manufacturing industries around the world are at a critical point of reshaping development concepts, readjusting unbalanced structures, and re-establishing competitive edges. Thanks to breakthroughs made in and the spread of new-generation information technology, flexible manufacturing, networked manufacturing, green manufacturing, smart manufacturing, service-oriented manufacturing and the like are becoming important directions for the transformation of the modes of production. Thus, extensive discussions and deep thoughts have been triggered among the international community on a series of development concepts and models, such as the third industrial revolution, energy Internet, industrial Internet, and digital manufacturing.

Developed countries are actively implementing their "reindustrialization" and "return of manufacturing" strategies in response to the challenges brought about by a new round of technological revolution

[3] *2016 China Statistical Yearbook.*

and industrial transformation. The drafting and enactment of a series of strategic plans, such as the Advanced Manufacturing Partnership of the USA, Industry 4.0 of Germany, and the New Industrial France, are fundamentally oriented at establishing new competitive edges in manufacturing against other countries in the context of informatization. This not only shows a thorough rethinking of traditional development concepts of the manufacturing industry by developed countries but also reflects their strategic intent and determination to seize high grounds in a new round of international competitions in manufacturing and readjust the unbalanced industrial structure.

There Is Huge Value in the Integration of the Internet into Manufacturing

China is a manufacturing powerhouse with the largest manufacturing industry and the most sophisticated industrial system. China is also a major power in terms of the Internet with a large Internet industry featuring a large number of enterprises and application terminals. In terms of the overall strength of the Internet industry, China is second only to the USA. The rapid expansion of the Internet economy is demonstrating its increasing prominence in stimulating economic growth. The penetration and application of the Internet in the consumer market have spurred a series of new technologies, products, business formats and models, and inspired the unlimited potentials in innovation and vitality in the innovation of the whole society. In general, however, the integration of the Internet into the manufacturing industry is still at an early stage, with great potentials in the industrial Internet which serves the transformation and development of manufacturing enterprises. Due to the late start and weak foundation of informatization in China's manufacturing enterprises, there is a lack of in-depth application of the Internet in the manufacturing processes that create value. As a result, there is an urgent need to quicken the pace of putting the Internet into application in the field of manufacturing.

The integration of the Internet into the manufacturing industry will give better play to the dual advantages of China as a manufacturing powerhouse and a power in the Internet, resulting in addition, aggregation, and multiplication effects. Addition is the buildup of industrial competitive edges, aggregation is the qualitative change catalyzed by the fusion of competitive edges built up while multiplication is the amplified new impetus for economic development generated by such qualitative change, which is a key source of new drivers for China's economic development.

As compared to other fields of "Internet Plus," "Internet Plus" manufacturing has three unique characteristics:

First, the process of integrating the Internet into manufacturing is not just a one of value transfer, but also one of value innovation.

Second, the integration of the Internet into manufacturing has not only made transactions in the manufacturing industry more efficient but also improved the efficiency of production.

Third, the integration of the Internet into manufacturing is a comprehensive integration involving development concepts, technologies and products, production systems, and business models.

Manufacturing is a segment featuring value innovation. Such characteristics of the integration of the Internet into manufacturing are the reason that promoting digital transformation in the manufacturing industry has great value.

Accelerating the Promotion of Digital Transformation in the Manufacturing Industry Is a Requirement of National Strategies

China attaches great importance to the transformation and upgrading of its manufacturing industry. Since 2015, it has successively issued important documents to accelerate the promotion of digital transformation in the manufacturing industry, including *Made in China 2025*, *Robotics Industry Development Plan (2016–2020)*, *Guidelines for Deepening Integrated Development of the Manufacturing Industry and the Internet*, *Plan for Integrated Development of Informatization and Industrialization (2016–2020)*, and *Plan for the Development of Smart Manufacturing (2016–2020)*.

At the Symposium on Cybersecurity and IT Application held on April 19, 2016, General Secretary Xi Jinping emphasized, "It means making rigorous efforts to integrate the Internet more deeply into the real economy, using information flows to facilitate the flow of technology, capital, talent, and materials, and improve resource allocation and increase total factor productivity, so as to develop innovatively, transform the economic growth model, and restructure the economy."[4]

Guided by such policies, the digital transformation of the manufacturing industry will be further enhanced in the future, and the industry will become the main battlefield for the implementation of the "Internet Plus" action plan and the development of the digital economy.

The Internet Facilitates the Digital Transformation of the Manufacturing Industry

A key feature of the new round of industrial transformation in the world is the continuous innovation of a new generation of information technology represented by the Internet and its integration with traditional industries. After a transformation from partial penetration to full integration, from quantitative accumulation to qualitative change, and from production transformation to organizational innovation, such a process is promoting the integration of digital technologies, the Internet and artificial intelligence in R&D, products, equipment, production, management, and services, and accelerating the reconstruction of a new system for the development of manufacturing.

The Internet Is Increasingly Becoming a New Driver for the Transformation and Upgrading of the Manufacturing Industry

Such characteristics as openness, sharing, collaboration, and decentralization of the Internet are driving profound changes in entities, processes, and models of innovation in the manufacturing industry.

First, the application of new technologies, such as mobile Internet, industrial Internet of Things, open-source software and hardware, and 3D printing, has been pushing innovative organizations to become smaller and decentralized "makers." The emergence of various innovative and entrepreneurial platforms for large enterprises and small- and medium-sized enterprises is nurturing an industrial ecosystem that supports mass innovation.

[4] Speech at a Symposium on Cybersecurity and IT Application, Xinhuanet, April 16, 2016.

Second, the center of the way innovation resources are allocated and the process they are organized is shifting from producers to consumers. Building an innovation system that explores deeply, senses in real time, responds quickly, and satisfies customer requirements in a timely manner is increasingly becoming a new capability of enterprises.

Third, the interweaving and dynamic integration of technological innovation, business format innovation, and business model innovation are causing new innovation models such as collaborative innovation, iterative innovation, crowd innovation, crowdsourcing, crowdfunding, and online-to-offline (O2O) to mushroom.

The optimized allocation of innovation resources by the Internet has been constantly stimulating the vitality of innovation in the whole society, thus becoming a new driver for the transformation and upgrading of the manufacturing industry.

The Internet Opens New Space for the Development of the Manufacturing Industry

The integration of new-generation information technologies, such as the Internet, into traditional industries further improves the efficiency of the allocation of factors of production, including labor, capital, land, technology, and entrepreneurship, and enhances the capacity and standard of industrial supply. These are bound to continuously inject new vitality and new impetus into economic growth and open new space for industrial development.

The first aspect of the new space would be for economic growth. The accelerated integrated innovation of a new generation of sensing, transmission, storage, and computing technologies has greatly stimulated the vitality of technological innovation in ubiquitous access, mass storage, high-speed Internet, intelligent processing, data mining and the like. The cross-industry integrated innovation in such fields as smart manufacturing, biomedicine, new energy, and new materials is on the rise, and new economic growth drivers are constantly emerging.

The second aspect of the new space would be for industrial investment. Industrial cloud, industrial big data, industrial core software and hardware, cyber physical systems, Internet of Things, intelligent robots and the like are becoming key facilities and equipment to support the development of the manufacturing industry. As hot spots of industrial investment at present and in the future, they will further drive the construction of information infrastructure that is high-speed, mobile, secure, and ubiquitous, and the intelligent transformation of important infrastructure in such fields as energy and transportation.

The third aspect of the new space would be for information consumption. The popularization of the Internet is driving the formation of new consumption habits, patterns, and processes. New products, such as smart wearables, smart homes, smart cars, and service robots, are constantly emerging and continually stimulating consumer demands for new information products and services. The Internet has continuously spurred a large number of emerging growth drivers in terms of industry, investment, and demand, therefore opening new space for the development of the manufacturing industry.

The Internet Spurs New Models and Business Formats in the Manufacturing Industry

The in-depth integration of the Internet into the manufacturing industry can effectively stimulate the vitality of innovation, the potential for development, and the impetus for transformation of manufacturing enterprises. It is bound to engender many new models, business formats, and products.

The first would be networked collaborative manufacturing. This is not entirely a new concept, as it has been adopted by aviation, automotive and other industries for decades. The development of a new generation of information and communication technology has given new meaning to networked collaborative manufacturing. It now refers to enterprises using the Internet or industrial cloud platforms to develop new models, such as collaborative R&D between enterprises, crowdsourcing design, and supply chain collaboration. Thus, they could effectively reduce the costs of obtaining resources, greatly extend the scope of utilization of resources, break down boundaries, accelerate the transformation from fighting alone to industry coordination, and promote the improvement of the industry's overall competitiveness.

The second would be customization. Customization is an important mark of the transition from a traditional industry to the smart manufacturing stage. It means using Internet platforms and smart factory establishments to directly convert user needs into production orders, and conduct user-centered customization and on-demand production. This could effectively meet the demand of the market for diversity, solve the long-standing problems related to inventory and production capacity in the manufacturing industry, and strike a dynamic balance between production and sales.

The third would be service-oriented manufacturing. China's manufacturing industry has long been chiefly characterized by processing and manufacturing, which are at the medium- to low-end of the value chain. Accelerating the extension sideways from the traditional manufacturing link alone and increasing the added value of products are the key to the development of China's industry towards the high end. Promoting the transformation of the manufacturing industry from production-oriented manufacturing to service-oriented manufacturing is the key to facilitating the transformation and upgrading of the manufacturing industry.

Customization and service-oriented transformation have become new trends in the transformation of modes of production. Traditional products are going to be replaced by smart ones with sensing, storage, and communication functions. Consumers are becoming prosumers deeply involved in the whole manufacturing process as the traditional centralized mass production mode is accelerating its transformation towards the distributed and customized production mode. Product lifecycle management, integrated general contracting, precise supply chain management, Internet finance, online retailing and the like are accelerating the reconstruction of a new system of industrial value chain.

The Internet Reshapes New Advantages in International Competition

The accelerated integration of the Internet into the manufacturing sector has triggered continuous changes in infrastructure, modes of production, and the competitive landscape.

First, cloud computing and the Internet are gradually becoming the new infrastructure for the development of the manufacturing industry. The integrated utilization of industrial big data and industrial applications (apps) has been fueling the pressing demand for industrial clouds and steadily pushing industrial networks towards broadband, IP, and wireless development. Networked smart machinery has become a key element of the new manufacturing system.

Second, the fundamental role of software in supporting and defining manufacturing is being continuously highlighted. Industrial software in such fields as computer-aided design and simulation, manufacturing execution systems, and product lifecycle management are deconstructing and reshaping industrial activities. Those being redefined include industrial products, business processes, modes of production, new capabilities, business models, and the industrial ecosystem.

Third, building a smart manufacturing industry ecosystem is the focus of industrial competition in various countries. New technologies, such as the Internet, facilitate the ubiquitous connectivity of people, machines, products and other elements in the manufacturing process, thus forming a community of interests featuring collaborative research, standardized cooperation, capability adaptation, and joint rulemaking involving multiple parties, including manufacturers, device producers, network service providers, software companies, chipmakers, solution providers. The role of the Industrial Internet Consortium and Platform Industry 4.0 as initiators, promoters, and builders of the industrial ecosystem will be further consolidated and strengthened as new rules for competition are beginning to take shape.

Global Industrial Giants Are Leading the Development Towards Digitalization

Global manufacturing leaders are accelerating their development towards digitalization. Multinational companies, such as GE and Siemens, are rushing to acquire a stake in industrial big data platforms and the industrial ecosystem.

GE: Actively taking the lead in digital transformation

GE: The first to propose industrial Internet

GE was the first to propose the concept of "industrial Internet" eight months after Barack Obama, then president of the USA, announced the implementation of the "reindustrialization" strategy in February 2012. Following that, GE quickly launched nine industrial Internet projects in the fields of aviation, oil and gas, transportation, medicine, energy, and other industries.

The industrial Internet is an open, global network capable of systematically connecting people, big data, and sensors to break down the boundaries between intelligent beings and machines so as to realize the network-based, AI-oriented, and service-based transformation of industrial production.

In March 2014, GE founded the Industrial Internet Consortium together with four other industry giants, namely, AT&T, Cisco, IBM, and Intel, to redefine the future of the manufacturing industry. The consortium aims to break down industrial and regional technical barriers and accelerate the full fusion of the physical real world and the virtual digital world. It has now become one of the most influential international organizations for industrial Internet with more than 260 member organizations, including almost all leading enterprises in the field of industrial Internet of Things, such as Microsoft, Hewlett Packard, Accenture, Huawei, Bosch, EMC, SAP, and Siemens.

In addition, there has been official benchmarking between the concepts of "industrial Internet" and "Industry 4.0" since the Industrial Internet Consortium started to cooperate with Platform Industry 4.0 in 2016. As a broader concept, the industrial Internet encompasses Industry 4.0.

Predix: Building an Operating System in the Industrial Sector

GE launched Predix, an industrial big data analysis platform, in 2013 and opened it to global manufacturers in 2015. In October 2015, GE put all internal digital functions into "GE Digital" together, integrating software and analytical technology into the company's industrial products. It has set a goal to develop itself into "one of the world's top 10 software companies by 2020."

As an important platform connecting machines, data and people, Predix sorts out various types of data according to a unified standard, providing a platform that is accessible and capable of conducting analysis for cloud computing and big data technologies anytime. Engineers could develop programs and applications on Predix according to the needs of their respective enterprises. Various elements, including distributed computing, big data analysis, asset management, machine-to-machine (M2M) communications, and mobility, could be added on to those programs and applications.

Predix is sometimes placed in the same category as iOS (a mobile operating system developed by Apple) and Android operating systems. With that, GE hopes to establish an industrial ecosystem for the industrial Internet, and build an app store—the GE Store for industrial applications—on top of it.

Industrial Leaders Are Rushing to Seize High Grounds in Cloud Platforms

Apart from US-based GE, Germany-based Siemens launched MindSphere and China-based Haier launched COSMOPlat, both of which are industrial cloud platforms. MindSphere laid the foundation for the Plant Data Services of Siemens. Haier is building COSMOPlat, China's first and also the largest industrial Internet platform established with independent R&D and innovation. COSMOPlat has more characteristics of a platform. In addition to serving Haier's connected factories, it has started to provide society-oriented services to manufacturers, enabling users to participate in the whole process of mass customization. It provides eight industrial ecosystem services, including mass customization solutions, big data services, networked collaborative manufacturing, intelligent knowledge service, testing, and certification, to the whole society.

Successful Cases of "Internet Plus" Manufacturing Are Springing Up in China

The manufacturing industry is the main battlefield for developing the digital economy, and it is also the focus and a challenging part of "Internet Plus." A group of innovative industrial enterprises represented by Redcollar, Baosteel, CCAG, and Haier have made remarkable achievements in their active exploration for the way to digital transformation.

Apparel: Redcollar Offers "Internet Plus" Mass Customization

Established in 1995, Qingdao Redcollar Clothing Co., Ltd. is a large private apparel enterprise mainly producing and selling a series of high-end apparel and accessory products. Since 2003, Redcollar has invested

RMB 260 million into a suit production factory with more than 3,000 workers serving as a laboratory. Supported by such technologies as big data, Internet, and Internet of Things, the laboratory is dedicated to research and experiment on solutions for the whole process of mass apparel customization and production. With the flow of order information as the main clue, a massive template database and a management parameter system as the carriers, and the automation of the production process as the support, a unique "Redcollar model" has been shaped up, becoming a benchmark enterprise in China's "Internet Plus" industry.

The successful practices of Redcollar in the field of apparel customization have fundamentally changed the traditional operating model and shaped up a new business format for the development of industrial enterprises. It is a new paradigm for the operations of enterprises in which the Internet is to get deeply integrated into the industry. Main practices are as follows:

Establishing a C2M Factory Direct Selling Platform

Traditional apparel enterprises adopt a sales model of "manufacturer-wholesaler-retailer-consumer." On the one hand, the costs at various links have raised the final price of the product; on the other hand, it is difficult for producers to acquire timely information about the diverse consumer demands. Redcollar eliminates intermediate links by using Internet technologies, thus achieving a direct connection between consumers and producers, which constitutes a customer to manufactory (C2M) model. Consumers could log into the C2M platform via terminals, such as computers and mobile phones, and submit their orders online. The enterprise could produce according to the orders, which greatly reduces the overstocking of capital and goods and realizes "on-demand production with zero inventory." Consumers could get maximized discounts as they no longer need to undertake distribution costs. For the enterprises, the costs of customized production are only 10% higher than that of mass production, but the revenues are more than doubled.

Producing Personalized Products with the Means and Efficiency of Industrial Production

Personalization and efficiency are inherently contradictory to each other. Redcollar has, however, greatly improved the efficiency of mass customization through re-engineering the production process by means of information technology. Consumers could choose the fabrics, styles, production processes, and the like of their apparel online. The enterprise receives the orders in real time, and the information contained is automatically converted into production data after data modeling in a self-developed database. The C2M platform then divides the task and distributes it to various stations in the form of instructive push notifications, and the production is to be completed within seven days. In the process of production, each product has a separate electronic tag that accompanies it throughout the entire production process. Each station has a terminal device independently developed by Redcollar, which downloads from the cloud on the Internet and reads the order information on the electronic tag. Such a model not only meets the needs of apparel customization but also achieves industrial mass production.

Data-Driven Smart Production

An important reason for Redcollar's ability to achieve low-cost, high-efficiency customization lies in the support of big data. Redcollar attaches great importance to the integration and development of data from multiple sources. First, it builds up a database to collect available data. After more than a decade of exploration, Redcollar has accumulated data on the customization of more than 2 million customers, including data about templates, styles, processes, and designs. Then, it conducts data modeling. A data model is established on the system with 22 data entries of 18 body parts of each customer collected through the innovative "three points in one line" measurement method. It then conducts computer-aided 3D pattern making, achieving "one template for each person and one style for each garment." Finally, an algorithm is established; with that algorithm, the system would find the best match even for customer requirements not described clearly and calculate the most suitable garment production process.

At present, the customization system of Redcollar consists of over 20 sub-systems, all of which are data-driven. The system automatically schedules orders, cuts cloth, calculates data, and generates templates every day. Information is transmitted and shared in real time with no paperwork in the whole process.

Demand-Centered Restructuring of the Organization

With the central idea of "satisfying consumer requirements," Redcollar breaks down the old structure of departments and bureaucracy and transforms it into platform-based management, thus establishing a management model with node management as the core. The customer service center gathers all customer requirements, issuing point-to-point instructions to relevant posts, and mobilizing all resources to meet the needs. Redcollar has canceled such functional departments as the human resource department and the finance department, leaving only posts with specific responsibilities. The posts can be combined anytime according to customer requirements without the need for bureaucracy or departments to make decisions. As a result, all "barriers" between customer requirements and the company's capacity are completely removed, so that customers are put at the very center and the efficiency of decision-making and production is greatly improved.

Exporting Capabilities: SDE Aids Traditional Enterprises in Their Transformation and Upgrading

Redcollar has coded and programmed its successful experience in the field of apparel customization to form a standardized solution named as "SDE" (source data engineering), a methodology for the transformation and upgrading of traditional industries that can be converted into applications in other industries. At the same time, it provides customized software development, production process re-engineering, management consulting, and other services to enterprises with such needs. The injection of Redcollar's mass customization genes into traditional enterprises could help them achieve transformation and upgrading to varying extents. With varying levels of investment, over three months of upgrading and transformation could increase the efficiency by more than 30% and have the costs reduced by more than 20%, thus achieving the operating capabilities of "zero inventory, high profit, low cost, and high turnover."

In early 2016, Redcollar began to popularize its SDE solutions. Within only seven months, it had signed contracts with 38 enterprises covering such industries as apparel, shoes, and hats, home furnishing, furniture, casting, cosmetics, and electrical appliances.

Value and Benefits

Redcollar got connected to consumers directly through the Internet to realize one-click customization of personalized apparel. It had shortened the production cycle of customized apparel from 20–50 working days to no more than 7 working days and achieved mass production, thus making once-expensive apparel customization service an affordable, mass-marketed consumption for ordinary people. In short, the Redcollar model has realized the personalization of apparel manufacturing, disintermediation of apparel distribution, and zero inventory.

Redcollar itself had also achieved rapid growth. It now has a production capacity of 3,000 sets (or pieces) of customized products per day. In 2015, the business revenues of the apparel segment amounted to RMB 3.7 billion, among which the revenues and net profits from the online customization business grew by more than 130% year on year, with a profit margin of more than 25%.

Steel: Baosteel Builds an Ecosphere in the Whole Steel Industry Chain

Faced up with the tough situation of severe overcapacity and continuation of the trend of meager profit, Baosteel as a leader in the steel industry is exploring the way out. It has formulated three major directions for its transformation "from steel to materials, from manufacturing to services, and from China to the world" to accelerate the implementation of its "one body, two wings" strategy—with the steel industry as the main body while green, high-quality intelligent manufacturing and steel service ecosystem as the two wings. As the core carrier of the steel service ecosystem, "Ouyeel" is seen as a paragon for the Internet-based transformation of steel enterprises. It is leading the acceleration of Baosteel's transition from product competitiveness to industry chain competitiveness and that of its transformation from a manufacturer to a service provider.

Basic Information About Ouyeel

In view of the long-standing problems in the field of steel distribution, such as information asymmetry, high distribution costs, low trading efficiency, poor credit environment for steel trade, overlooking of the vast number of small- and medium-sized end-users, and difficulty in quickly responding to personalized needs, Baosteel had sensed the huge underlying room for improvement and potential value in the steel industry. On February 13, 2015, Baosteel Group and Baosteel Co., Ltd. made a joint investment of RMB 2 billion in the would-be Ouyeel Incorporation. Relying on such new technologies as the Internet, Internet of Things, big data, and mobile Internet, it strove to build an industrial service ecosystem with the industry chain e-commerce platform cluster as the core, featuring joint efforts and win-win collaboration between multiple parties. It aimed to restructure all business links along the production chain of the steel industry and drive the overall transformation and upgrading of the industry.

Main Practices and Characteristics of Ouyeel

Ouyeel has achieved rapid development right from the start by relying on Baosteel's strategic advantages. Such strategic advantages accumulated by Baosteel over years have laid a solid foundation for the development of Ouyeel. First, the advantage of its professional background has facilitated the rapid expansion of business fields. As the most competitive steel conglomerate in China, Baosteel boasts of comprehensive, systematic service capabilities in such aspects as steel production, technological R&D, information service, marketing network, and capital, which provides key support for the business development of Ouyeel in various directions. Second, the advantage of in-depth development in the industry has facilitated the quick aggregation of industry chain resources. Nearly 40 years of accumulation of Baosteel in the industry has enabled Ouyeel to get various parties upstream and downstream, including high-quality suppliers, steel manufacturers, traders, logistics providers, and processors to gather abundant offline resources for platform services quickly integrated into it. Third, the advantage of branding has facilitated a huge amount of financing. Backed by the Baosteel brand, Ouyeel obtained a credit line of RMB 162.7 billion from 15 banks, including China Construction Bank and Industrial and Commercial Bank of China, on

May 7, 2015, thus providing a solid capital reserve for expanding its financial services. Ouyeel strove to establish integrated services for online distribution steel with the industry chain e-commerce platform as the core. Focusing on all links of the whole steel industry chain, Ouyeel has gradually expanded in multiple dimensions across products, regions, and services to build an online service system with the industry chain e-commerce platform as the center, thus getting such functions as information, settlement, logistics and warehousing, processing and delivery, technical services, financial services, and data services integrated.

1. Starting from e-commerce. With the trading of products as the core, Ouyeel has formed a cluster of product trading platforms along the steel industry's production chain, including the bulk trading platform for raw materials and fuel, the trading platform for chemicals, the procurement platform for equipment and spare parts, the trading platform for steel products, and the trading platform for recycled resources. Those platforms are distributed along the lifecycle of products from raw materials to products, from products to use, and from use to recycling (Fig. 6.1).

Data Processing Service Platform

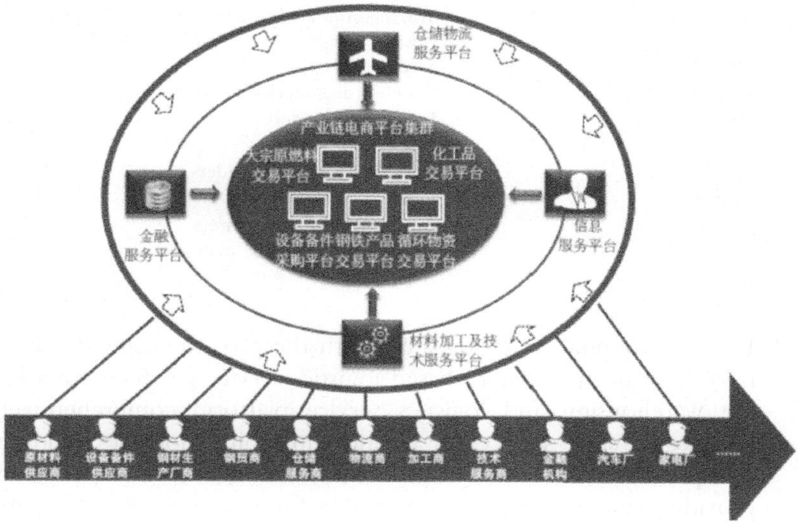

Fig. 6.1 Ouyeel as an ecosphere along the production chain (*Source* The First Electronic Research Institute of Ministry of Industry and Information Technology)

仓储物流服务平台	*Warehousing and logistics service platform*
产业链电商平台集群	Industry chain e-commerce platform cluster
大宗原燃料交易平台	Bulk trading platform for raw materials and fuel
化工品交易平台	Trading platform for chemicals
设备备件采购平台	Procurement platform for equipment and spare parts
钢铁产品交易平台	Trading platform for steel products
循环物资交易平台	Trading platform for recycled resources
金融服务平台	Financial service platform
材料加工及技术服务平台	Material processing and technical service platform
信息服务平台	Information service platform
原材料供应商	Raw material suppliers
设备备件供应商	Equipment and spare parts suppliers
钢材生产厂商	Steel manufacturers

(continued)

(continued)

仓储物流服务平台	*Warehousing and logistics service platform*
钢贸商	Steel traders
仓储服务商	Warehousing service providers
物流商	Logistics providers
加工商	Processors
技术服务商	Technical service providers
金融机构	Financial institutions
汽车厂	Automobile manufacturers
家电厂	Household appliance manufacturers

2. Laying a foundation in logistics. With the goal to create standardized, high-quality, and IT-based logistics service products for steel, the warehousing and logistics service platform comprehensively engages in such services as business matching, logistics bidding, transportation scheduling, payment, and financing supervision, providing one-stop logistics solutions for steel traders, end-users, carriers, warehousing service providers and others.
3. Developing based on finance. With its three financial licenses, namely, payment, mortgage, and factoring, the financial service platform has launched a series of Internet finance products, such as payment and settlement, wealth management, supply chain finance, billing services, and mortgage, providing full support for the closed-loop operation of the business system of Ouyeel.
4. Featuring technologies. On the one hand, the material processing and technical service platform have realized the online trading of such steel processing services as blanking, cutting stock, and press working, the first to do so in China; on the other hand, tapping into Baosteel's technical accumulation over years, it provides customers with comprehensive knowledge of steel and convenient technical solutions for steel to form special services.
5. Expanding in information. By pooling think tanks resources in the whole industry, the information service platform has established a comprehensive service system integrating information products, consulting products, and conference and training products tailored to the metallurgical industry to provide one-stop solutions for personalized information requirements of users.

6. Succeeding in data. With the vast amount of data resources accumulated in the operations of the service system, the data service platform will fully open such application services as data storage, data mining, demand forecasting, precision marketing, price forecasting, and logistics optimization to realize the sharing and exchange of data value.

Ouyeel has built a support network for the whole offline industry chain by following the guiding principles of cooperation and opening up. Though its development is based on Baosteel, Ouyeel does not limit itself to serving Baosteel but strives to become a third-party steel service platform that truly serves the whole industry while adhering to the development concepts of cooperation and opening up. It aims to fully open up to the whole industry chain ranging from business operations to equity investment.

In terms of business operations, Ouyeel attracts upstream and downstream business entities along the industrial chain to settle in by use of multiple modes of cooperation such as hypermarkets, exclusive shops, and e-commerce alliances, thus resulting in a rapid aggregation and integration of high-quality supply-side resources in various business sectors to rapidly expand the influence and prosperity of the platform. In terms of equity cooperation, a number of investing parties, such as steel mills, steel traders, logistics providers, and other strategic investors, are introduced to truly realize joint construction and sharing in the industry. Such measures have not only quickly built a physical support network featuring offline products, warehousing, logistics, processing and the like for the online service system but also boosted the transformation of all parties in the industry, forming a steel service ecosphere featuring the integration of online and offline, the collaboration between upstream and downstream of the industry chain, and hand-in-hand development of large-, medium- and small-sized enterprises, so as to truly realize the joint development of logistics, product flow, information flow, and capital flow.

Successful Development of Ouyeel

In less than two years, Ouyeel has basically completed its preliminary strategic layout. In the first ten months of 2016, Ouyeel traded a total volume of 24.24 million tons, with a maximum daily trading volume of more than 497,000 tons. The amount settled exceeded RMB 84.4 billion, up by 48.3% compared with the whole year of 2015. The amount financed on the financial service platform reached RMB 11.81 billion, an increase of 689% over the whole year of 2015. In June 2016, its logistics services deployed the "Baosaas" warehousing management system in 1,000 warehouses nationwide, marking the preliminary completion of the layout for the offline storage network of Ouyeel and the completion of its logistics neural network.

At the same time, Ouyeel has also brought benefits for the optimization and innovative development of the steel industry chain. By realizing the large-scale exchange of information flow with the e-commerce platform, the information asymmetry in the steel trading link has been broken down, therefore making all products along the industry chain transparent and reducing transaction costs. Through optimizing the layout of warehousing and logistics networks, logistics resources have been matched and integrated efficiently, logistics costs cut down, and transportation made more efficient. Through processing and delivery and professional technical services, the resolution of the problems of inadequate technical capabilities of small- and medium-sized terminal customers and failure to meet innumerable personalized needs has been accelerated. Through the collaboration between the data service platform and financial service platform, responses have been quickly made to the personalized financial needs of various parties along the industrial chain, thus forming a multi-layered financial service structure and reshaping the credit system of the steel industry chain.

Problems and Prospects

At present, various business sectors are still in a relatively fragmented state though Ouyeel has formed a preliminary integrated service system for steel. In the future, how to accelerate the interconnection between various business sectors and realize the collaborative sharing of data and resources will become the key to giving full play to the Ouyeel's ecological advantage.

Besides, Ouyeel is also going to facilitate in-depth cooperation between the upstream and downstream of the industry chain, and reversely drive profound changes to the steel manufacturing and processing links from the user side with the steel distribution problems and the open sharing of industry chain information gradually solved. Responses shall be made dynamically and sharply to diverse personalized requirements of end-users in real-time, realizing innovative development of the whole industry.

Automobile: CCAG Builds a Global Collaborative R&D System with Independent Innovation

With a history of 155 years, China Changan Automobile Group (CCAG) has accumulated its experience in automobile manufacturing for over 34 years. It is now one of the four automobile conglomerates in China, boasting of 12 production bases and 32 whole vehicle and engine factories worldwide. It has set a new record as the first passenger vehicle brand in China has managed to produce and sell more than one million vehicles in a year. Centering on its grand vision of building itself into a first-class automobile enterprise in the world, CCAG has gradually explored and taken a path of progressive development from "absorbing imported technologies" to "a leader in joint development" and then to "a leader in independent development." In such a development process, it has always been adhering to independent innovation while being based on a global vision, powered by processes, and driven by data, regarding the organization as the carrier, and reserving 5% of its annual sales revenue as a guarantee. For eight consecutive years from 2009 to 2015, it has been ranking the first in terms of capabilities for technological research and development in China's automobile industry.

Main Practices

Integrating its superior resources globally based on independence. By combining its technological and talent advantages in various regions, CCAG has built up its global R&D system distributed at "nine places in five countries, each with its own focus": the Turin R&D Center in Italy focusing on styling and design, the Yokohama R&D Center in Japan focusing on automobile interiors, the Nottingham R&D Center in the UK focusing on powertrain design, the Detroit R&D Center in the USA focusing on chassis design, and the five local R&D centers respectively located in Chongqing, Shanghai, Beijing, Harbin and Jiangxi geared to the domestic market. Those R&D centers have achieved the synergy of resources with complementary advantages.

Focusing on processes with strict control over R&D progress. CCAG's practice over years has enabled it to continuously sum up, extract and draw on international successful experience, thus creating a "4 + 1" system of R&D processes that integrates new technology development, platform development, product development, product introduction, and technical documents. Thanks to such a system, the key issues of "what to do" and "how to do" in the R&D process can be addressed; and it is possible to implement comprehensive control over the progress, risks, costs, quality, and benefits of R&D.

Among them, product development is at the core of the R&D processes as a whole covering the lifecycle of the product. CCAG has defined the classification standards, cycles, and stages for product development, setting 14 milestones and their corresponding acceptance conditions. In doing that, it has established a three-level process system of harmonograms, flowcharts, and working documents as important clues for accurately guiding product development (Fig. 6.2).

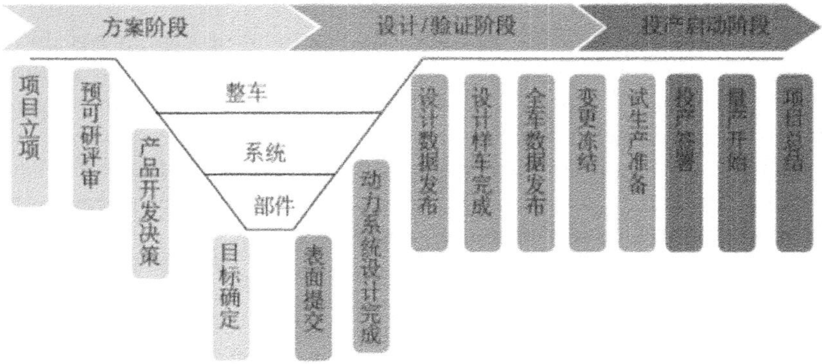

Fig. 6.2 Milestones of the CCAG product development process (*Source* The First Electronic Research Institute of Ministry of Industry and Information Technology)

方案阶段	Planning stage
设计/验证阶段	Design/Verification stage
投产启动阶段	Production initiation stage
项目立项	Project proposal
预可研评审	Review of pre-feasibility study
产品开发决策	Product development decision-making

(continued)

(continued)

整车	Whole vehicle
系统	Systems
部件	Parts
目标确定	Determination of objectives
表面提交	Submission of surface design
动力系统设计完成	Completion of powertrain design
设计数据发布	Release of designed parameters
设计样车完成	Completion of prototype
全车数据发布	Release of all vehicle parameters
变更冻结	Finalizing all changes
试生产准备	Preparation for pilot production
投产签署	Signing production documents
量产开始	Beginning of mass production
项目总结	Summary of the project

Changing the structure to conduct multiple segments of R&D simultaneously. In order to establish an efficient R&D institution oriented to the market and customers and ensure the smooth execution of the R&D process, CCAG has gradually transformed its R&D organizational structure. With the step-by-step evolution from a weak matrix structure to a strong matrix structure, CCAG has formed a "one vertical and two horizontals" organizational structure, with the vertical focusing on the enhancement of professional capabilities and the horizontals focusing on product development and research into generic technologies. By virtue of that, CCAG achieves the simultaneous advancement of multi-project R&D, professional technology research, and generic technology research. At the same time, in order to give full play to the impetus given by a strong matrix, CCAG has established its project director responsibility system and signed assignments and letters of authorization with the project directors to give them the authority concerning such issues as research funding, procurement approval, and performance evaluation, so as to maximize the efficiency of R&D.

Building a platform for conducting fully collaborative online R&D. CCAG has established an online collaborative R&D platform and mechanisms globally distributed to achieve the internal collaboration in various departments of the enterprises and the external collaboration with suppliers in multiple locations around the world based on a single data source (Fig. 6.3).

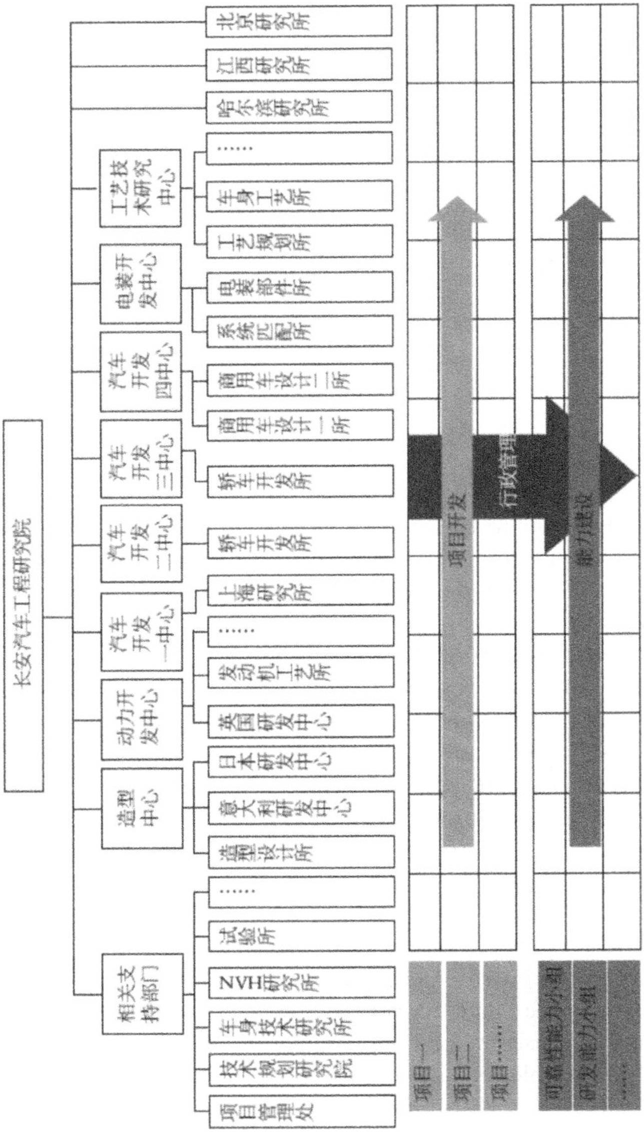

Fig. 6.3 Project management matrix of CCAG (*Source* The First Electronic Research Institute of Ministry of Industry and Information Technology)

长安汽车工程研究院	Changan Automotive Engineering Institute
相关支持部门	Relevant supporting departments
造型中心	Modeling Center
动力开发中心	Powertrain Development Center
汽车开发一中心	Automotive Development Center (I)
汽车开发二中心	Automotive Development Center(II)
汽车开发三中心	Automotive Development Center (III)
汽车开发四中心	Automotive Development Center (IV)
电装开发中心	Electrical Equipment Development Center
工艺技术研究中心	Process Engineering Research Center
项目管理处	Project Management Office
技术规划研究所	Technical Planning Research Institute
NVH研究所	NVH Research Institute
试验所	Testing Laboratory
造型设计所	Modeling Design Institute
意大利研发中心	R&D Center in Italy
日本研发中心	R&D Center in Japan
英国研发中心	R&D Center in the UK
发动机工艺所	Engine Process Engineering Institute
上海研究所	Research Institute in Shanghai
轿车开发所	Sedan Development Institute
商用车设计一所	First Design Institute for Commercial Vehicles
商用车设计二所	Second Design Institute for Commercial Vehicles
系统匹配所	System Matching Institute
电装部件所	Electrical Equipment Parts Institute
工艺规划所	Process Planning Institute
车身工艺所	Bodywork Process Institute
哈尔滨研究所	Research Institute in Harbin
江西研究所	Research Institute in Jiangxi
北京研究所	Research Institute in Beijing
项目一	Project 1
项目一	Project 2
项目……	Project…
可靠性能力小组	Reliability Capability Team
研发能力小组	R&D Capability Team
项目开发	Project development
行政管理	Administration
能力建设	Capability building

1. Building a product data management (PDM) system to realize data-driven R&D. Since CCAG first started to deploy the PDM system early as in 2003, it has gradually established its global distributed

collaborative framework. Within the framework, the master server of the PDM system is set up locally in Chongqing, which stores and manages the accounts and permissions of users in the whole network and controls all engineering data. Slave servers of the PDM system are set up in remote research institutes to store relevant engineering data of the institutes. Securing network connection between various local systems is achieved through using routers, firewall devices, VPNs, or private line networks and by virtue of such means as encryption, authentication, and access control.

After years of practice and upgrading, the R&D management mechanism based on the PDM system has gradually matured, truly contributing to the realization of multi-site, multi-user, and full-process collaborative data-driven R&D. First, the comprehensive application and control of data has been achieved by adopting online R&D standards and norms represented by the Online Research and Development Working Mechanism as guidelines and relying on R&D processes. In the planning stage, the part designers are required to work by using professional 3D design software and save the data in the PDM system from time to time. In the design/verification stage, after the design is completed, it is required that the data be entered into the system to support such work as checking, iteration, and approval by the chief system engineer and other engineers before releasing all parts of the system. At the beginning stage of mass production, it is required that verification data be introduced for verification and confirmation before entering the process for changes to the design. As a result, the generation, uploading, modification, storage, and utilization mechanisms of data are all clearly defined to ensure the uniqueness of the data source and collaboration based on the data source. Second, the extension of data management to multiple parties has been achieved by using user rights as the portal. With the continuous expansion of fields involved in R&D, the data management of CCAG is gradually extended to production bases and partners. For example, in terms of collaborative data management with suppliers, a hierarchical authorization system for suppliers is implemented according to their relationship with CCAG. Among the suppliers, core suppliers have direct access to the PDM system for sharing, general suppliers exchange data through the supplier distribution system, while suppliers outside the system use emails for data transmission, thereby achieving data sharing between internal departments and external organizations and the collaboration in supply chain R&D.

2. Strengthening IT-based assistance to achieve efficient and lean R&D. With a focus on collaborative R&D, CCAG has also comprehensively implemented multi-dimensional IT-aided construction, which effectively solved a series of key bottleneck problems, thus greatly improving R&D abilities.

    First, CCAG uses digital technologies extensively to readily improve its R&D efficiency. In the design and development processes of new products, it adopts digital technology extensively, using more than 1,000 sets of digital software falling into 50 categories. At the same time, it is also engaged in the secondary development of many digital tools and standardizing the design process, so as to better integrate design methods, standards, and norms into the digital tools and accumulate them as corporate knowledge.

    Second, CCAG establishes its high-performance computing system to provide strong computing support. With independent optimization, the total computing capacity of the high-performance computing platform of CCAG has reached over ten trillion times per second, becoming one of the core systems supporting automobile R&D that has been carrying out computing at full load for long. In addition to providing effective support for the rapid extension of computer-aided engineering (CAE) software, it also provides key support for strength analysis, collision analysis, multibody dynamics simulation, analysis of external aerodynamics of the whole vehicle, analysis of external aerodynamics of the engine, air conditioning system analysis and the like.

    Third, CCAG introduces and promotes the lightweight technology to facilitate its R&D visibility. In order to track the progress of R&D and design and identify project risks, CCAG has introduced and promoted the lightweight digital mock-up (DMU) technology to automatically convert the mathematical models of professional 3D design software stored in the PDM system into lightweight data formats (with the file size being only 1/10 of the original). Thus, such technical difficulties as the compatibility of heterogeneous data and matching of whole vehicles and engines under different locomotive coordinate systems have been solved, thus realizing real-time viewing of visual models of vehicles under R&D and ensuring highly compatible collaboration across departments, professions, and regions.

Outcome of Development

Through accumulation and in-depth cooperation with multiple parties over years, CCAG has successfully acquired most of the key technologies in the field of automobile R&D and successfully launched a series of independently developed products, including Star 4500, Benben, Jiexun, Zhixiang, Yuexiang, Raeton, Eado, Honor, Eulove, and Oshan. In terms of new energy vehicles, CCAG has been granted more than 30 patents, with breakthroughs made in such fields as heavy-duty hybrids, plug-in hybrids, and battery-powered electric vehicles. So far as smart vehicles are concerned, it has acquired more than 60 intelligent technologies falling into three categories, such as smart connected devices, smart interaction, and smart driving. In particular, the 2000-km driverless test of CCAG has set the record for the longest unmanned journey among first-time driverless tests performed by whole vehicle enterprises in China.

The enhancement of R&D capabilities directly brings a brand effect. From January to August 2016, CCAG sold a total of 1.901 million vehicles, a year-on-year increase of 5.2%. Within such a figure, 1.088 million Changan brand passenger vehicles were sold with a year-on-year increase of 5.8%, which exceeded one million half a month earlier than the time in 2015; some 784,000 Changan brand passenger vehicles were sold, registering a year-on-year increase of 17.8%, maintaining its leading position in the passenger vehicle industry of China.

Future Prospects

With the rapid penetration of the Internet and the steady progress of informatization, the R&D system of CCAG is bound to expand in-depth in the future. In terms of participants, CCAG would rely on the Internet to attract a vast number of potential users to participate in product design and development, so as to fully unleash the initiative of users, enhance the user experience, and drive product innovation. In terms of coverage, CCAG would gradually build a collaborative R&D platform that covers product lifecycle management (PLM), extending from "PDM-based collaborative R&D" to "PLM-based collaborative R&D" to achieve full integration of R&D and manufacturing.

Household Appliance: Haier Leads a Revolution of the Times with All-Round Internet-Based Transformation

After more than 30 years of innovation and development, Haier has transformed itself from a small collectively-owned factory on the brink of bankruptcy into today's No. 1 white goods brand in the world. Faced with waves of the rapid development of the internet, Haier is actively promoting its internet-based transformation, with comprehensive reforms in such aspects as strategic direction, management model, R&D system, manufacturing system, service system, and entrepreneur incubation system. It aims to transform from a traditional manufacturer of household appliances to a platform that incubates makers for the whole society, building new production relations among enterprises, employees, users, and partners in the internet era and leading the transformation of the manufacturing industry.

New Requirements of the Times: Fully Implementing the Networking Strategy

Haier Group is committed to providing the best user experience. Since its establishment in 1984, it has been through four stages of development with different strategies, namely, brand building, diversification, internationalization, and global brand. In response to the requirements put forward by the internet era for development and the new challenges and opportunities brought to enterprises by the era, Haier fully implemented the networking strategy in 2012, and proposed the "three no's" development concept of "enterprise with no boundary, management with no leader, and supply chain with no limit." In 2014, the content of the strategy was expanded to gradually achieving "enterprise as a platform, employee as makers, and customization for users" (see Fig. 6.4) based on integrity. With that, Haier has been actively integrating the internet thinking into all facets of production organization and operations management of the enterprise, making itself a node on the internet that connects various resources. It creates and shares a user-centered business ecosphere in cooperation with partners to achieve win-win added value for all parties concerned.

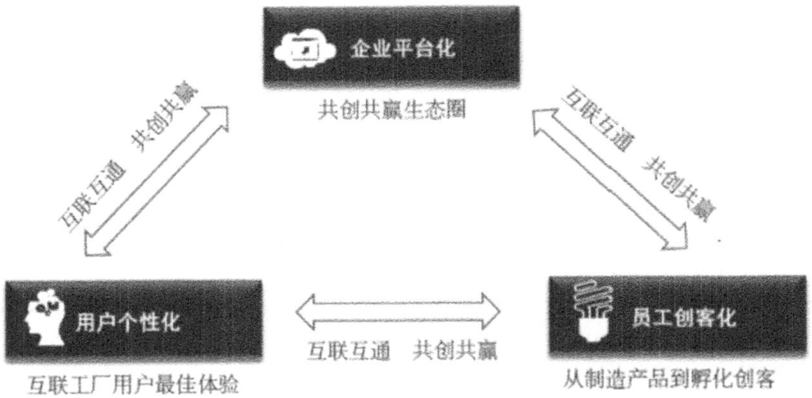

Fig. 6.4 Transformation of Haier under the networking strategy (*Source* The First Electronic Research Institute of Ministry of Industry and Information Technology)

企业平台化	Enterprise as a platform
共创共赢生态圈	Ecosphere featuring cooperation for a win-win outcome
互联互通 共创共赢	Interconnection and cooperation for a win-win outcome
用户个性化	Customization for users
互联工厂用户最佳体验	Connected factory delivering the best user experience
员工创客化	Employees as makers
从制造产品到孵化创客	From manufacturing products to incubating makers

New Management Model: Fully Stimulating the Vitality of the Enterprise

In order to respond to its networking strategy quickly, Haier has changed its management model profoundly. By such means as pioneering a win-win model called "Rendanheyi" and building investment-driven platforms and user payment platforms, Haier effectively breaks the traditional bureaucratic management model by directly connecting employees and users. This deconstructs the "aircraft carrier" in the traditional household appliance market into a parallel "fleet," which quickly transforms the corporate culture from execution to entrepreneurship, from enterprise payment to user payment, and from an accelerator for manufacturing products to an accelerator for incubating makers. At present, Haier has no hierarchy but only three kinds of people—platform owners, microenterprise owners, and makers. The former department leaders of the Group have become platform owners, transforming from managers to service providers. Employees have become entrepreneurs and makers, transforming from following instructions from superiors to directly creating value for users. Microenterprise owners, who are elected by makers, form microenterprises with the makers to fully tap into innovation and entrepreneurship resources provided by platform owners and the society. They jointly create user and market demands to form an ecosphere with platforms in parallel (Fig. 6.5).

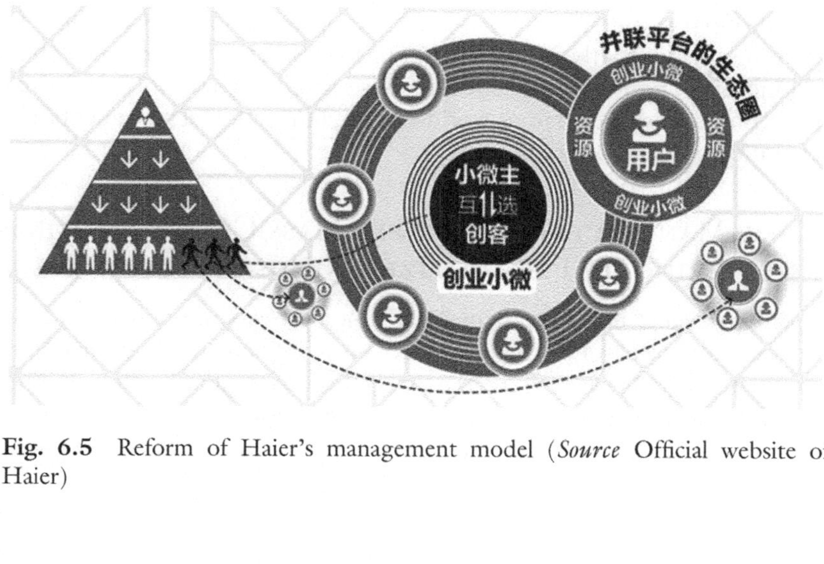

Fig. 6.5 Reform of Haier's management model (*Source* Official website of Haier)

并联平台的生态圈	Ecosphere with platforms in parallel
创业小微	Entrepreneurial microenterprises
资源	Resources
用户	Users
小微主	Microenterprise owners
互选	Two-way selection
创客	Makers

New R&D System: Building the Largest Open Innovation System in the World

Haier has created the Haier Open Partnership Ecosystem (HOPE) platform, the world's largest open innovation ecosystem and interactive community for whole-process innovation, with a vision of "making the world its R&D center" and learning from the best practices for technological innovation globally. Adhering to the idea of openness, cooperation, innovation, and sharing, Haier is actively building win-win sharing mechanisms such as co-construction of patent pools, profitable sharing, and incubation investment, which have attracted a wide range of parties globally including users, technical talents, and solution providers. It has realized the coverage of innovation resources for the whole industry chain from creative output to prototype design, technical solutions, structural design, rapid prototyping, small-batch trial production, and the like. In this way, it has properly solved difficult problems in the resource allocation of innovation and entrepreneurship sources and innovation transformation, continuously generating world-leading innovation achievements and revolutionary user experience.

New Manufacturing System: Mass Customization Centering on Personalized Needs of Customers

In order to meet the users' demand for the best experience in the whole process, comprehensive changes have been implemented in manufacturing at Haier. It has realized the integration of standardization, modularization, automation, and AI-oriented transformation, and ushered in a new era of mass customization that connects users, suppliers, and connected factories. First, taking "diy.haier.com"—the first interactive customization platform in the industry—as a bridge, Haier fully gathers the personalized needs of users to transform them from purely buyers into designers, supervisors, and beneficiaries by relying on the three customization models of modular, bespoke, and crowd innovation customization. Second, based on the "Haidayuan" platform, Haier has restructured suppliers into module vendors to achieve modularization of product manufacturing. At the same time, it matches module vendors directly to user demand and conducts corresponding adjustments to design and product R&D to upgrade the modules, thereby transforming the game in the traditional supply chain into a win-win relationship. Last but not least, with the connected factory as the mainstay, Haier carries out automatic scheduling according to the real-time user order information received. The information is transmitted to the production lines of various processes and all module vendors, with instructions for the production of corresponding product modules and eventual assembly on the final assembly line, hence realizing data-driven flexible production.

New Service System: Constructing a New Ecosphere for Product Promotion, Marketing, and Financial Services

Relying on diversified platforms, Haier has integrated various forms of services into all links of the product lifecycle, pushing service-oriented manufacturing towards becoming online, networked, and collaborative, and effectively expanding the service scope and potential for added value.

With the "U+" open platform as the core, Haier strives to create a smart home ecosphere. Haier released its U+ system, the world's first smart life operating system, in 2014. With U+ smart home platform, U+ cloud service platform and U+ big data analysis platform as technical support, Haier has integrated a full range of household appliances, such as electrical appliances, lights, curtains, and security devices, through the establishment of unified standards for smart protocol and full openness, whole industry chain, and full compatibility features. It provides consumers with a complete set of smart life solutions, effectively solving the problems of interconnection and interoperability among smart products and services in different categories and produced by different brands and greatly expanding the scope of products and services (Figs. 6.6 and 6.7).

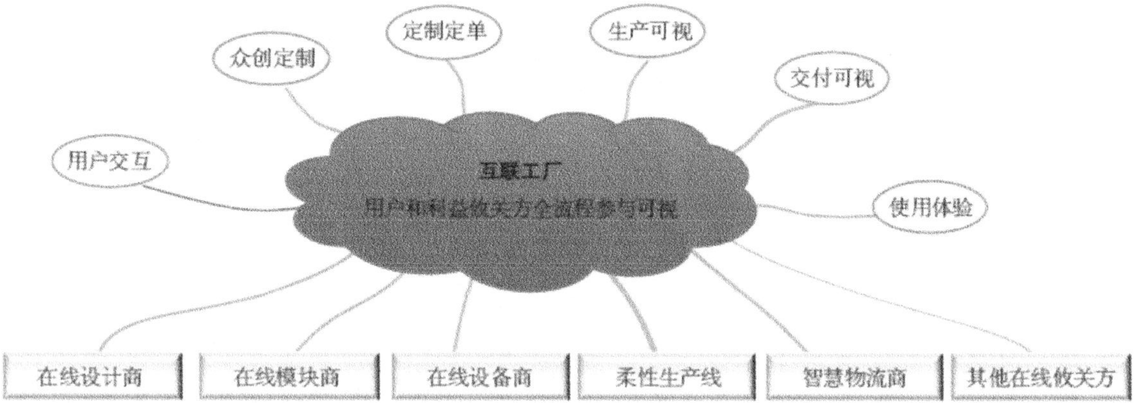

Fig. 6.6 Haier connected factory (*Source* The First Electronic Research Institute of Ministry of Industry and Information Technology)

用户交互	User interaction
众创定制	Crowd innovation customization
定制定单	Customized ordering
生产可视	Visualized production
交付可视	Visualized delivery
使用体验	User experience
互联 工厂	Connected factory
用户和利益攸关方全流程参与可视	Participation of users and interested parties with visibility in the whole process
在线设计商	Online designers
在线模块商	Online module vendors
在线设备商	Online equipment suppliers
柔性生产线	Flexible production line
智慧物流商	Smart logistics providers
其他在线攸关方	Other online interested parties

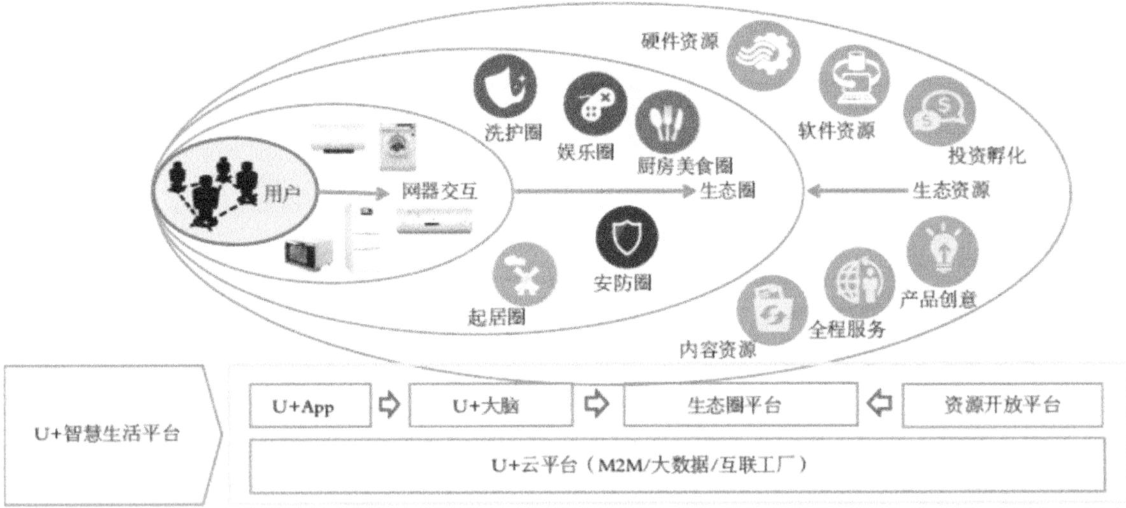

Fig. 6.7 Haier U+ smart home ecosphere (*Source* The First Electronic Research Institute of Ministry of Industry and Information Technology)

用户	Users
网器交互	Interaction with IoT-enabled devices
洗护圈	Personal care sphere
娱乐圈	Entertainment sphere
厨房美食圈	Kitchen and gourmet sphere
生态圈	Ecospheres
安防圈	Security sphere
起居圈	Living sphere
硬件资源	Hardware resources
软件资源	Software resources
投资孵化	Investment and incubation
生态资源	Ecosphere resources
产品创意	Creative ideas for products
全程服务	Whole-process services
内容资源	Content resources
U+ 智慧生活平台	U+ smart home platform
U+ 大脑	U+ brain
生态圈平台	Ecosphere platform
资源开放平台	Open platform for resources
U+ 云平台(M2M/大数据/互联工厂)	U+ cloud platform (M2M/big data/connected factory)

With the three major e-commerce platforms as the core, Haier strives to create a new marketing ecosphere. By now, Haier has established three major e-commerce platforms, namely, jushanghui.com, a professional factory direct sales service platform for household appliances targeting dealers; RRS.com, an e-store focusing on the water purifier market; and ehaier.com, a platform dedicated to one-stop sales services of all series of Haier's products. It has also set up corresponding supporting service systems for such aspects as logistics and warehousing, finance, after-sales support, and online training, effectively optimizing supply chain management services and greatly raising the added value of the trading of products.

With financing platforms such as hairongyi.com as the core, Haier strives to build an internet finance ecosphere. Relying on its rich ecosphere resources, Haier has quickly established a series of financial platforms including hairongyi.com, Haier Financial Services, Haier Money, and haiercash.com to engage in multiple types of financial services such as supply chain finance, financial leasing, consumer finance, and financial factoring. It provides customized financial solutions for various interested parties, transforming from product finance to financial ecosphere and exploring new space for product-based value-added services.

New Entrepreneurship System: Transforming from "Manufacturing Products" to "Incubating Makers"

Driven by the online incubation platform "Hai Chuanghui (HCH)" and supported by offline entrepreneurship incubation spaces such as HCH incubators and Haier-Peking University Entrepreneurship Base, Haier has fully incorporated industrial park resources of the government, channel resources, processing and manufacturing resources, financial service resources and the like to achieve a systematic combination of innovation and entrepreneurship, online and offline, and incubation and investment. It provides makers with one-stop incubation services including investment, consulting, counsel, supply chain and channel acceleration, space, factories, and innovative technologies, fostering Haier's new ecology of open entrepreneurship.

Outcome of Development

In an environment characterized by greater downward pressure on the macro economy and sluggish overall demand in the household appliance industry of China, Haier has boldly reformed and forged ahead to achieve steady growth in profits and coordinated optimization of multiple business segments during the in-depth transformation. Achievements in innovation are quickly emerging, effectively cultivating new impetus for the development of the enterprise.

According to the *2016 Market Innovation Report* released by Haier Group, Haier's global turnover is expected to reach RMB 201.6 billion in 2016, an increase of 6.8% year-on-year, with a profit of RMB 20.3 billion, up 12.8% year-on-year. The growth rate of its profit is 1.8 times that of turnover. At present, the HOPE open platform for innovation has established a resource network of more than 2 million first-class enterprises for the whole world, among which more than 100,000 have registered on the platform. More than 500 ideas are generated through interactions per month, and more than 200 innovation projects are successfully incubated per year. The entrepreneurship platform of Haier has gathered 3,600 startups for incubation, and 1,333 venture capital institutions with a total fund pool of more than RMB 12 billion. It has successfully incubated emerging brands such as Thunderobot, Xiaoshuai Theater, RRS Lejia express delivery lockers, youzhu.com, and jiawayun. There has been explosive growth in customized products, as Haier sold 330,000 customized products in Q3 2016, a year-on-year increase of 667%. In the future, as the Metcalfe's Law of online platforms gradually takes effect and the marginal benefit increases, Haier's networking transformation will usher in a new peak, making it truly a pioneer and leader in industrial internet.

Achievements and Challenges of the Digital Transformation of China's Manufacturing Industry

Preliminary Achievements of the Digital Transformation of the Manufacturing Industry

In recent years, the digital transformation of manufacturing enterprises in China has made some preliminary achievements, and the application of the internet in manufacturing has increased significantly. According to data from the Contemporary Service Platform for Integration of Informatization and Industrialization, the internet-based index of China's manufacturing enterprises was 32.7 in 2016, up 7.5% from 30.4 in 2015. The four sub-indicators of the index, namely, data application, user participation, organizational innovation, and enterprise interconnection, have also improved steadily as compared to those in 2015. In particular, the organizational innovation indicator has increased by 15%, with the greatest percentage increase. More and more enterprises are beginning to recognize the importance of organizational reform in digital transformation (as shown in Fig. 6.8).

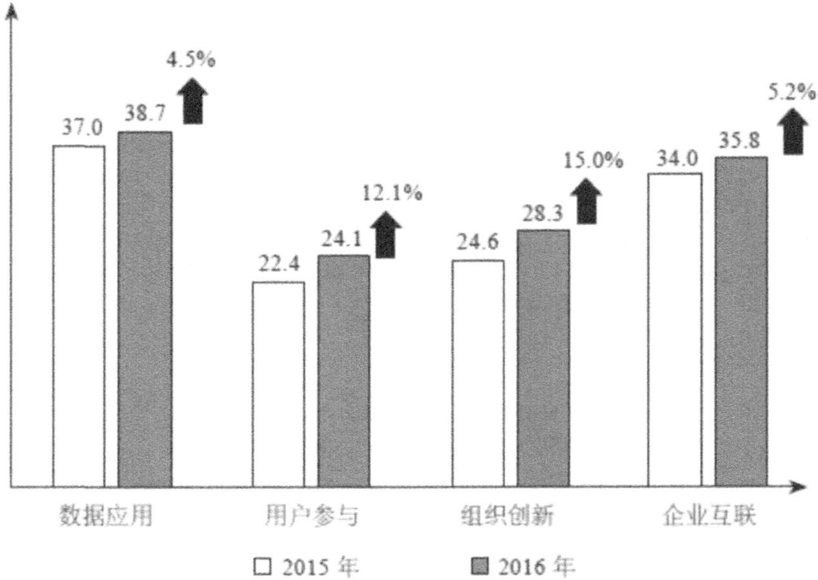

Fig. 6.8 Internet-based index and level one indicator scores of enterprises from 2015 to 2016 (*Source* Contemporary Service Platform for Integration of Informatization and Industrialization)

数据应用	Data application
用户参与	User participation
组织创新	Organizational innovation
企业互联	Enterprise interconnection
2015年	2015
2016年	2016

Challenges Faced by the Digital Transformation of the Manufacturing Industry

Unlike developed countries in the world which experienced industrialization before informatization, China is experiencing waves of informatization before industrialization is completed, and is facing the dual historical tasks of completing industrialization and accelerating informatization. This has brought challenges to promoting the digital transformation of the manufacturing industry.

Heavy Reliance on Other Countries for Key Technologies

Despite the large size, China's manufacturing industry is far from strong, with weak independent innovation capabilities, heavy reliance on foreign countries for key technologies and high-end equipment, insufficient inter-disciplinary and cross-sectoral collaboration between the government, industrial entities, educational institutions, and research institutes, and inadequate manufacturing innovation system with enterprises as the main-stay. The structural contradictions between the supply and demand of technology are apparent: there is insufficient effective supply of technology with poor quality of supply. It is difficult to apply many of the technological achievements directly to production, as many technologies lack conditions for systemic application and there are insufficient core technologies with independent intellectual property rights. The heavy reliance on other countries for key technologies has become the Achilles heel in the transformation and upgrading of China's traditional industries and the cultivation and development of emerging industries.

Lack of Inter-Disciplinary Talents

The accelerated integration of digital technology in the manufacturing industry has placed great demands for inter-disciplinary talents with mastery of both internet technology and industry expertise. Industrial enterprises lack talents who are proficient in the new generation of information technologies such as cloud computing and big data, while most internet-based software companies have limited knowledge of the industry, processes, and business. The shortage of inter-disciplinary talents, applied talents, and leading talents who are suited to industrial integration and development is hindering the digital transformation of China's manufacturing industry.

Insufficient Conditions for Popularizing Industrial Applications

The overall informatization of China's manufacturing enterprises is low, with varying stages of development. There is inadequate informatization as a basic foundation for the comprehensive promotion of digital transformation and development. Due to the lack of effective models and paths, many of the enterprises do not have a sufficient understanding of what industrial Internet of Things is or what smart manufacturing is. More of them, especially small- and medium-sized enterprises, have no motivation or capacity to apply digital technologies due to various constraints such as high costs and lack of talents.

CHAPTER 7

Vigorously Promoting the Digital Transformation of the Real Economy

Digital Agriculture

Agriculture is one of the oldest industries. With relatively primitive production methods, there is an urgent need to seize the opportunities brought about by the digital revolution and accelerate the development of modern agriculture.

Development of Digital Agriculture in China

The Application of Such Equipment as Smart Agriculture Devices and Unmanned Remote Sensing Aerial Vehicles Has Realized Smart Monitoring, Smart Spraying, Smart Fertilization, and Smart Surveying in Agriculture

China has successfully integrated and applied modern electronic technologies, control technologies, sensor technologies, and agricultural machinery and equipment technologies in smart equipment for precision agriculture. Typical smart equipment technologies frequently used in agricultural production mainly include automatic navigation, sowing monitoring, precision land leveling, smart yield monitoring, variable rate fertilization, and variable rate spraying. Apart from those, the application of unmanned aerial vehicles (UAVs) has gradually shifted from the military to agriculture. In present-day China, in addition to the traditional use in aerial pesticide spraying for crop protection, UAVs are being

M. Huateng et al., *The Chinese Digital Economy*,
https://doi.org/10.1007/978-981-33-6005-1_7

used in increasingly broader fields in land rights confirmation, standardized farmland management, aerial crop protection, and farmland damage measurement.

Standardized Tracing of Agricultural Product Quality and Safety

The quality and safety of agricultural products have become issues of concern to the government and consumers. Since 2005, China has started to construct a traceability system for the quality of agricultural products. Pilot projects were first initiated in some provinces and municipalities including Beijing, Jiangsu, Shaanxi, Fujian, Tianjin, and Zhejiang, with a lot of efforts in establishing the coding of agricultural land, production base files, standardized packaging and labeling, and other systems. It has created a whole-process quality traceability system, and established technical standard systems corresponding to stages before, during, and after the production of agricultural products together with raw material bases, logistics bases, and retailers. In recent years, the continuous development of automatic identification technologies, sensor technologies, mobile communication technologies, smart decision-making technologies, and Internet of Things technologies has laid the foundation for building a whole-chain traceability system for agricultural and food products that integrates comprehensive monitoring, real-time transmission, and smart decision-making. At present, it has not only achieved whole-chain traceability before, during and after production that includes pre-production reminders, in-production early warning and post-production testing for organic production, but also attained key technologies for traceability of different agricultural products based on the characteristics of vegetables, fruits, livestock, and aquatic products. With these, it has realized scientific and safe production with "environmental monitoring, production standards, operating procedures, product inspections, emergency plans, and brand integrity." After more than a decade of development, the overall pass rate of the routine monitoring of major agricultural products in China reached 97.5% in 2016, an increase of 0.4 percentage points year on year. There were no major agricultural product quality and safety incidents throughout the year, thanks to the digitalization of quality and safety tracking for agricultural products. Taking the "safe vegetables" quality and safety supervision and traceability system of Tianjin as an example, the municipality has built a total of 186 "safe vegetables" bases,

10 district/county-level supervision centers, and 72 township-level supervision centers. The project has been promoted on 354,700 mu of land for an annual output of more than 1.8 million tons of high-quality vegetables, with an average increase in benefits of RMB 1461.6 per mu.

Rural e-commerce is Spreading like Wildfire

In 2015, "the first year of rural e-commerce," e-commerce giants led by Alibaba, JD.com, and Suning started to take root in the rural market by opening rural outlets nationwide. In the following year, online retail sales in rural areas of China amounted to RMB 894.54 billion, accounting for approximately 17.4% of the online retail sales nationwide, of which online retail sales of goods amounted to RMB 579.24 billion while that of services amounted to RMB 315.3 billion. The quarterly year-on-year growth rates of rural online retail sales were higher than those in urban areas in the whole year. The development of rural e-commerce has entered a new stage, and e-commerce and express delivery enterprises have begun their more in-depth layout in the rural market.

In March 2016, JD.com announced that its household appliances department would open brick-and-mortar franchises as a move to establish its presence in the rural market. It aims to gather approximately 10,000 franchisees to open "JD.com household appliances stores" in township markets of China, and expand the number to 20,000 by 2017 to cover 400,000 administrative villages.

At the same time, Cainiao Network, a socialized collaborative logistics platform established by Alibaba together with express delivery enterprises such as SF Express, STO Express, YTO Express, ZTO Express, and Yunda Express, announced that it would join hands with logistics partners to form the Cainiao Alliance, which shall play an especially prominent role in the "cun.taobao.com (Taobao for villages)" plan. Administrative divisions below the county level are a weak part of China's logistics system. The task of the Cainiao Alliance is to get through the "last kilometer" of logistics in rural areas by selecting logistics enterprises and building a logistics network.

Suning followed their actions. In May 2016, Suning announced its "five-local model" of "sales, tax payment, employment, service, and wealth creation." The goal is to build an e-commerce ecosphere for rural economic development and facilitate the development of various regions characterized by agricultural industrialization, brand building of agricultural products, and professionalization of talents. It is reported that by now, Suning has established more than 2000 suning.com service stations, and has launched more than 400 local specialty stores.

A framework of coordinated development of various economic entities and major e-commerce enterprises in rural areas is beginning to take shape, which is bound to play an active role in the economic development of rural areas, especially poverty-stricken areas, increasing farmers' incomes and improving people's quality of life.

Case Study: The "Running Chicken" Project of JD.com

The "Running Chicken" project is an innovative e-commerce poverty alleviation project carried out by JD.com. Chicks are given to poor households for free-range raising provided that they are registered at the poverty alleviation office and have a good credit record. The natural growth cycle of each chick is recorded in a scientific manner during more than four months of raising before the chickens are sold on the market. Combined with such links as smart monitoring, mass slaughtering, processing, and transportation, the project provides consumers with the green, healthy food "running chicken." It not only lifts poor households out of poverty to become affluent, but also reflects the corporate social responsibility of JD.com and its philosophy of high-quality life. In May 2016, the pilot of the "running chicken" poverty alleviation loan project was launched in Wuyi County, Hebei Province. Currently, some 10,000 "running chickens" have been sold to the market. Preliminary calculations show that poverty-stricken households could earn about RMB 30 from each chicken after subtracting the costs, adding an average of RMB 3000 of income to each household.

"Running chicken" for poverty alleviation is marketed as a type of broiler chicken raised and slaughtered in a pure natural and pollution-free environment. Each is sold for RMB 188 in the self-run stores of JD.com. The "running chickens" were quickly sold out upon release to the market despite a price five or six times that of ordinary broilers in the market. On the one hand, consumers trust JD.com for its vision of quality e-commerce and believe that its "running chicken" is safe in quality. On the other hand, with the spread of the concept of poverty alleviation via consumption, more and more consumers recognize that "poverty alleviation has no bystanders" and are willing to support the poverty alleviation efforts of the state by purchasing and consuming products from poverty-stricken areas.

The pilot project of "running chicken" for poverty alleviation has proven that the model of cultivating green and safe food, building well-known agricultural brands, and giving back to poor families is effective. Next, guided by the State Council Leading Group Office of Poverty Alleviation and Development, JD.com plans to continuously expand the coverage of the "running chicken" for poverty alleviation pilot project in Jiangsu, Hebei, and Guizhou provinces. Base on this project, it will pilot more targeted poverty alleviation projects such as "swimming duck" to cover more poverty-stricken families and establish a new model of poverty alleviation in the whole industrial chain.

Great Demand for Rural Finance

For farmers, in addition to their yearning for convenient basic financial services, they are also eager to solve the lack of funding, technology, and skills in industrial development. In order to let all kinds of agriculture-related clients, especially poverty-stricken farmers, gain access to financial services, get loans, complete formalities quickly, and be able to pay back, the "No. 1 Central Document" 2014 proposes to accelerate innovations in the rural financial system as a key task for comprehensively deepening the rural reform. It clearly proposes to strengthen the awareness of financial institutions of their responsibility to serve "agriculture, rural areas, and farmers," develop new types of rural financial cooperatives, and step up support for agricultural insurance.

Currently, financial models for rural areas are mushrooming. Since the official establishment of the Postal Savings Bank of China (PSBC) in 2007, it has established a collaborative platform between the bank and "the government, guarantors, insurers, enterprises, and associations" to address the problems of difficulty in getting loans and high interest rates of loans. At the same time, it adopts localized innovative mortgage and pledge guarantee methods, successively bringing large-scale agricultural machinery, large agricultural orders, agriculture-related direct subsidies, land transfer income and the like into the scope of collateral and pledges. With that, it has formed ten product lines, including loans for farmers, new types of agricultural business entities, agriculture-related merchants, agriculture-related small and micro businesses in counties, and loans for leading agricultural enterprises.

In addition to PSBC, there have been other enterprises providing targeted financial services coming into being. Deeply rooted in the fields of rural production, distribution, and consumption for many years, these enterprises have accumulated vast amounts of trading data of farmers, which has now become big data resources—a vital asset of the enterprises. Relying on the ability to assess the credibility of farmers with big data, these large agriculture-related enterprises have successively ventured to internet financial services for rural areas. They provide credit loan products to farmers, such as Nongyindai and Nongfudai of Da Bei Nong Group, and Cuncundai and Cuncunrong of Cuncunle. These platforms have built a major channel between thousands of farmer households and the market, and addressed their difficulty in connecting to the market after production.

Trends in the Development of Digital Agriculture

From Individual Digital Agriculture Technologies to Digital Integration and High Degree of Atomization

Digital agriculture has become an important means of transforming the development models for agriculture from individual digital agriculture technologies as of now towards digital integration and a high degree of automation. Data analysis and processing capabilities are the core of the development of digital agriculture, while research on the system of smart learning and analysis models of agricultural big data is one of the keys to the future development of digital agriculture. Such technologies as artificial intelligence, data mining, machine learning, and mathematical modeling could be used to address actual problems in the field of digital agriculture in China, eventually forming a digitally integrated, highly automated decision-making system for digital agriculture.

From Scattered Information Resources to Sharing and Collaboration of Agricultural Data Resources

Agricultural big data is the foundation for the development of digital agriculture. Learning from the development of digital agriculture in foreign countries, the collaborative sharing of agricultural data resources is a trend for the future development of digital agriculture. Innovative collection, processing, handling, and collaborative sharing mechanisms systematically integrate the information resources of various agriculture-related institutions for unified planning and unified formulation of standards and norms, gradually forming an open, shared, circulating, and connected system of digital agriculture resources to provide agricultural production and management entities with more authoritative, accurate and diversified services.

From the Monotonous Agricultural Service Mode to Customized Services of Digital Agriculture

The ultimate goal of R&D, application, and promotion of digital agriculture technologies is to serve the vast number of agricultural production and operation entities. Therefore, the customization of digital agriculture services is one of the trends for the future development of digital agriculture. With the needs of agricultural production and operation entities as a starting point, the service functions of the digital agriculture platforms have been continuously improving for an order-based digital service model for agriculture and rural areas, so as to provide service packages tailored to the actual needs of farmers and promote the development of agricultural service modes towards convenient, personalized and interactive ones.

Online Retail

China's Online Retail Started Late but Developed Quickly

China is not one of the earliest to start developing online retail. As early as 1995, Amazon and eBay were already online in the United States, while retailers such as Otto and Argos in Europe also began to engage in online retail in the same year. By contrast, the earliest batch of e-commerce ventures in China (dangdang.com, 8848, eachnet.com, etc.) came into being in 1999, four years later than developed countries in the West. Taobao and JD.com, the two leading e-commerce companies in China, were not established until 2003 and 2004 respectively.

Despite the late start, China's online retail has developed rapidly to get ahead of others. At present, China has the largest population of internet users in the world, and its online retail sales surpassed the USA to rank first in the world for the first time in 2013. According to data from the National Bureau of Statistics, China's online retail sales reached RMB 4.2 trillion to account for 12.6% of the total retail sales of consumer goods in 2016, an increase of 25.6%. eMarketer expects that China will gradually increase its advantage over the USA in terms of scale, increasing its share of global online retail sales to 40% by 2018.

The Internet Facilitates Quality and Efficiency in the Development of the Distribution System

The internet is an advanced productive force. By empowering the retail industry, it could greatly reduce distribution costs and improve the efficiency of economic operations.

Online Retail Has Lower Operating Costs

Compared with brick-and-mortar retailers, online retailers enjoy lower operating costs. Looking at the comprehensive operating expense ratio figures in 2014, the figure of JD.com based on a pure e-commerce model is only 12%, while the average of five offline retailers (including retailers that mainly adopt an offline model), namely, Gome, Suning, Yonghui Superstores, Dashang Group, and Sun Art, is as high as 17%. Among them, Gome and Suning have a certain proportion of e-commerce business, hence their comprehensive operating expense ratios—16 and 15% respectively—are relatively lower than the average of the five. Among the other three offline retailers, Yonghui Superstores and Sun Art have combined operating expense ratios of 17 and 19% respectively.[1]

It could be seen that the internet is a key element in reducing the operating costs of retailers. From low to high, the comprehensive operating expense ratios of retailers could be generally ranked as pure e-commerce retailers < mainly offline retailers < offline retailers. Similar conclusions could be drawn from analyses into other years, indicating that the cost advantage of online retailing is evident. The costs saved could be translated into benefits for upstream suppliers and downstream consumers, promoting the common prosperity of the industrial chain.

[1] Source of data: "The Advantages of e-Commerce Compared to Brick-and-Mortar Stores," *IChina*, 2015, Vol. 7.

Online Retail Has Higher Operating Efficiency

For retailers, days of inventory on hand and payment days are the two most important indicators to measure the operating efficiency of an enterprise. The performance of online retailers on these two indicators far exceeds that of offline brick-and-mortar stores.

JD.com and Amazon, based on a pure e-commerce model, have low days of inventory on hand, which were respectively 34.2 days and 45 days in 2013. Gome and Suning perform the best among offline retailers, yet their days of inventory on hand are 60 days and 72 days respectively, which are much higher than pure e-commerce retailers.

Online retailers have shorter payment days and faster capital turnover. The payment days (days payable outstanding) of JD.com and Amazon, based on a pure e-commerce model, were respectively 42.2 days and 95 days in 2013, while that of Gome and Suning, mainly offline retailers, were respectively 136 days and 142 days, exceeding that of online retailers by a large margin.[2]

Online Retail Has Advantages Unmatched by Offline Brick-and-Mortar Stores

In addition to lower costs and higher efficiency, online retail has some other unique advantages reflected in the following three aspects:

1. Online retail is conducive to forming a nationwide unified market. Due to such constraints as bureaucracy and regional protectionism, China's offline retailers tend to be regional, with few retailers operating nationwide. For example, Jingkelong, an affiliate of the State-owned Assets Supervision and Administration Commission of Chaoyang District, has its stores mainly located in Chaoyang District, with more than half of its stores located in that area. CSF Market, formerly Beijing Haidian Non-staple Food Company, has a similar distribution, with most of its stores located in Haidian District. Regional division is obvious even in one city like Beijing; it would be even more difficult to establish a nationwide

[2] The accounts payable of Gome and Suning include both accounts payable and notes payable.

unified market. The internet could effectively overcome geographical constraints. Taking JD.com as an example, it has covered 2660 districts and counties across the country with its self-run business with 13 years of operation in e-commerce.[3] Online retail could accelerate the formation of a nationwide unified market, which helps retail enterprises in China to become bigger and stronger.

2. Online retail has an infinitely large "shelf," with a vast number of commodities available for sale. The stock-keeping units (SKU) of an online retailer could reach 10 million or even hundreds of millions, which is unmatched by any brick-and-mortar store. Therefore, online retailers can meet people's needs on a broader scope.
3. The rental costs of online retailers are lower. The basic logic of a brick-and-mortar store is to open a store in a crowded area, which is conducive to boosting sales. However, the rental costs of such locations are relatively high, with other problems such as traffic congestion. Online retailers do not have brick-and-mortar stores; they usually build large warehouses in the suburbs with lower rental costs.

The Existence of a Large Number of Natural Person Online Stores is a Unique Phenomenon in China

Business-to-customer (B2C) is the mainstream in the development of online retail internationally. Due to the inadequate development of China's retail entities, customer-to-customer (C2C) has long been occupying the lion's share of the online shopping market. With the improvement of people's standard of living and the acceleration of consumption upgrading, consumers are beginning to shift their focus from price to quality and user experience, hence B2C has experienced rapid growth. However, C2C still has a 45% share of the market.[4]

The existence of a large number of natural person online stores has become a unique phenomenon in China. A large number of consumer complaints, coupled with illegal activities such as the sale of counterfeit and shoddy goods, infringement of intellectual property rights, and click

[3] Source of data: Official website of JD.com, March 2017.

[4] Source of data: Analysys Qianfan.

farming are rampant in these natural person online stores, with a lot of international intellectual property disputes and criticism caused. Though opening a natural person online store requires real-name registration on a third-party platform, collection of evidence and law enforcement are often not possible even if an illegal operator is found. This is because regulatory authorities have long been unable to obtain the information of relevant subjects, and law enforcement personnel from the administration for industry and commerce do not have the right to enter private homes. The extremely low cost of breaking the law and the extremely high cost of law enforcement have resulted in the long-standing inadequate control of illegal behaviors of natural person online stores. The mix of good and bad players in the market has intensified the price war at the expense of quality, resulting in bad money driving out good money.

Natural person online stores, which do not need to be registered at the administration for industry and commerce, played a positive role in the initial stage of the development of online retail. After more than a decade of development, major changes have taken place in the situation and conditions of the development of China's online retail, entering a new stage of standardized development from the nurturing period of the market. The reform of the commercial system has specifically lowered the restrictions on the business premises for online operations. The registered capital is now subscribed rather than paid in full, saving the need to pay capital verification fees and making the registration of online stores more convenient. The natural person online stores have fulfilled their historical mission of breeding players and cultivating a market. At the same time, a large number of online stores engaged in online retail as businesses but in the name of natural persons. They have evaded the duty to pay taxes and their corporate responsibilities, resulting in an unfair market environment.

Faced with the new situation, focusing on long-term development, and based on building an online market environment characterized by fair competition, online and offline rules should be set equal, and special regulations for online stores to evade licensing should not continue to exist for long. It is recommended to set a reasonable threshold for registration at the industrial and commercial. For small merchants who have not reached the threshold yet, they may not immediately register, but those who meet the threshold must be registered in accordance with state requirements.

New Direction for the Development of Online Retail

Through the transformation of the traditional distribution system, online retail has achieved rapid development. In the future, it would further break the boundary between online and offline and the constraints of time and space to achieve greater development.

O2O Promotes the In-Depth Integration of Online and Offline Retail, Facilitating the Transformation and Upgrading of the Distribution System

In the past ten years, China's retail industry has basically taken a path that separates online and offline retail. Pure e-commerce and brick-and-mortar retail are two parallel lines. E-commerce and brick-and-mortar stores have their respective advantages and disadvantages. Only when they are closely combined could they better serve consumers. The in-depth integration of online and offline retail has become a general trend, and the O2O era is coming.

In the O2O model, online retail could fully tap into the experience and guaranteed high-quality services that traditional retail brings to consumers, thereby increasing its attractiveness to traffic. At the same time, traditional retail could also make full use of the advantage of big data of online retail to achieve precision marketing, providing consumers with more convenient services and solving the problems of parking and queuing for users. This model achieves coordinated development of online and offline retail by integrating online and offline resources, complementing advantages, providing users with a better shopping experience, and adapting to changes in consumer demand.

Fresh Produce Has Become a Prioritized Category for Development

The development of categories of online retail basically follows a path from standardized products to non-standardized products. In the field of online retail, books are the most standardized products. Early e-commerce businesses, such as Amazon and dangdang.com, mostly started by selling books. Currently, books, mobile phones, computers, household appliances, dried food, beverages, daily chemicals, clothing, and other more standardized products have a higher penetration of online retail. There are still opportunities associated with non-standardized, personalized products. Fresh produce is characterized by a low level of standardization and high loss in distribution, posing very high requirements for product selection and distribution capabilities of teams. It is one of the areas that has not witnessed effective internet-based development. Fresh produce is also a high-frequency product with rigid demand, which has determined the great potential for the development of e-commerce in this field. After years of market cultivation, the external conditions are ripe for the rapid development of e-commerce for fresh produce. E-commerce giants are beginning to go all out in the fresh produce market one after another. Innovative models based on the supply chain are emerging, fueling the explosive growth of e-commerce for fresh produce.

In order to adapt to fresh produce, a special type of commodity, e-commerce retailers have made a lot of changes to their operations, such as developments in the cold chain and increasing the speed of delivery, but in general, they still used the sales model of traditional commodities to do the fresh produce business. With the rapid development of the mobile internet, a brand-new e-commerce model for fresh produce quickly emerged around 2014 to achieve much progress. The most distinctive feature of this model is the extremely fast delivery, increasing the delivery speed from same-day or one-day delivery of traditional goods to delivery in 1–2 hours.

There are two different approaches behind the extremely fast delivery: the asset-light model and the asset-heavy model. The asset-light model is the fast delivery of fresh produce to nearby consumers based on the existing inventory of offline brick-and-mortar stores. It is a purchasing agent service with Instacart and JD Daojia as examples. The asset-heavy model develops the industrial chain extensively to ensure good quality and user experience. It achieves so through controlling the whole distribution process of fresh produce by means of direct procurement from production bases, strict quality control, and self-operated cold chain. An example would be Missfresh.

Rural e-Commerce Aids Targeted Poverty Alleviation

Rural e-commerce is playing an increasingly important role in poverty alleviation and poverty reduction. Farmers in poverty-stricken areas are quickly getting rid of poverty and becoming affluent by means of online retail and similar tools relying on the unique resource advantages of the rural areas. The Chinese government attaches great importance to this. In October 2016, the Cyberspace Administration of China, the National Development and Reform Commission, and the State Council Leading Group Office of Poverty Alleviation and Development jointly issued the *Internet Poverty Alleviation Action Plan*, which is met with the overwhelming response from companies such as JD.com, Alibaba, and Suning, and poverty alleviation with the internet has been in full swing.

In the practice of poverty alleviation with e-commerce across the country, many successful cases have been explored. These cases have driven the economic development of poverty-stricken areas, effectively improved the quality of life of poor people, and provided valuable experience for other poverty-stricken areas to get rid of poverty and become affluent. For example, Longnan, a national pilot city using e-commerce to alleviate poverty, opened 1715 new online stores in 2016 with the online sales of agricultural products reaching RMB 3.035 billion, contributing RMB 620 of per-capita income to the poor. In the process of poverty alleviation with e-commerce, various business entities in Longnan directly created 57,000 jobs for the city, including more than 14,000 for those from poor households, which effectively alleviated the difficulties of the poor in finding a job. Longnan has gradually formed rural e-commerce construction patterns such as entrepreneurship for poor farmers, leadership of capable people, leadership of enterprises, and service by rural officials. Through the establishment of an interest sharing mechanism with poor households, the "Longnan Model" of poverty alleviation with e-commerce characterized by "one village led by one store" and "multiple villages led by one store" has taken shape.[5]

Social Commerce Such as WeChat Microbosses and Internet Celebrities Is Booming

The advantage of social commerce is that it could timely know the needs of users, achieve precision marketing, and thus achieve a high traffic conversion rate. Due to the social connections between buyers and sellers, consumer stickiness and loyalty are greatly increased, and the repurchase

[5] "The Gansu Model of Poverty Alleviation with e-Commerce: The Secrets Behind Longnan's Experience in Poverty Alleviation with e-Commerce," Targeted Poverty Alleviation of Gansu, February 13, 2017.

rate of products is also increased accordingly. The emergence of social commerce has made shopping scenario-oriented, generating and meeting demands in people's social and entertainment interactions. This greatly improves the shopping experience of users, and allows better adaptability to changes in the consumption concepts of consumers.

The typical examples of social commerce are WeChat microbosses and internet celebrities, with rapid development of both models in 2016. WeChat microbosses and internet celebrities represent two current directions for the development of social commerce. Most of the WeChat microbosses are based on strong ties: their social relations are mostly online counterparts of offline relations known as the "acquaintance economy," with relatively close connections between users and strong stickiness. Internet celebrities represent weak ties: the relationship between internet celebrities and fans is an open, interactive one. In decentralized dissemination of information, internet celebrities attract and gather fans relying on their unique characteristics, thereby accumulating traffic. Both economic models rely on social relations to generate traffic, and then divert the traffic to e-commerce to reap benefits.

Technological Logistics is Leading the Revolution in e-commerce Logistics

Technology constantly promotes revolutions in the field of logistics. At present, high technology represented by artificial intelligence is leading revolutions in logistics.

Robotics is transforming the labor-intensive industry of warehousing, with Amazon at the forefront of its applications. Amazon acquired Kiva Robotics in 2012 to gain advanced warehouse robotics technology. It changed the name of the acquired company to Amazon Robotics, and has been using Kiva robots in logistics centers to work together with employees on cargo handling jobs in the warehouse since 2014. In the future, Amazon will enable this robotics technology in all newly-built logistics centers. Though Kiva robots are expensive, they could greatly improve the efficiency of warehouses. MWPVL, a logistics consulting company, claims that by using Kiva robots in warehouses, Amazon could save USD 21.3 cents for each item sent, cutting costs by 48%. Analysts from UBS estimate that Amazon Robotics could save about USD 900 million in labor costs for Amazon each year. Apart from Amazon, fresh produce e-commerce retailer Ocado, Wal-Mart, and JD.com also announced their warehousing robot projects.

In distribution, unmanned aerial vehicle (UAV) is the most promising technology. Following Amazon and Google, such companies as JD.com, SF Express, and Singapore Post also announced their plans for UAV in 2015 in a bid to improve delivery efficiency and reduce delivery costs. In terms of other technologies, Amazon has filed a patent application for a delivery truck with on-the-way 3D printing services, while Google has obtained a technology patent for a self-driving truck for express delivery.

CHAPTER 8

Vigorously Promoting Digital Transformation in Public Services

Digital technology not only promotes the transformation and upgrading of traditional industries such as manufacturing, agriculture, and retail, but also accelerates and empowers the transformation of public service industries with high barriers to entry, such as education, healthcare, and transportation, to improve people's livelihood.

Digital Education

With the development of information and communication technology and the gradually expanding scope of its application, the characteristics of inclusiveness, convenience, and sharing of the internet have gradually penetrated the education sector. The internet is facilitating the comprehensive sharing of education for all, promoting equity in education, stimulating individualized education, and reshaping the business format in education.

Digital Technologies Drive Waves of Development in Digital Education

The development of education in various countries varies due to varying standards of economic development, population development foundation, popularization of education, and infrastructure and facilities. On

M. Huateng et al., *The Chinese Digital Economy*,
https://doi.org/10.1007/978-981-33-6005-1_8

a global scale, driven by new technologies represented by the internet, the education industry is gradually developing towards digitalization and integration of artificial intelligence.

Artificial Intelligence + Education: Opening a New Model for Digital Education

As artificial intelligence technology continues to mature, it is becoming more closely integrated into the education sector. Education technology with artificial intelligence as the core is starting its in-depth fusion with and application in the education sector from the three aspects of data collection (voice recognition, image recognition, sensors, etc.), data processing (semantic interpretation, big data, adaptive ability, cognitive computing, emotional computing, etc.) and human–machine interface (AR/VR, robotics, and 3D printing), gradually improving the smartness and interactivity of teaching. Integrated applications are mainly manifested in the four directions of automatic homework correcting, online question answering with photo searching, smart assessment, and personalized learning. Although the points of fusion are now scattered, and most of the products are still being experimented, some products have been put into application to be tested by the market, with remarkable results achieved.

In addition, there are more dimensions and greater amounts of data collection and data aggregation, more efficient data processing methods, and more interactive human–machine interfaces being developed. With those, artificial intelligence is going to form a product evolution model characterized by the combination of points and areas and a product application trend that is systematic and smart, constantly revolutionizing the learning paradigm of traditional education and opening new models of digital education. For example, an adaptive learning system geared to learners could generate smart learning content for students, and develop personalized learning plans through big data analysis and data feedback. For teachers, they could achieve such applications as oral evaluation, smart assessment of academic standing, and virtual learning assistants relying on artificial intelligence, effectively improving feedback for teaching and improve the quality of teaching.

VR/AR + Education: Promoting New Changes in Digital Education

The future development of education faces challenges in both the learning environment and the learning methods. In terms of the learning environment, the attention and focus of people are shifting to higher-level learning experience, such as whether there is long-term appeal in teaching and dynamic, friendly learning content, and whether multi-dimensional interactions between teachers, students, and the environment could be realized. In terms of learning methods, the progress of offline courses is rigid with slow updates to content, which limits the initiative and vitality of innovation of learners, while the fragmented learning information online often cannot form a complete learning system.

The increasingly maturing VR/AR technology and its applications could seamlessly integrate the digital environment to establish a balanced, in-depth learning framework, bring a more immersive experience, and provide a richer, more vivid online education scenes and opportunities for "practical experience." This improves the learning methods of learners, changes their learning habits, and even changes their way of thinking, influencing their perceptions of themselves, the world, and time and space. For example, when teachers talk about the universe and galaxies, students could better experience the scene and perceive it intuitively wearing virtual reality helmets. Immersive teaching greatly improves the efficiency of learning, as VR devices could reduce the costs and risks of practical training in medical surgeries, simulated driving, and on-site rescue. VR/AR could also perfectly replicate three-dimensional stereoscopic images, greatly improving the learning efficiency of people who study contents related to design and architecture.

STEAM Education: Spreading New Concepts of Digital Education

STEAM education is a comprehensive type of education that integrates the interdisciplinary development of science, technology, engineering, art, and mathematics and promotes a "practical exploratory" learning process. The emphasis on practice, interdisciplinary development, and innovation is a prominent characteristic of STEAM education. The combination of artificial intelligence, VR/AR, and 3D printing technology with the educational methods advocated by STEAM enables students at various stages of elementary school, junior high school and senior high school to practice logical thinking, improve practical abilities, and cultivate the innovative spirit in more intelligent scenarios, opening a new model of education for all-round development.

In the future, simulation laboratories based on artificial intelligence and VR/AR, companion and teaching robot products based on advanced robotics and 3D printing technology, and complex assistance systems for decision-making based on cognitive computing are all going to help students cultivate logical thinking and practical abilities in a learning experience resembling games, and truly complete a multidisciplinary, crossover exploratory learning process from the perspective of intelligent interactions. For example, there are now STEAM education products that provide programming applications in the market. Students could program the actions of a robot with the simplest visual programming language by dragging, clicking, drawing, and the like, and give instructions to the robot.

Various Countries Are Placing Great Emphasis on the Development of Digital Education

Guided by new technologies, the digitalization of the education industry is becoming an important indicator of the popularization of digitalization in various countries. Improving the digitization of education is an important measure for all countries to benefit people's livelihood and reform and innovate the education industry. In OECD countries, digital education is a key component of the digital strategy. Its goal is to promote the use of information and communication technology in education, improve the effectiveness of the education system, and ensure the development of basic and advanced information and communication skills. The focus is on the development of infrastructure to promote ICT-related courses, the training of teachers, and the development of online learning environments.

In the USA, the e-learning of the mainstream K12[1] curriculum is basically being promoted by the competent authorities of various states or

[1] The basic education stages in 12 years of kindergarten, primary school, and secondary school education are collectively called K12.

school districts, with corresponding regulations and standards. The "Universal Service Program for Schools and Libraries" plans to invest USD 3.9 billion annually in providing schools and libraries with stable high-speed broadband. In 2014, the Federal Communications Commission of the USA provided huge funding to a project aimed at narrowing the gap between schools and libraries in broadband connection and hardware supporting personalized learning, especially in rural areas, and attempts to increase the number of affordable high-speed broadband connections.

The National Digital Economy Strategy of Australia aims to provide connections to registered training organizations (RTOs), universities, and more professional educational institutions to engage in development and collaboration on innovation and providing flexible educational methods. It aims to extend e-learning resources to homes, workplaces, and public facilities to provide online virtual learning opportunities for students and other learners. Its specific content includes completing the development of digital courses, working with companies to promote the development of digital education, and encouraging people to use virtual courses to learn or teach students.

The Information Economy Strategy of the UK describes a series of measures to promote the application of information and communication technology in education to ensure that people have a basic understanding of such technology. It also calls for the establishment of a technical team connecting supply and demand to formulate a digital technology strategy, including expanding the benefits of massive open online courses (MOOCs), retraining workers, and increasing digital literacy. In addition, it also encourages the private sector and educational institutions to help boost the employment of graduates studying courses related to computer technology and shorten the apprenticeship of electronic technologies.

With the Indian government vigorously promoting the "Digital India" initiative, the growth rate of India's digital education ranks first in the world. The emergence of mobile technologies and cloud computing, coupled with the growing emerging population and the huge market demand for skilled labor, has been driving the rapid development of the digital education market of India. Digital education is the next focus of the development of India's internet industry after online retail, which is expected to reach USD 40 billion in size from 2017 to 2018.

Digital Technologies Help with the Rapid Development of Education in China

The education system of China has long been facing the problems of uneven distribution of resources, unbalanced input and output, and low standard of education for all-round development. With the strong support and guidance of national policies, the facilitation and driving of the digital economy, among other factors, the internet and the education sector have been gradually penetrating and integrating into each other, forming new business formats of digital education. The internet has also made remarkable achievements in optimizing the allocation of educational resources, promoting equity in education, respecting individual differences between students, meeting the individualized needs of students, breaking the limitations of space and time in learning, accelerating the transformation of teaching/learning methods, and enriching the content of subjects. With the concepts of learning for all, lifelong learning, and personalized learning becoming more and more popular, information and communication technology with the internet as the carrier has brought new opportunities for innovation and reform of traditional education.

The Government Encourages the Development of Digital Education

A series of policy documents such as the *Education and Information Technology Ten-Year Development Plan (2011–2020)*, the *Guiding Opinions on Actively Promoting the "Internet Plus" Action Plan*, and the *"Thirteenth Five-Year Plan" for Educational Informatization* show that informatization of education is gradually becoming an important indicator of the indicator system for education modernization. For now and in the future, China will continue to advance education informatization, using the internet to promote comprehensive reform in the field of education and actively developing new business formats of digital education. China's current efforts in the construction of education informatization and digital education continue to maintain a development model led by the government with schools and enterprises as the mainstay. Schools are actively applying the "three connections and two platforms" and the latest digital education resources, while traditional educational institutions, education technology companies, internet companies and the like are focusing on the R&D of digital education platforms and digital education applications.

Digital Education Is Exploring Rational Development Models

The rapid development of internet technologies, especially mobile internet, has enabled more and more internet companies to enter the education sector, which has significantly stimulated the vitality of the market. In 2014, online education entered a booming period. At the end of 2015, nearly 70% of these enterprises registered losses, severely quenching the fever over O2O for education and bringing rationality back to the industry. In 2016, as the government continued to strengthen the construction of infrastructure for the informatization of education, enterprises were also gradually exploring the development models for online education and seeking innovation and breakthroughs. According to data from iResearch, China's online education market amounted to RMB 156.02 billion in 2016, a year-on-year increase of 27.3%. In the next few years, online education is expected to maintain a stable growth rate of about 20% annually. The application of new technologies represented by big data, cloud computing, artificial intelligence, and AR/VR is bound to break through the extension of education and promote the deepening of the integration of online and offline applications, gradually making it possible for the internet to reshape traditional education.

Significant Growth of Mobile Digital Education

With the popularization of applied internet technologies, the number of online education users in China continues to grow steadily. Especially with the widespread application of mobile internet technology and the in-depth popularization of the 4G network, the mobile sector of internet-based education still has potential after achieving significant growth. The 39th *Statistical Report on Internet Development in China* released by the China Internet Network Information Center shows that as of December 2016, the number of online education users in China reached 138 million, with an annual growth rate of 25.0%; the utilization rate of online education users was 18.8%, an increase of 2.7 percentage points as compared to that in 2015. Among the users, the number of mobile online education users was 97.98 million, with an annual growth rate of 84.8%;

the utilization rate of mobile online education users was only 14.1%, with much room for growth.

Live Streaming for Education Is Gaining Impetus

Live streaming is gradually becoming a mature technology and gradually integrating with the applications in the field of education, becoming a new trend in the innovation and development of digital education. Major traditional educational institutions, digital education platforms, and internet companies are making plans in this area, injecting fresh vitality into the exploration of digital education models. Compared with traditional education, digital live streaming for education is more conveniently and efficiently assessable, and is more suitable for fragmented learning. Such means as one-to-one live streaming, one-to-many live streaming, and a combination of live streaming and recordings are also constantly striving to meet customized learning needs, while immersive learning scenarios are bringing interactions between teachers and learners. Content is king in the field of education, as excellent, experienced teachers are always scarce. Live streaming for education allows for more extensive dissemination and sharing of professional, high-quality teacher and content resources, providing everyone with the opportunity to meet excellent teachers face-to-face and engage in online interaction with them.

The Path for the Future Development of Digital Education in China

The development of digital education plays a huge role in promoting equity for education, achieving education for all and lifelong education, and pursuing personalized education. There is a need for China's digital education to further strengthen exploration and innovation in multiple dimensions such as system, technology, and model, so as to achieve the long-term goal of digital education to improve people's livelihood and enhance social well-being relying on new internet technologies.

Fostering a Healthy, Dynamic Atmosphere for Innovations in the Market

China shall speed up the formulation of standards for the quality of digital education and digital education resources, promote the establishment of access and supervision mechanisms for digital education resources, and improve the intellectual property protection mechanism for digital education resources. It shall encourage enterprises and other social forces to develop digital education resources and develop digital education products and applications to form a fair, orderly, healthy, and dynamic market environment. It shall encourage the innovation and development of new internet technologies and applications in the field of education, cultivate a socialized service market for digital education resources, explore the establishment of digital education management standards, and develop new business formats for digital education services. It shall also promulgate regulations on educational data management, improve the security management system, and form an open sharing mechanism for educational data resources, so as to ensure network security and security of the content of educational resources.

Expanding the Coverage of Digital Education Resources

China shall increase investment in education in remote and underdeveloped areas, optimize resource allocation, and gradually establish a mechanism for joint construction and sharing of high-quality digital education resources, so as to improve the coverage of such resources. It shall accelerate the coverage of high-quality education resources to rural, remote, poverty-stricken, and ethnic minority areas and let the convenience and sharing of the internet truly benefit the people, gradually realizing equity in education. It is necessary to continue to promote the construction of "three connections and two platforms," consolidate the achievements of the "full coverage of digital education resources in teaching sites" project, improve information facilities for formal schooling, strengthen the construction of "wireless campus," and further popularize the full coverage of network teaching environment and wireless networks. It shall also improve the national education resource public service platform, promoting the formation of a nationwide, interconnected digital education resource public service system featuring collaborative services.

In addition, for areas with high levels of digitalization and networking in education, schools shall be encouraged to use big data technology to collect, analyze, and provide feedback on education and teaching activities and student behavior data to support the promotion of personalized learning and targeted teaching. China shall continue to promote and support various schools at all levels in building smart campuses, and comprehensively use the internet, big data, artificial intelligence, and virtual reality technologies to explore new models for education and teaching in the future.

Promoting the Integration of Online and Offline Education

In digital education, the internet is the main carrier, while online and internet-based development is the means and tools. At the same time, offline teaching interactions are still the focus, as content is king and high-quality teaching content and teachers are the key in the education industry. It is necessary to perfectly integrate online and offline education, and encourage schools and local authorities to cooperate with qualified enterprises to promote the construction of online open resource platforms and the development of mobile education application software. China shall integrate various types of high-quality education resources, promote the general open sharing of resources, and accelerate the reform of the online and offline education service models and learning methods.

Looking at the subdivisions of online education, the market for primary and secondary school education is developing rapidly, while the demand for online vocational education is strong. According to the 39th *Statistical Report on Internet Development in China* released by the China Internet Network Information Center, as of December 2016, among the key subdivisions of online education, the user utilization rate of primary and secondary school education was the highest at 53.4%, an annual increase of 15.7%, with the number of users reaching 73.45 million, an annual increase of 76.9%. China shall continue to improve the internet facilities in primary and secondary schools, provide a basis for online teaching methods such as high-definition live streaming of courses, so as to increase the utilization rate of online education products. It shall promote offline training supplemented by effective methods such as online question reserves, online assignments, and online revision, achieving better training results with the integration of online and offline education. In addition, with the transformation and upgrading of China's economy, the structural contradictions of talents are becoming more and more prominent. The number and structure of high-level technical and skilled talents fall short of market demand by a large margin. Given the unlimited potential of online vocational education, personalized courses shall be designed according to the actual needs of employers, so as to meet their demand for knowledge and skills of employees, improve training efficiency, and reduce training costs.

Digital Healthcare

As the most basic need of people, healthcare has a direct impact on the health and safety of the people, with a unique position in the field of digital public service. The penetration of new information technology into the traditional healthcare industry is bound to bring about a revolution and reshape a new ecology for healthcare.

Six Major Trends in Digital Healthcare Globally

Taking Improving the Workflow as the Foundation

In the short to medium run, achieving the digitization, AI-based development and automation of medical services via information technology, optimizing the service workflow in the process of medical treatment, releasing labor resources of doctors from the supply side, and alleviating the imbalanced supply and demand of medical resources to a certain extent are the main directions for the development of the digital healthcare industry.

In the USA, it usually takes several weeks or even months for patients to make an appointment for a medical service. The "difficulties in seeing a doctor and making an appointment" is also a very prominent problem in China. The shortage of medical resources is one of the reasons, but the imperfect traditional workflow is also a big killer consuming medical resources. According to the statistics of the American Medical Association (AMA), doctors need to take twice as much time as the diagnosis to enter the patients' data into the electronic medical record. In the future, digital healthcare technologies will provide smarter data entry methods, more flexible communication channels between doctors and patients, and more comprehensive data monitoring methods, completely revolutionizing the traditional model for medical work. Streams, a product of Google's DeepMind team, could view the blood test results of patients at risk of acute kidney injury and optimize the treatment plan in just a few seconds. Augmedix uses Google Glass to enter patient data into electronic medical records remotely, HealthTap enables interactions between doctors and patients anytime and anywhere, while WelkinHealth promotes the formation of a platform for chronic disease monitoring and care, which all help to improve the communication model between doctors and patients. Alipay and WeChat have also realized online appointment for many hospitals, while Guangzhou Women and Children's Medical Center has implemented a "diagnosis first, payment later" process to shorten the time for medical consultations. In the future, digital healthcare technologies are also going to provide more comprehensive and scientific decision-making support and artificial intelligence analysis tools, reducing the costs of the medical workforce and realizing the full automation and AI-based development of medical services.

Taking Open Healthcare Data as the Means

Data, as an underlying resource of the information society, is playing an increasingly fundamental role in the future of the digital economy. Opening up healthcare big data resources and stimulating the vitality of innovation in all sectors of society is of great significance for tapping into the value of data and truly releasing the vitality of data-based healthcare.

In the past few years, digital health data collection by such means as hospital institutions, electronic medical records, and intelligent terminals has taken shape in the process of promoting medical informatization. It is predicted that by 2020, medical data resources will reach 40 trillion gigabytes (GB), of which 80% will be unstructured data. How to integrate, analyze, and apply the massive data and tap into the value behind the data will be the focus of future research conducted by digital healthcare practitioners. The U.S. Food and Drug Administration (FDA) launched the openFDA program in June 2014, making hundreds of millions of adverse drug reactions, medical treatment error reports, drug recalls, drug labels and other types of information submitted to the FDA from 2004 to 2013 public. Mobile terminal application developers, web developers, data visualization experts, and researchers could easily gain access to data for in-depth analysis through the application programming interface (API). The openness of data resources has greatly activated the vitality for innovation in all sectors of society. Social capital, scientific research organizations, and individuals have actively taken part in the analysis of medical data with such innovative models as crowdfunding, crowdsourcing, and collective wisdom. Google DeepMind has collaborated with Imperial College London and Royal Free Hospital to promote the application of machine learning technology in the healthcare sector. IBM Watson has been cooperating with the world-renowned MSKCC, with 21 Chinese hospitals currently applying IBM Watson's oncology solutions. Startups such as Evidation Health, Human API, and Validic are also attempting to integrate third-party medical resources to promote large-scale and efficient clinical trials. It can be seen that the open sharing of medical data resources is not only the openness of information resources, but also a collaborative innovation that combines the efforts of experts and social forces from all walks of life.

Taking the Medical Value-Oriented Approach as the Guidance

For any healthcare system, the pursuit of a better quality of medical service is a basic need of all people for medical support. The market competition rule of obtaining the best therapeutic effect at a fixed cost will reshape the value system of the global healthcare market and safeguard the healthy and sustainable development of the digital healthcare industry.

In the current healthcare system, the medical value is equal to the number of patients treated, with a highly fragmented payment and supply system based on surgeries, drugs, or fee-based services. There is a lack of coordination between public spending and private payments, or between hospitals and the industry, resulting in about 20 to 40% of medical resources being wasted annually on a global scale. Under the general trend of countries putting in efforts to control medical costs, the future healthcare system will pay more and more attention to medical "value," that is, to obtain the best therapeutic effect at a fixed cost, and push the medical market towards the direction of "competition based on therapeutic effect." Compared with competition over quantity, the advantage of competition based on therapeutic effect is that the focus of competition is on things truly important to patients. The root of the existence of all healthcare systems is providing cost-effective and high-quality medical services. In 2015, the U.S. Department of Health & Human Services (HHS) set a goal to base 50% of traditional medical expenses or fee-based services and medical social security on quality or value through replacing payment models by the end of 2018. The new incentive measures will be used to reward high-quality medical services instead of focusing solely on quantity. The National Health System (NHS) of the UK also brings together the efforts of the government, medical and related supporting service providers, housing services, public health, and other institutions to take further measures in providing better comprehensive medical services. By achieving transparency of the data on the therapeutic effect on patients and optimizing the incentive mechanisms, it enables payers, providers, manufacturers, and patients of medical services to work together for the same goal, and also allows the market to effectively balance between management costs and service quality.

Taking Digital Platforms as the Focus

As the global digital healthcare industry is still growing, and rules in the market and players in the industry are still unstable. Relying on the platform economy, we should integrate industrial resources and market resources, build a virtuous ecosystem, and provide a broader space for the development of digital healthcare enterprises.

Although it is a major trend for digital healthcare to revolutionize traditional healthcare, the path ahead remains tortuous. In 2017, the amount of financing for digital healthcare in the USA is expected to reach USD 6.5 billion. As digital healthcare startups accelerate their financing, a large number of companies are becoming zombie companies. There are fewer and fewer new startups that stand out, and perhaps even fewer could survive in the future. Accenture predicts that of the 900 digital healthcare projects it has studied, more than half would not be able to obtain a new round of financing in the next 20 months, thus facing the risk of shutdown. With an undecided current situation of the market, the key to success lies in going out of your way to put yourself at the center of the digital healthcare ecosystem, and integrating digital healthcare users, business models, and devices into your own platform by expanding the company's business. At present, digital healthcare startups in the USA hold nearly 1,700 patents, with top technical personnel from Google, Microsoft, and Yahoo. Traditional technology giants in healthcare information are eyeing this field, becoming vulture investors that buy innovative products of financially difficult startups to expand their business and profit from these products. St. Jude Medical obtained the

FDA-approved patent for a heart failure monitoring product through the acquisition of CardioMENS. Qualcomm Life obtained numerous technological talents by acquiring HealthyCircles. In the future, if any enterprise wishes to gain a strong footing in the digital healthcare industry, it must gather more talents, technologies, products, and innovative resources. It shall also attract more participants to join the network by taking the platform economy as the focus, and build a virtuous ecosystem featuring collaborative innovation and win–win outcomes. Only that could bring huge returns.

Taking the Multi-site Practice of Doctors as a Breakthrough

The multi-site practice of medical personnel is in line with the trend of virtualization and decentralization in the healthcare industry. Promoting the flow of professional labor resources could alleviate the imbalanced supply and demand of medical resources in the short to medium term.

With external challenges such as an aging population globally and an increase in the prevalence of chronic diseases, coupled with internal challenges such as high barriers to entry of medical professions, limited number of practitioners, unclear salary incentive mechanisms, and intensified doctor-patient conflicts, the supply of human resources in healthcare falls short of demand by a large margin. Improving the multi-site practice system for doctors could effectively alleviate the pressure of talent supply, and healthcare companies would also have more opportunities to come in contact with excellent talents and partners.

Currently, the Federation of State Medical Boards of the USA has enacted legislation in 18 states across the country to allow medical personnel to apply for licenses to practice in multiple states. The multi-site practice of British physicians is a "four plus one" model. Doctors of public hospital work in the hospital for four out of the five working days of a week, while they may choose to practice in other hospitals or community medical institutions for the remaining day. Non-fulltime doctors in public hospitals of Australia are permitted to practice part-time in national hospitals and private hospitals, allowing one doctor to practice in three or four hospitals at the same time. German law allows acting physicians to engage in services at the practice locations of the physicians they are acting. Practitioners could also provide outpatient and emergency services at specific times (such as after hours).

With the improvement of the multi-site practice systems of doctors in various countries, the power of the new medical models relying on the internet and social media will truly break out. Internet-based telemedicine will overcome the restrictions of the system and laws to effectively alleviate the current imbalance between supply and demand of medical resources.

Taking the Security of Personal Information as a Safeguard

In order to promote the stable, healthy, and sustainable development of the digital healthcare industry, it is essential to ensure the security of private information as a basic safeguard, clarify the definition of rights and responsibilities, improve the traceability system, and cultivate digital trust and moral responsibility of enterprises.

The informatization of digital healthcare is bound to break data islands and move towards open data sharing, so that data could bring real value while "flowing." However, how to drive the orderly flow, rational use, and safe sharing of data is an issue of concern for the industry. According to a survey, since 2013, more than 85% of the healthcare industry has encountered disclosure of patient data due to hacking. Both the European Union and the USA have extended legislative protection to personal healthcare information. In the past decade, due to the rapid development of internet technologies, both have promulgated new laws to adapt to new scenarios and needs. These laws mainly include the 2003 Privacy Rule and the Security Rule of the *Health Insurance Portability and Accountability Act* (HIPAA) and the 2013 HITECH Omnibus Rule of the USA, and the 2015 General Data Protection Regulation (GDPR) promulgated by the European Union, emphasizing that individuals have the right to dispose of, discretion and control over their own healthcare information. The *Cybersecurity Law of the People's Republic of China* was also passed on November 7, 2016, which came into effect on June 1, 2017. Behind the flow of data are huge business profits, making it necessary to improve data protection legislation, clarify the definition of rights and responsibilities in the process of data usage, and improve the traceability system for violations of laws and regulations together with the construction of credit systems in various countries. At the same time, enterprises should also strive to cultivate moral responsibilities in the process of data usage and improve the construction of their own network and data security. Brand reputation and credit in the market are hard to come by. Once an enterprise is found to have passed on personal information to third-party brokers for profit, the enterprise will completely lose the trust of consumers.

New Directions for the Development of Innovation in China's Digital Healthcare

Encouraging Innovation in the Application of Information Technology and the Cultivation of New Business Formats

China shall actively encourage the R&D of digital healthcare technologies, promote product innovation and clinical application, and strengthen research in key areas such as complicated diseases. It shall promote the application of DNA chips and gene sequencing technologies in the diagnosis of genetic diseases, early diagnosis of cancer, and disease prevention and detection, and promote the application of healthcare-related technologies and products such as artificial intelligence, biological 3D printing, medical robots, wearables, and related microsensors in disease prevention, health emergency response, health preservation, and daily care. It shall also actively encourage the private sector to engage in and innovation and development of the healthcare business, promote the in-depth integration of big data technology in the healthcare business, accelerate the construction of the digital healthcare industry chain, and continuously promote the coordinated development of healthcare and nourishment, elderly care, housekeeping, and other service industries.

Establishing a Sound Hierarchical Diagnosis and Treatment System

Considering the realities of China, we should make progress in the construction of a hierarchical diagnosis and treatment system to promote the orderly and effective sinking of high-quality medical resources. China shall improve the construction of grassroots healthcare talents with the focus on general practitioners, enhance the service capabilities of grassroots healthcare personnel, optimize the hierarchical diagnosis and treatment model of primary diagnosis, two-way referral, division of treatments for acute and chronic diseases, and linkage among levels. It shall facilitate the sharing of data resources and collaboration of services between large hospitals and grassroots healthcare institutions as well as that between general practitioners and specialists relying on the integrated service platform for healthcare. It shall also improve remote consultation, remote imaging, remote pathology, and remote ECG diagnosis services, and expand the service capabilities of healthcare institutions, so as to promote "downward shift of focus and sinking of resources" in a targeted manner.

Improving the Standard System and Data Protection System for Digital Healthcare

We shall speed up the construction of security systems for healthcare data, establish a responsibility system for data security management, and formulate rules for labeling, scientific classification, risk rating, and security review. Relevant institutions shall evaluate the reliability, controllability, and security of big data platforms and service providers, as well as the security evaluation and risk assessment of applications, so as to establish software evaluation and security review systems such as security protection, system interconnectivity and sharing, and privacy protection for citizens. At the same time, we shall strengthen big data security monitoring and early warning, establish a linkage mechanism between security information notification and emergency response, establish a sound working mechanism for "Internet Plus Healthcare" service security, improve risk mitigation and response measures, strengthen the protection of national interests, public safety, patient privacy, business secrets, and other important information, and tighten up the security of medical schools, scientific research institutions and others.

Digital Transportation

By creating a fair, efficient, safe, convenient, and environmentally friendly transportation system, digital transportation strives to meet the growing travel and transportation needs of people in the digital economy and society. It is a current hotspot and frontier for the development of transportation in the world and an important branch of the digital economy.

Digital Transportation Has Become a Trend in the Development of the Transportation Industry Worldwide

The core of the digital economy is data, a factor of production, while the key for smart transportation to play its role also depends on data-driven traffic management and services. Digital transportation includes not only detailed, dynamic, and smart management and control of transportation, but also convenient and safe transportation services. It is the manifestation of the digital economy in public services and social governance, and also a characteristic sector in the transition process from an industrial society to an information society. The ideal state of digital transportation is to achieve an all-round comprehensive smart connection of people, vehicles, roads, and environments. Specifically, digital transportation is a service system for transportation based on modern information and communication technology. It is composed of multiple sub-systems such as people, vehicles, roads, and environments, which focus on the collection, processing, distribution, exchange, analysis and utilization of information on transportation vehicles, roads, and services to provide efficient interconnection, optimal matching, and diversified services for participants of transportation and passengers, goods, transportation vehicles, and practitioners through multi-level, multi-mode, and smart means.

Traditional Automobile Manufacturers and Technology Enterprises Are Entering the Field of Digital Transportation from Different Directions

Digital transportation, an information system with integrated application of multiple technologies, is a technology derived from the intersection of the two basic industries of the transportation and automobile industry and the information and communication industry. Automobile enterprises and information and communication enterprises are shaping the future of smart transportation through different paths with efforts from their respective positions. On the one hand, the development of digital technologies has lowered the technical barriers to entry for the production of core components such as automobile engines and gearboxes. Information technology enterprises are entering the automobile industry from the aspects of creating smart, dynamic interactive vehicle operating systems, assisted driving, automated driving systems, and factory communication systems. In 2016, a report released by Forbes revealed that Tesla, Google, Apple, and Uber are widely recognized as the four giants of the future automobile industry of the world with their powerful computing and communication capabilities as well as algorithms and data mining capabilities. They have gradually been exerting pressure on traditional automobile enterprises. On the other hand, traditional automobile manufacturers are focusing on driverless technology and automobile electronics relying on their advantages in such fields as power and maneuverability. In 2017, BMW is going to test a fleet of 40 driverless vehicles in Munich, and subsequently expand this test project to other cities.

Countries Are Comprehensively Planning for Smart Vehicles and Digital Transportation

The USA is the bellwether of the development of digital transportation and smart vehicles. Its digital transportation, automated driving policies, and legislation on mandatory installation of vehicle-to-everything (V2X) systems have attracted attention from various countries. In 2015, the U.S. Department of Transportation issued the *ITS Strategic Plan 2015–2019*, which proposes the two strategic priorities of realizing connected vehicle implementation and advancing automation. At the same time, it proposes to create safer vehicles and roads, ease traffic pressure, enhance the flow of traffic, build a green digital transportation system, and comprehensively promote the development and innovation of digital transportation technologies. At the end of 2016, the U.S. Department of Transportation issued mandatory regulations on vehicle-to-vehicle (V2V) communication, requiring all light-duty vehicles produced in the future to be equipped with V2V communication devices.

Europe also attaches great importance to digital transportation, especially the R&D and industrial layout of the Internet of Vehicles, with the focus on developing new technologies represented by the Internet of Vehicles as the core competitiveness of the industry. In Horizon 2020, the EU Framework Programme for Research & Innovation, the EU proposed to develop smart, green, and integrated transportation, and accelerate the R&D on the Internet of Vehicles. *The Future Development of the*

Common Transport Policy: A Global Approach to the Construction of a Community Framework for Sustainable Mobility—White Paper of the EU focuses on the rational allocation and interconnection of various transportation networks such as highways, buses, railways, and water transport, and proposes the construction of efficient, coordinated, and environmentally friendly digital transportation systems and integrated transportation hubs.

The*Basic Act on Transport Policy* of Japan outlines a blueprint for the future of digital transportation. It points out that Japan must pay attention to the intensive and seamless connection of transportation planning and modes of transportation, closely integrate modes of transportation such as highways, navigation, aviation, and high-speed railway, with a focus on effectiveness of the allocation of transportation resources and environmental impact, so as to create a convenient, comfortable, green and safe comprehensive transportation network covering the whole of Japan.[2] At the same time, in order to present the world with a highly efficient and technologically advanced Japan at the Tokyo 2020 Olympic Games, the Japanese government is actively encouraging automobile enterprises such as Toyota and Honda to vigorously support the development of driverless vehicles so that they can be used in large numbers at the Olympic Games.

Trends in the Development of Digital Transportation Globally

Automated Driving Based on Smart Vehicles Has Become a Rising Star

Smart vehicles are no longer a means of transportation in the traditional sense, but a comprehensive technological product that integrates various capabilities such as smart interaction, automatic control, external communication, and artificial intelligence, and a new carrier for the hardware of innovative car services. Smart vehicles collect information inside and outside the vehicle (which are now measured in GBs) through built-in lidar, ultrasonic sensors, millimeter-wave radar, cameras, and the like, and build an automobile smart hub to realize intelligent operation and

[2] Strategies for the Development of Smart Transportation Systems Geared to the AI-based society in the Future, 2016.

automatic control of vehicles by using graphics processing units (GPUs) and neural network calculation methods. After small-scale demonstration, R&D, testing, and other stages, smart vehicles have begun to be driven and tested on actual roads, and some commercial vehicles have begun actual road tests on highways in the West. For example, Melbourne has realized the operation of driverless mini-buses in urban areas. According to predictions of relevant research, there will be 18 million vehicles worldwide with driverless functions by 2035, of which 12 million will have full driverless functions.

Although driverless technology is constantly being piloted and commercialized on a global scale, it still faces a series of unresolved problems in terms of technology and legislation. First, the massive data collected by smart vehicles and the Internet of Vehicles requires dozens of digital signal processing (DSP) chips to process, which is too costly. Due to the extensive access to various types of connected sensing devices and modifications done to existing control systems, there is a greater possibility of hacking of smart vehicles. Second, in addition to technical issues, the judgment of liabilities for traffic accidents is also going to restrict the commercial application of driverless vehicles. Recently, a self-driving vehicle of Google collided with a bus when the auto-driving mode was turned on. It has become a landmark event in the development of driverless vehicles, as the liability of the accident is yet to be clearly defined. In addition, many people still have doubts about whether driverless vehicles could realize their vision. As *Scientific American* puts forward in the latest issue of the magazine, driverless vehicles could not improve the efficiency of commuters; they only increase the density of vehicles, potentially making traffic even more congested.

Various Countries Are Conducting Research on Legislation for Automated Driving

The UN *Convention on Road Traffic* is an important international treaty for solving road and automobile traffic problems, with basically no major amendments over the past 50 years. In March 2016, the *Convention on Road Traffic* changed the original stipulation that "every driver of a vehicle shall in all circumstances have his vehicle under control" to "allowing those vehicles that have applied autonomous driving technology to participate in road traffic activities." This has paved the way for the integration of smart vehicles, especially driverless ones, into the daily life of human beings. At the same time, the National Highway Traffic Safety Administration of the USA issued the ***Preliminary Statement of Policy Concerning Automated Vehicles*** as early as 2013. Four states, including Nevada, have passed legislation for automated vehicles, with a focus on the testing licenses and testing supervision of automated vehicles.

In the past two years, relevant agencies of the United Nations have been formulating international safety regulations for automated vehicles. It is expected that relevant regulations will be passed in the first half of 2017. In 2016, the National Highway Traffic Safety Administration of the USA stated that it agreed to treat computers as drivers for Google's driverless vehicles. Moreover, the U.S. government has begun to develop a federal policy involving driverless vehicles, and has pledged to invest USD 4 billion in the next ten years. In addition, legislative bodies of countries such as Germany, Japan, and the UK have initiated legislation for automated vehicles.

The Internet of Vehicles Has Become an Important Direction for Development

Internet of Vehicles and AI-based development are the two major directions for the future of digital transportation, especially smart vehicles. Among them, the Internet of Vehicles uses the new-generation information and communication technology to realize comprehensive connections in vehicles, between vehicles and people, between vehicles and vehicles, between vehicles and roads, and between vehicles and service platform, promoting the transformation and upgrading of industries such as information and communication, automobile and transportation and solving outstanding social problems. The wireless communication technology of the Internet of Vehicles extends sensing to a range out of the reach of onboard sensors, and effectively improves the driving assistance functions.

At present, there are two types of standards for the wireless communication technology of the Internet of Vehicles. The first is based on the 802.11P wireless communication technology of the Institute of Electrical and Electronics Engineers (IEEE), which has been adequately tested as it was released quite early. Chipmakers such as NXP Semiconductors and Qualcomm have launched mature products. However, they could not fully meet the needs of people especially in terms of capacity and anti-interference as the technical conditions and business requirements way back then were different from the current ones. The other is the LTE-V2X technology based on cellular communication technology. With the development of demand, it has been evolving to V2X based on 5G communication technology on a clear path of technological evolution, becoming one of the many application fields of the Internet of Things with the greatest potential in the market.

Precise Sensing of Urban Traffic Conditions and Smart Navigation Have Become Possible

Traditional digital transportation mainly relies on cameras, inductive-loop traffic detectors, and other equipment to monitor traffic flow. With the deployment of the Internet of Things in the main urban road sections and parking lots and the popularization of smart devices, the full integration and accurate sensing of traffic data within the city limits realized with diversified and multi-dimensional data such as mobile phone communication data, parking data, Electronic Toll Collection (ETC) tolling data, and weather data is helpful for the AI-based control of urban traffic. In 2016, the U.S. Department of Transportation and Google's Sidewalk Labs jointly launched a development plan for a traffic information platform called Flow. The platform collects traffic information through sensors deployed on the streets, and uses Wi-Fi-enabled phone booths and geographic data from map service companies to realize real-time traffic monitoring of future "smart cities." The Flow platform gathers information on vehicles such as shared cars, taxis, bicycles, and buses, as well as the flow of traffic on the roads, providing citizens with the best travel suggestions based on urban traffic conditions and available parking lots, with active, positive guidance on the flow of urban traffic.

AI as a Service Has Become a New Service Format

With the comprehensive application and penetration of information technology, transportation has gradually become a new type of service, forming multiple types of transportation planning based on big data analysis that facilitates the abundant choices of the means and routes of transportation from departure to arrival at the destination. Europe took the lead in proposing the new concept of "Transportation as a Service" at the World Congress on Intelligent Transport Systems, which has received responses from the transportation industries in the USA, Japan, and South Korea, planning and designing transportation as a service. The quality of transportation services is defined according to such indicators as the time taken for each trip, the number of transfers, expenses, and carbon emissions, which depends heavily on the collection, analysis, and mining of transportation data.

Internet enterprises are more actively embracing the concept of "Transportation as a Service," creating a variety of "Transportation as a Service" such as shared taxi, tailored taxi service, vehicle and cargo matching, customized bus, O2O parking, and comprehensive traffic information service application through the prototype of "Internet Plus Transportation." For example, Uber, as a latecomer to digital transportation, uses its software platform to provide services such as smart travel and shared transportation. It also delivers flu vaccination services to people's homes in 35 cities of the USA. People only need to open the Uber mobile phone application at specific hours and click "UberHEALTH" to receive the home delivery service for flu vaccination.

Trends in the Development of Digital Transportation in China

As an important direction of the digital economy, the digital transportation industry has maintained rapid growth in recent years. Grand View Research has pointed out that by 2020, the global digital transportation industry will exceed USD 38 billion in size. As a key branch of digital transportation, the automated driving industry has emerged out of the blue, with its development far exceeding market expectations and the average growth rate of digital transportation. An annual report of HIS, an automobile information consulting company in the USA, pointed out that by 2035, the global sales of driverless vehicles will exceed 21 million units; China will become the world's biggest market for driverless vehicles in the future with its vast consumption and huge population size, taking up more than 25% of the global market.

After a period of rapid development of China's digital transportation industry during the "12th Five-Year Plan," the amount of investment in the field has increased rapidly at an average annual growth rate of over 25%. As of the end of 2015, the size of China's comprehensive digital transportation market exceeded RMB 65 billion. Meanwhile, more than 30 enterprises engaged in the Internet of Vehicles and digital transportation have been listed on stock exchanges.

Ministries and Local Governments Are Actively Engaging in Pilots and Demonstrations

In recent years, relevant ministries and commissions of China such as the Ministry of Transport and National Development and Reform Commission have successively introduced policies for digital transportation, "Internet Plus Transportation" and the like, forming an adequate policy environment for vigorously promoting the development of digital transportation. In 2016, the Ministry of Transport released the *IT-based Development Plan for Transportation in the 13th Five-Year Plan.* In the same year, the Ministry of Industry and Information Technology released the *Work Plan for the Innovation and Development of Internet of Vehicles*, the first development plan specifically targeting the Internet of Vehicles. It proposes the goals and key tasks for the development of China's Internet of Vehicles, with a focus on key generic technologies, standards, basic conditions, experimental verification, application and promotion, cyberspace information security and other fields. At present, the Ministry of Industry and Information Technology has signed cooperation agreements with Zhejiang, Beijing, Baoding, and Chongqing on the construction of the Internet of Vehicles demonstration zones.

In January 2017, the Ministry of Transport issued the *Action Plan for Promoting the Development of Smart Transportation (2017–2020).* In March of the same year, the State Council issued the *Development Plan for a Comprehensive Modern Transportation System in the 13th Five-Year Plan*, which proposes the five tasks of facilitating the AI-based transformation of the transportation industry, promoting the upgrading of smart transportation services, optimizing operations and control of transportation, improving smart decision-making support and supervision, and strengthening the AI-based construction of transportation development. At the same time, the *Specifications for Testing of Smart Connected Vehicles on Public Roads* prepared by the Ministry of Industry and Information Technology, Ministry of Public Security and Ministry of Transport will be released soon. The Internet of Vehicles has become the focus of the "Internet Plus" action plans of most provinces and municipalities, with 20 provinces embarking on the construction of the Internet of Vehicles nationwide.

Infrastructure and Technical Application and Promotion of Digital Transportation is Progressing Steadily

On the one hand, there is great progress made in smart infrastructure supporting digital transportation. The comprehensive application of information technologies such as wireless communication networks, sensing facilities, and smart computing in highway infrastructure has greatly improved the safety guarantee and smart sensing and interaction in the operation of vehicles. Based on the corresponding geographic information public platforms, Zhejiang Province has completed the plotting of 800 km of high-grade electronic navigational charts, collecting data of important landmarks such as basic navigational information, water service facilities, ship locks, and buoys. In terms of the basic network for transportation information, the Datong-Xi'an High-speed Railway has completed the testing for the interconnection of the public mobile communication system and the satellite communication technology in the carriages. On the other hand, significant progress has been made in the application and promotion of digital transportation technologies. Early digital transportation technologies mainly focused on detection, verification, and scheduling. With the widespread implementation of such technologies as the Internet of Things and mobile internet and the full application of big data, the current digital transportation system places more emphasis on supporting decision-making in traffic scheduling through data analysis. Hangzhou has built an "urban data brain" to automatically optimize and effectively allocate transportation resources through comprehensive monitoring and active use of the government's open big data resources for transportation. It has achieved the favorable outcome of increasing the speed of vehicles on the road by 3 to 5% on average, with an 11% increase in some road sections.

Smart Connected Vehicles and Smart Driving Have Become Important Directions for the Development of Digital Transportation

In 2016, China's development plan for the automobile industry in the "Thirteenth Five-Year Plan" proposed that smart connected vehicles are one of the eight major directions for development. *Made in China*

2025 proposed to establish preliminary independent R&D and production support systems for smart connected vehicles by 2020. With the introduction of policies for the Internet of Vehicles and other related fields, Shanghai, Shenzhen, Zhejiang and other provinces and municipalities have successively launched automated driving demonstration zone projects. China has already launched demonstrations for driverless automated driving vehicles in some cities and several road sections, with emerging new cooperative smart transportation modes. In 2016, Shanghai set up a closed test zone named "National Smart Connected Vehicle Pilot Demonstration Zone (Shanghai)" to provide more than 20 testing and verification scenarios for smart connected vehicles, driverless technology, and autonomous driving. The People's Government of Wuhu, Anhui Province has cooperated with Baidu to jointly build "operation areas for fully driverless vehicles." The Wuzhen Water Town of Zhejiang Province has piloted fully automated driverless vehicles on some roads in the scenic area.

Applications of Technologies Such as Electronic Vehicle Identification and Smart Parking Have Become New Highlights of Digital Transportation

Electronic vehicle identification is the extended use of IoT-based passive radio frequency identification (RFID) in the field of smart transportation. In recent years, China has made positive progress in the implementation and promotion of electronic vehicle identification. Chongqing is the first in China to adopt electronic identification to promote the development of smart transportation. About 2 million electronic plates have been issued so far, with nearly 150 road surface information collection points constructed to covering major urban roads and key checkpoints of the city. The Traffic Management Research Institute of the Ministry of Public Security has drafted six national standards including *General Technical Specification of Electronic Registration Identification of Motor Vehicles* upon sufficient investigation and carried out demonstration projects in Wuxi, Beijing, and Shenzhen. At the beginning of 2016, Wuxi and Shenzhen have become the first demonstration cities in China to begin using electronic vehicle identification in digitalized traffic management, with

31,000 and 60,000 key vehicles installed with electronic identifiers respectively. Shenzhen is expected to expand the number of vehicles install with electronic identifiers to more than 200,000 in 2017.

"Smart parking" relies on information technology to effectively integrate parking space resources, expand parking spaces, optimize links of parking management, and reduce the time needed for parking, thereby effectively solving the problems of difficulty in finding parking spaces and expensive parking fees. In 2016, the National Development and Reform Commission issued the *Notice on Printing and Distributing Key Points for Construction of Parking Lots in 2016*. Six cities including Beijing and Shenzhen were used as pilots to encourage the application of intensive three-dimensional garages and the simultaneous construction of charging piles. By the end of the year, Guiyang had started the pilot work of smart parking management. By sorting out, counting, and fully utilizing public parking resources in the city, it has built a basic parking database, and encouraged citizens to check and reserve parking spaces before traveling to achieve green travel and smart parking. In addition, Yunxi Township of Zhejiang Province has cooperated with such enterprises as Huawei and China Mobile to deploy a narrowband IoT smart parking demonstration. By providing smart mobile apps, it realizes the whole process services of status query of all parking lots, parking navigation, reverse car search, and self-service payment.

CHAPTER 9

Vigorously Promoting Digital Transformation in Finance

Finance is a data-intensive industry. From the early use of punched cards to assist data processing to the use of computers to achieve computerized accounting, and from the use of mainframes for integrated business processing to the use of the internet to develop various new business models, financial institutions have been the most active in the application of information technology in the course of their development.

The Ecosystem of Digital Finance

Digital finance constantly develops as an ecosystem. Within the ecosystem, technology enterprises have gradually penetrated into the financial industry and actively entered the territory of traditional financial companies. At the same time, traditional financial institutions have also accelerated the application of new technologies and the pace of financial innovation through modern technologies. For example, Goldman Sachs of the USA claims to be a technology company, with the total number of technical engineers accounting for 1/3 of all employees, exceeding that of Facebook.

M. Huateng et al., *The Chinese Digital Economy*,
https://doi.org/10.1007/978-981-33-6005-1_9

Payment

Payment is an important field of innovation in fintech. The payment business of fintech companies is different from that of traditional financial institutions. The former relies on cloud computing, big data, blockchain, and other technologies to create a more scenario-based and convenient payment platform, and conducts other related services through accurate analysis of massive transaction data. Today, whoever has control over the payment interface would be able to likewise control the financing and investment scenarios, forming a closed loop of financial ecosystem integrating foreign exchange, lending, and deposit. At present, non-traditional financial institutions such as Baidu, Alibaba, and Tencent (collectively referred to as BAT) and third-party payment account for a large market share of front-end customers. These institutions include WeChat Pay, Alipay, JDPAY, Baidu Wallet, and 99Bill.com. Banks, on the other hand, has been turning into back-end channels for payment. With the development and application of blockchain technology, banks may even lose the back-end channel of payment.

Online Lending

Online lending facilitates the direct connection between the demand side and the supply side of capital, which unleashes the financing needs of SMEs and individual consumers. The advantages of online lending are flexible and convenient borrowing methods, limited restrictions on borrowing, and low barrier. Online lending breaks the credit business model and framework of traditional financial institutions. By collecting more extensive data and using big data analysis and machine learning algorithms to perform credit ratings, it could provide customers with more convenient and personalized credit services.

Wealth Management

Wealth management manages the assets, liabilities, and liquidity of customers by providing customers with a series of financial services such as cash, credit, insurance, and investment portfolio, so as to meet their financial needs at different stages, helping them reduce risks and realize growth in wealth. With the application of emerging technologies such as cloud computing, big data, and artificial intelligence, wealth management is gradually shifting from traditional financial institutions such as banks to technology companies. Business model innovation in the field of wealth management mainly focuses on lowering investment thresholds and transaction costs, simplifying decision-making processes for investment, and ensuring the convenience and security of transactions. For example, smart investment consultants automatically provide users with asset allocation suggestions through algorithms applying the most basic asset portfolio theory and other derivative models, using market information obtained quickly and accurately at low cost with cloud computing, big data, and other technologies, and considering the risk preference, financial conditions and wealth management goals of investors. Smart investment consultants have changed the traditional service model of face-to-face contact between customers and financial consultants. Its advantages include low cost and easy operation, which could avoid the interference of the emotions of investors, spread investment risks, and obtain information in a relatively transparent manner, so that ordinary customers could also enjoy services previously only available to senior financial institutions.

Insurance

The development of emerging technologies represented by the Internet of Things, cloud computing, big data, and artificial intelligence plays a huge role in promoting and facilitating development and innovation in the insurance industry. The application of the Internet of Things technology has nurtured new models of Internet of Things insurance, such as Internet of Vehicles insurance. Cloud computing provides a safe, reliable, and efficient basic technology platform for internet insurance. By applying big data analysis to business processes such as the design of insurance products, automated ordering, settlement of automobile insurance claims, precision marketing, and risk management, personalized internet insurance products could be customized for netizens. Artificial intelligence has comprehensively improved such processes as marketing, service, operations, and risk control in insurance.

Retail Banking

In traditional banking, retail banking has always been one of the most profitable services in the banking industry. In recent years, innovative fintech companies are gradually invading retail banking. A significant part of the reason is that the return on investment of brick-and-mortar branches is gradually declining due to rising labor costs, while most business costs could be saved through automation. Targeting consumers and SMEs, retail banking is characterized by small and scattered transactions, which are conducted mainly via such means as bank branches, automated teller machines (ATMs), online banking, and mobile banking. Under the current technological and institutional environment, technology is deeply integrated into finance, and new retail bankers are exploring purely online digital banking without setting up any physical branches, enabling remote account opening, and using modern technology to deliver a better experience in financial services.

Digital Technologies Have Extensive Applications in the Financial Industry

Fintech mainly refers to the application and innovation of modern technology in the financial field, especially the application and innovation of modern information technologies such as cloud computing, big data, artificial intelligence, Internet of Things, and blockchain.

The Applications of Cloud Computing

Cloud computing is a revolution in the establishment, delivery, and use of IT resources. In recent years, China's financial regulatory authorities have gradually clarified their support for cloud computing. Public cloud service providers have been further increasing their investment in the financial field, as more and more cloud service providers have built financial industry public clouds that specifically serve financial institutions. At the same time, more and more financial institutions are considering using public cloud services or building proprietary cloud platforms, and the cloud computing market in the financial industry is gradually expanding. For various reasons, many financial institutions still have concerns over public cloud services.

The Applications of Big Data

With the rapid development of big data technologies, the application scenarios of big data in the financial industry are gradually expanding, with extensive applications in such segments as risk control, operations management, sales support, and business model innovation. Due to the characteristics of the industry itself, the financial industry has been an active player in the fields of data management and data analysis before the concept of "big data" was proposed, and has conducted fruitful practices in data warehousing, data analysis platforms, and data mining, among other fields. In recent years, the industry has actively absorbed and learned the concept of "big data" and relevant technologies, and pushed existing data analysis to a new level in its own business. For example, among internet finance services companies, the areas where big data applications are prominent include fast credit, risk control and anti-fraud, big data marketing, user portrait, and dynamic pricing.

Fast Credit

Internet finance has lowered the cost of credit rating and marketing through big data and other technical means, so that a wider group of people could have access to loans or investments. Currently, the time taken for approval of small loans in the industry has generally been lowered to ten seconds or even one second.

Risk Control and Anti-fraud

Fraud activities include forging information to gain more credit, arbitrage using loopholes in procedures, and even getting loans with stolen or forged identities. Due to the non-contact nature and convenience of the internet, this kind of fraud is more concealed and quicker to complete. Anti-fraud measures with big data usually require multiple risk control models to work together, including models based on the personal application information of the user, the social relations of the user, and historical transactions made by the user. At the same time, machine learning models could also be used to automatically detect non-linear combinations of features, improving the accuracy of recognition. An obvious advantage of anti-fraud efforts using big data is that when there are a great many models and a significant amount of calculation, the relationship between conclusions and data can no longer be interpreted by human experience.

Big Data Marketing

Big data solutions in marketing include analyzing credit products, gaining insight into target customer groups, and forming user portraits; predicting customer desires through desire prediction models; dividing customers into different tiers and adopting different marketing methods for different value tiers; designing marketing templates considering common characteristics of customer groups; optimizing and updating models with real-time data feedback; helping risk control modeling and cross-marketing through dynamic analysis of customers. Due to the introduction of precise marketing models of big data, the overall response rate and compliance rate are significantly improved compared to the traditional models. With the gradual optimization and updating of models, the effect of marketing at various links is also showing an upward trend.

User Portrait

Be it lending or investing money, enterprises need to understand customers in-depth, including their income, ability to pay back, consumption preferences, and allocation of assets, and even psychological conditions, social relations, and trends in their professions. These are of great significance for the prediction of investment or borrowing behaviors of customers. Through big data analysis, internet finance companies could expand the labels for customer attributes from dozens to hundreds or even thousands, thus comprehensively describing a customer with nothing missed out.

Dynamic Pricing

Dynamic pricing refers to abandoning the traditional fixed pricing model centering on products to relate prices to service scenarios and recipients, and achieving the purpose of improving returns using price leverage to deal with risks more accurately. A typical example of this application is freight insurance: through big data analysis, insurance companies could set prices according to specific people and commodities.

The Applications of Artificial Intelligence

Artificial intelligence has broad prospects for application in the financial industry. At present, the four major types of services arising from the integration of artificial intelligence in finance include automatic generation of reports by investment banks and securities research institutions, AI-assisted quantitative trading, securities research conducted by financial search engines, and wealth management by smart investment consultants. These have shown the unlimited possibilities of smart finance as a result of the integration of artificial intelligence in finance in the future.

The Applications of the Internet of Things

The combination of the Internet of Things technology and finance involves multiple business directions such as banking, insurance, financing, and leasing. There are both improvements to the internal operations management of these institutions and innovation in financial models.

For example, the financial Internet of Things could also enhance the ability of financial companies to manage key internal data, such as the electronic labeling of file boxes adopted by some banks and insurance companies, which not only realizes service progress queries, reading and writing of handling opinions, and process time management, but also provides supporting evidence for internal service pricing and risk accountability.

As another example, with the full popularization of online commodity trading, the authenticity issue of trade has become a major factor restricting the development of supporting financial services for trading. Internet of Things technologies such as electronic trading platforms, warehousing and logistics companies, and financial institutions relate the IT-based online transaction process with the actual delivery of offline commodities to match commodity trading and delivery with services provided by financial institutions such as fund supervision and payment clearing, achieving the unity of information flow, logistics and capital flow of transactions.

The Applications of Blockchain

Blockchain is effectively a continuously growing distributed ledger maintained by multiple parties. Its core concept lies in establishing a mutual trust relationship between parties through the cryptographic ledger and distributed consensus mechanisms characterized by distributed network and non-tamperable time sequence. It uses smart contracts composed of automated script codes to program and manipulate data, eventually realizing the evolution from information interconnection to value interconnection. The reason why the blockchain has attracted widespread attention from the financial industry is that it has the great potential to transform finance, and that it may bring new opportunities and new challenges to the financial industry.

The Blockchain Technology Has the Potential to Improve the Collaborative Service Capabilities of Financial Institutions

Services such as syndicated loans, supply chain finance, and trade financing may involve multiple financial institutions and multiple enterprises in different countries, requiring a long period of coordination among parties and complicated processes to complete the services. Many services are still using paper documents, which need to be manually checked and processed with the participation of multiple parties. For this type of financial services involving many participants and complicated processes, blockchain technology has the potential to enhance the level of automation, simplify collaborative processes, and accelerate collaborative efficiency of services conducted between different financial institutions.

The Blockchain Technology Has the Potential to Lower the Costs of Financial Operations

Various business systems and background jobs of financial institutions tend to have long processes and many links. Nowadays, Visa, MasterCard, and Alipay are all operated by centralized institutions. The transfer of funds must be conducted through third-party institutions, which results in excessively high costs arising from cross-border transactions, currency exchange, internal accounting and the like, and brings risks to capital. Blockchain technology could optimize the business processes of financial institutions, reduce the interactions between the front office and the back office, and save a lot of manpower and material resources, hence reducing costs of financial operations.

The Blockchain Technology Has the Potential to Improve the Business Audit System

In the current business audit process, it takes a lot of manpower and material resources to check the authenticity of such data as the balance of funds and transaction contracts of the audited entity. The technical characteristics of the blockchain allow all transaction data to be recorded in blocks in an open, transparent, and tamper-proof manner. Any transaction data could be queried and traced, thereby improving auditing efficiency, reducing auditing costs, and improving the reliability of auditing results.

The Blockchain Technology Is Helpful to Financial Regulation and Compliance Checking

The characteristics of openness, transparency, and non-tamperable time sequence of the blockchain technology could help financial regulators monitor every inflow and outflow of funds. This helps to control financial assets and step up efforts to crack down on illegal and criminal activities such as money laundering and black-market transactions, preventing systemic risks in the financial market. The smart contract technology of the blockchain could automatically verify the compliance of transactions and users, hence improving the efficiency and reducing the costs and probability of errors of compliance checks.

Innovating the Regulation Models of Digital Finance

Regulators in various countries are most concerned about how to promote the healthy development of digital finance and ensure the stability of the financial system. Digital technologies are undoubtedly helpful to the development of the financial industry, but at the same time, the strong power and influence displayed by it have a revolutionizing effect on the entire financial industry, which might be destructive. Nowadays, most countries and regions require that innovations in digital finance follow the basic principles of existing financial supervision to ensure consistency. Therefore, in the face of constantly advancing financial technologies, governments of various countries are also actively adjusting their regulatory strategies to ensure the healthy, rapid development of digital finance.

There Is No Consensus Among Regulatory Policies Yet

There are huge differences in regulation on specific fintech categories on a global scale. On the one hand, this is due to the uneven development of digital finance in various countries and regions; on the other hand, it is because a consensus on the definition of digital finance is yet to be formed. It is common to see a "race" between the development of digital finance and the promulgation of regulatory policies by countries. With increasing AI-based and technology-driven development of fintech, there is an increasing need for appropriate governance and supporting mechanisms to ensure that "technology" is properly integrated into "finance," thereby improving the efficiency of financial services.

Cooperation in Regulation Lags Behind the Globalization of Digital Finance

At present, digital finance has gathered entities such as traditional financial institutions and innovative fintech enterprises, with head-on competition going on in some fields. This situation has now spread to the international financial market, but the cross-border regulatory cooperation on digital finance has clearly lagged behind the development of the industry. On March 16, 2016, the Financial Stability Board (FSB) held its 16th plenary session in Japan, during which it formally discussed the systemic risks of digital finance and global regulatory issues for the first time. This marked the end of individual regulation of digital finance by various industries and countries and the beginning of a new stage characterized by global coordination and cooperation, with financial stability becoming an important factor for consideration.

Regulatory Authorities Are Exploring Regulatory Models for Digital Finance

Faced with rapid technological development, governments of various countries are actively adjusting their regulatory strategies to ensure that digital finance is developing rapidly in the right direction. Generally speaking, there are three main types of regulatory methods that governments of various countries have explored with the times.

The first is restrictive regulation represented by the case of the USA. The financial system of the USA has a long history. Its financial regulations and supervision are relatively sophisticated after enduring multiple financial crises over the past 100 years. Faced with a new fintech sector, although the existing laws and regulations could not cover it, the government is able to timely adjust the legislation for it to operate within the prescribed scope by virtue of sound regulatory and legislative systems. The USA adopts functional supervision, that is, grasping the essence of fintech regardless of the form taken by digital finance, and integrating financial services associated with the fintech into the existing financial supervision system according to their functions. For example, as the business of Lending Club, a typical company in the peer-to-peer (P2P) lending industry, involves asset securitization, the relevant business of it is regulated by the U.S. Securities and Exchange Commission (SEC). In 2012, the US government enacted the Jumpstart Our Business Startups Act to fill the gap in the regulation of equity crowdfunding. Overall, digital finance is under strict regulation in the USA.

The second is active supervision represented by the cases of the UK and Singapore. The typical characteristics of countries adopting this type of supervision are sound financial systems, abundant financial talents, and sophisticated corresponding regulations. Without market and technology as drivers, government policies have become the major force in the development of digital finance in these countries. Both London and Singapore are competing to become the new digital financial center of the world, so they are constantly updating regulatory means to guide and promote the development of digital finance in the country. The Financial Conduct Authority (FCA) of the UK has launched "Project Innovate" aimed at promoting financial innovation. In November 2015, it pioneered the implementation of the "regulatory sandbox" plan for finance, which was later officially launched in May 2016 after six months of planning. After studying the FCA plan, the Monetary Authority of

Singapore launched the Singapore version of the "regulatory sandbox" in June 2016. Any fintech company registered in the "sandbox" could engage in business that conflicts with current laws and regulations as long as the business is reported in advance, and will not be legally prosecuted even if the business is officially terminated in the future. Australia and Hong Kong and Taiwan regions of China are also eagerly preparing their own versions of the "regulatory sandbox" following the examples of the UK and Singapore. With this "sandbox" mechanism, the government is able to carry out a variety of financial innovations within a controllable range, and allow entrepreneurs to rest assured when trying various relevant innovative businesses. Through this "regulatory sandbox" mechanism, regulatory authorities have changed their passive, lagging image of the past to actively participate in the development of digital finance, providing key help in shortening the innovation cycles and saving compliance costs of related companies. At the same time, it also allows regulatory authorities to monitor and guide the potential risks of digital finance to the financial system from the very beginning, eliminating systemic risks right after they appear rather than fixing the loopholes after incidents.

The third is passive supervision. In some developing countries, laws and regulations regarding the financial system are inadequate compared to the West. Driven by capital and the market, the development of digital finance is mainly fueled by the market and business models. Most of the time, regulatory authorities are forced to release corresponding regulatory measures after trial and error by fintech companies.

PART IV

Suggestions: Actively Responding to Revolutions in the Digital Economy

CHAPTER 10

Development of the Digital Economy: Problems and Countermeasures

Problems in the Development of the Digital Economy

According to the experience of foreign countries and the practice of China, the following potential problems and risks require attention during the development of the digital economy.

The Digital Divide and the Quality of Data

The digital divide includes both the divide in terms of access to infrastructure and that in terms of digital literacy. In terms of access, there are still 4 billion people in the world without access to the internet. Although most of them are located in developing countries, developed countries in the West have yet to completely overcome the digital divide. In terms of digital literacy, there is a general shortage of digital skills in all countries. Statistics from the European Union in 2014 show that up to 47% of the EU's population lacks adequate "digital capabilities," constituting the biggest obstacle to digital development in Europe. The digital divide has also been a stubborn problem in China for many years. In recent years, although the penetration of the internet in China has continued to increase and the number of internet users has continued to increase, the digital divide between urban and rural areas and that between East China and West China have been expanding.

M. Huateng et al., *The Chinese Digital Economy*,
https://doi.org/10.1007/978-981-33-6005-1_10

The quality of data is another important issue. Data is as important as personnel, technology, and capital, becoming the core, strategic asset of many companies and countries. Therefore, many countries are promoting the openness of data and driving the development of many enterprises. However, a lot of the open data are not under the same standard, affecting the efficiency of use. The World Bank found that the quality of data is the number one problem in a survey conducted on data-oriented enterprises in low- and middle-income countries. The improvement of the quality of data depends on the release of general standards and procedures by government departments to improve the standardization of data; otherwise, a "digital divide" will be formed on the data supply side.

Cyberspace and Information Security Problems

With the development of the digital economy, threats related to digital security are on the rise, the number of high-risk vulnerabilities is ever-increasing, cyber-attacks are intensifying, and critical infrastructure is facing serious threats, with the financial sector and the energy industry being the hardest-hit areas. According to data from Arbor Networks, an internet monitoring company, in just three years from 2011 to 2014, the number of distributed denial of service (DDoS) attacks globally increased by more than 30 times. According to the 2015 global cybersecurity survey report released by consulting firm PricewaterhouseCoopers, a total of 42.8 million cyber-attacks were detected in all industries around the world, an increase of 48% over the previous year.[1] According to a 2014 report released by the Washington Center for Strategic and International Studies, computerized crime and cybercrime activities cause more than USD 445 billion in losses to the world economy each year. In recent years, the rapid development of the Internet of Things has also brought unprecedented challenges to cybersecurity. The Internet of Things is a combination of software and hardware, which involves many parts and related components. It is not possible to respond to potential security threats through simple upgrades, modifications, and replacements, which makes it far more difficult to safeguard the security of the Internet of Things than that of the internet. In particular, many developers of smart

[1] Cybersecurity Ventures. Cybersecurity Market Report [R]. 2015.

devices are small start-ups that do not have the resources or experience to provide complex security functions.

The research on trends in cybersecurity conducted by the National Computer Network Emergency Response Technical Team/Coordination Center of China shows that the number of incidents that threaten China's cybersecurity has also increased significantly. There has been further subdivision and upgrading of cybersecurity combats, frequent occurrence of major security incidents, and more advanced cyber-attack techniques. In addition to the increasing number of traditional threats such as phishing websites and DDoS attacks, smart mobile products have also become targets of cybercrime. At the same time, the investment of Chinese users in cybersecurity is far lower than that in developed countries, which makes the cybersecurity situation in China more severe.

The Problem of Laws and Regulations Lagging Behind

Digital technologies and the digital economy are developing very fast, yet the laws of various countries are generally lagging behind. For example, data is a key factor of production in the digital economy, but the proliferation of data has caused the phenomenon of "data flooding" to a certain extent, which has brought us great challenges. For instance, in terms of property rights in data, who owns the data? Who manages it? How to manage it? How to use it? How to determine the responsibilities, rights, and interests of the owners, controllers, users, and managers? As another example, in terms of digital intellectual property, the attitudes of digital technology enterprises and traditional enterprises are generally different, and the policies of various countries are also different. Some countries are committed to strengthening the protection of intellectual property rights. An example would be the *Digital Economy Act 2010* of the UK, which clarifies the procedures for the protection of copyright for digital content such as music, media, and games, with detailed stipulations on initial notification and reporting obligations of internet content providers and the government's technical measures for remedy and punishment. However, many countries and research institutions believe that technological revolutions have broken the boundaries of traditional intellectual property rights, and the original intellectual property system has departed from the development of the digital economy, creating a parasitic system composed of patent trolls and patent holders that hinders innovation. For instance,

New Zealand passed an act in 2013 prohibiting the granting of patents to software. In another example, countries have not reached a consensus on the protection of user privacy and the "right to be forgotten." These issues have led to a wide variety of digital economy regulatory policies in various countries, and the emergence of conflicts between traditional and emerging industries from time to time. In addition, many relevant laws in China need to be further improved. For example, there is no specialized legislation on the protection of personal information in China. The provisions on the protection of personal information in the existing legislation are scattered in various laws, regulations, and rules without an established system.

The Problem of Structural Changes in Employment

Digital technologies have a huge impact on the employment structure and the number of jobs. The World Economic Forum estimates that 65% of children in primary school today will end up in new occupations not yet in existence. The current trend will lead to disruptive changes in the labor market from 2015 to 2020. There are mainly four possible impacts of digital technology on the number of jobs, namely, the creation of new jobs, transformation of employment, globalization of employment, and reduction of jobs. The final impact of technology on total employment depends on the combined outcome of the above effects, and such impact will also affect the corresponding income distribution.

Artificial intelligence has the greatest impact on employment in digital technologies. According to research conducted by the World Economic Forum, increasing automation and introducing artificial intelligence into the workforce will cause 15 major economies to lose 7.1 million jobs over the next five years, while technological advancements would bring only 2 million new jobs over the same period. In 2013, Oxford University studied the computing power of 702 occupations and found that 47% of all occupations in the USA could be replaced by automation; follow-up research indicates that 35% of all occupations in the United Kingdom could be replaced, while this proportion is 49% for those in Japan. Some other researchers believe that by 2030, 90% of the jobs as we know today will be replaced by AI-based machines. As a result, economists worry about the risk of "job polarization," that is, mid-level technical jobs are disappearing while low-end and high-end jobs are expanding.

Differences in digital capabilities and digital literacy among different industries and different people within a country will also have varying effects on their employment and income distribution. In general, individuals and enterprises with better digital literacy and digital skills are more likely to benefit from the development of the digital economy. Obviously, individuals and enterprises with better financial standing are more likely to receive digital education and training to improve their digitalization standards. Therefore, market forces alone would only widen the existing gap between the rich and the poor in the digital era. To change this situation, the government and society need to put in more effort.

The Problem of Applicability of Economic Theories and Organizational Management Mechanisms

The development of the digital economy has challenged the existing economic theories and organizational management systems. According to the existing accounting methods for the national economy, non-market and non-profit activities could not be counted in GDP, and the calculation of GDP only takes into account the amount of consumption but not whether the consumption is effective or wasteful. Activities in the digital economy, such as the sharing of resources emphasized by the sharing economy and the concept of conservation, are different from existing economic theories. Many sharing activities are carried out directly between buyers and sellers, which are usually not counted in GDP statistics. With the increase in this kind of economic activity, we could no longer use traditional economic accounting methods to measure the digital economy and formulate targeted policies. In another example, in a perfectly competitive free market according to the market economic theory, as long as the information of both the supply side and the demand side is completely transparent, equilibrium could be reached at a price that is most beneficial to consumers. However, under the conditions of the digital economy, the use of public information and certain algorithms could achieve a "non-collusive" oligopoly. This means that "complete information," the cornerstone of the market economy, does not improve consumer benefits but may harm them instead.

Certain activities in the digital economy may also increase the difficulty of regulatory enforcement. For example, by coding customized algorithms, prices could be kept high artificially, thereby manipulating the market. Software that tracks the price of gasoline at gas stations could instantly detect a price reduction at a certain gas station and take corresponding price reduction actions to avoid losing customers. Therefore, there is no incentive for any supplier to lower prices first, resulting in prices constantly being kept above the reasonable price. However, this kind of "non-collusive" oligopoly is almost impossible to be found out or prosecuted. Such activities are named "anti-trust challenge in the digital era."

For organizations, the process of digital transformation brought about by the application of digital technologies is inevitably accompanied by changes in organizational management. A few decades ago, when digital technologies were gradually being applied to various fields, the revolution in organizational management brought about by digitalization has begun. In particular, since the 1990s, western enterprises have carried out business process optimization and organizational reengineering across the board, continuously promoting the integration of information technology (IT) and operational technology (OT). Following this trend, Stanford University and other well-known institutes of higher education have also set up courses on business intelligence, digital-led decision-making, and digital competition derived from data to help graduates adapt to the needs of digital economic management. However, not all enterprises could succeed in the transformation of organization and management, as it is a systematic project involving many factors. According to research conducted by McKinsey & Company, 50% of companies would end up unsuccessful in their digital transformation attempts. The digital transformation process of the government is also dependent on business optimization and organizational management reforms. This process may or may not succeed, and requires systemic design and meticulous arrangement.

Suggestions for Promoting the Sound Development of the Digital Economy in China

The problems and risks faced by the development of the digital economy are inevitable as it promotes economic and social transformation. When the transformation is completed, these challenges will gradually subside or even disappear, the original economic and social theories, systems, and models will be gradually replaced new ones, and the economy and society will also take on a new form. In this process, various parties including the government, enterprises, and people must actively participate and play their respective roles.

Establishing Systemic Rules and Regulations Targeted at the Effective Use of Data

Data is the core asset of the digital economy. There should be corresponding regulations for every link and aspect of the development and utilization of data, such as who shall own the data, what are the standards for data, how to trade, use, manage, and protect data, and the like, so that data can be used on a larger scale and with a higher standard. Therefore, the state should attach great importance to the data issue from a strategic perspective, gradually promote openness of data, and formulate data-related regulations. At the same time, various sectors and enterprises should also formulate their own data management standards to jointly improve the standard of data development and utilization.

Comprehensively Improving the Security of the Digital Economy

The digital economy involves a wide range of fields and aspects, hence ensuring the security of the digital economy is a very difficult systemic project. Looking at international experience, developed countries have issued a large number of laws, policies, and strategies on security strategies, protection of critical infrastructure, protection of personal information, and sharing of security information over the years. Based on the realities of the development of China's digital economy, the Chinese government should also unite domestic forces to continuously formulate and improve the security system for the digital economy to safeguard its development.

Gradually Improving Legislation on the Digital Economy

The innovation and development of the digital economy will inevitably make it impossible to completely apply the traditional legal system and supervision methods. To this end, on the one hand, it is necessary to constantly improve China's legal system and enhance the contemporary nature of legislation, such as the formulation of laws on digital property rights, digital intellectual property rights, and digital taxation, providing the necessary institutional guarantee for the development of the digital economy; on the other hand, there should be necessary space reserved for innovation in the digital economy to avoid shackling innovation due to over-regulation. At the same time, we should make use of platforms such as G20, APEC, BRICS, and SCO to strengthen exchanges and cooperation with international organizations and foreign governments, and promote the development of international trade, investment, and judicial rules as required by the development of the digital economy, so as to promote the healthy development of the transnational digital economy.

Timely Implement Organizational Management Reforms

The digital transformation of any organization or industry will inevitably require corresponding organizational management reforms for support, which include optimizing business and operating models, adjusting organizational structures, and forming a collaborative and shared business system in order to flexibly respond to user needs. For the Chinese government, on the one hand, it should strive to build a digital government by optimizing the business processes and organizational structures of government departments in conjunction with streamlining administration and delegating power, so as to promote the shift of the focus of China's e-government construction from information and interaction to service and perception; on the other hand, it is necessary to gradually standardize the regulatory policies of various industries, break down local protectionist barriers, and form a unified and unobstructed large national market to create conditions for the healthy development of the digital economy. For enterprises, they should actively apply tools such as the Contemporary Service Platform for Integration of Informatization and Industrialization to achieve the matching of information technology applications with the organizational structure, management, and processes of the enterprises. For educational institutions and individuals, they should timely grasp the relevant knowledge and concepts of organizational management reforms in the process of digital transformation and apply them to specific work.

Comprehensively Improving the Digital Literacy of All People

The digital literacy of the people directly affects the severity of the digital divide in a country and the corresponding structural unemployment and the gap between the rich and the poor, as well as the overall development of the country's digital economy. In order to improve the digital literacy of all people, on the one hand, the government should cooperate with various parties to provide digital literacy education for all. For example, the European Union has issued policies such as the *Riga Declaration on eSkills* and *New Skills Agenda for Europe—Employment, Social Affairs and Inclusion*, proposing the plan to improve the digital skills of all people in Europe. For specific groups such as laid-off and unemployed people, corresponding digital literacy training and vocational skills training could be provided to help them switch to other jobs. On the other hand, the government should comprehensively strengthen digital literacy education in schools to improve the digital abilities of students. For schooling students in particular, internet and computer courses could be established in all primary and secondary schools and even kindergartens drawing from foreign experience, so that digital literacy could become a mandatory quality for the young generation. High-end talents in digital technology could be cultivated by hosting contests, training camps, and school-enterprise cooperative courses in universities.

Encouraging the Innovation and Development of the Digital Economy and Relevant Theoretical Research

Only through continuous development could digital enterprises create more jobs for people and make major contributions to overall economic prosperity. Digital technologies are rapidly upgrading, and the corresponding business models and operation models are also quickly changing. Therefore, the government should encourage R&D of digital technologies and innovation and entrepreneurship in digital enterprises, and provide systems and policies for innovation and development according to the characteristics of the development of the digital economy. For example, the U.S. Department of Commerce proposed that the Department and other federal government agencies must formulate forward-looking policies and adopt innovative technology-oriented measures. The government should explore innovative solutions, discover challenges, and turn challenges into opportunities with personal and corporate interests in mind.

At the same time, the government should guide professors at institutes of higher education and scientific researchers to actively engage in theoretical research aimed at exploring and solving basic economic theories, social theories and moral, ethical, and legal issues related to the digital economy, so as to provide theoretical guidance for the digital transformation of the whole economy and society. Among these efforts, some basic and operational work could be carried out as early as possible under the leadership of the government. For example, in response to the challenges in measuring the digital economy, the U.S. Department of Commerce is promoting the collection of information on the "size of the digital economy" to assess the trends in the development of different digital activities such as digital consumption and digital work, conduct "technical classification" and timely update the classification framework to identify emerging areas of economic activities, and develop standards for measuring new economic activities and use these standards to track the impact of related activities on the economy. These measures are actually laying the foundation for establishing a national economic classification and GDP accounting system that meets the needs of the development of the digital economy.

The above aspects are not the only measures to be taken to promote the sound development of the digital economy. There are more to it. For example, addressing the problem of digital divide due to infrastructure is also dependent on the gradual implementation of the "Broadband China" strategy and other informatization strategies; likewise, the problem of structural unemployment caused by the development of the digital economy could not be solved by strengthening digital literacy education and training alone.

In conclusion, the sound development of the digital economy is a huge social project, which could not be achieved without the concerted efforts and collaboration among the government, enterprises, social organizations, and people. In this process, the government should focus on providing a good institutional and policy environment for the development of the digital economy. Industry organizations should promote the formulation of solutions and standards at the industry level. Social organizations should play their role in educating and training people. Enterprises should actively transform towards digitalization. Individuals should strive to improve their digital literacy and hence their ability to participate in digital activities.

CHAPTER 11

How Enterprises Go About Digital Transformation

In the digital era, all organizations must actively engage in digital transformation. This is the process from adapting to relying on digital technology and gradually forming digital thinking. It is a complete evolution of the organizations and an important part of modernizing social governance. Within the process, the most important type of organization is enterprises.

Background of the Digital Transformation of Enterprises

Digital technologies are reshaping the business world. New business models and revolutionary innovations are constantly emerging, while boundaries between industries are fading away. The digitization of the external environment determines that digital transformation is the only way for traditional enterprises.

Rapid Changes in the Consumer Market

In the digital era, more and more business activities are taking place online. Innovations such as e-commerce platforms, community marketing, virtual goods, online services, electronic payment, and O2O are emerging one after another. Consumers have more channels and

M. Huateng et al., *The Chinese Digital Economy*,
https://doi.org/10.1007/978-981-33-6005-1_11

means to compare, choose, and purchase commodities, with more attention to consumer experience. They are no longer merely passive recipients of commodities and advertisements, but active participants willing to discuss and express their understanding and expectations of commodities, and participate in the business activities of enterprises. The lifecycle of commodities is getting shorter and shorter, the market is becoming more and more segmented, and consumer loyalty is getting lower and lower.

Competition Among Digital Enterprises

The first type of competition is among a new generation of native digital enterprises that have emerged in traditional industries. For example, digital media is completely revolutionizing traditional forms of media. Social networks such as Twitter, Weibo, Facebook, and WeChat and news aggregators such as Toutiao have changed not only the way news is disseminated, but also reader perceptions of news brands and news generation processes. Pure digital media in vertical subdivisions do not need specialized content distribution channels and reader analysis departments. They only need to focus on the content in their own field, and the internet could direct their content to interested readers. E-Commerce vendors such as Alibaba and JD.com are directly competing with players in traditional retail industries such as shopping malls and large supermarkets, while Uber and Airbnb are putting tremendous pressure on the taxi industry and the hospitality industry.

The second type of competition is the cross-sector competition between enterprises in the digital sector. Through Project Loon and Google Fiber, Google has made forays into the manufacturing of communications equipment and the market for internet access, while its self-driving cars project has entered its eighth year. In addition to launching Amazon Books and Amazon Go, Amazon has also clinched the Best Actor and Best Original Screenplay Academy Awards in 2017 for *Manchester by the Sea*, while *The Salesman* won the award for Best Foreign Language Film. Netflix, which had its beginnings in DVD rentals, is currently active in the streaming and video-on-demand markets, providing TV shows to more than 93 million users in more than 190 countries and regions around the world through the internet. Netflix has also produced its own movies and TV programs, well-known examples of which include House of Cards and Making a Murderer. The Netflix documentary The

White Helmets also won the 2017 Academy Award for Best Documentary (Short Subject).

Competition Among Traditional Enterprises During the Course of Digital Transformation

Competition among traditional enterprises during digital transformation is a competition in the speed and effect of transformation. Traditional enterprises that achieve better, faster digital transformation can more rapidly and effectively adapt to the digital era, and maintain their strengths in human resources, financial capital, and branding. For instance, the BBC has promoted comprehensive digital transformation encompassing content production and platform distribution to brand development and organizational management, continually providing high-quality content suited to market demand and improved user experiences. Competition among traditional enterprises during the course of digital transformation is also reflected in business transformation or business expansion through digital technologies. For instance, GE and Simens have respectively pursued softwarization and digitalized (analytical) transformation through the Predix software platform and MidSphere cloud platform. COFCO has extended its operations to fields other than cereals and oil, such as household chemicals, home textiles, furniture, and household appliances through its womai.com portal.

The Substance of Digital Transformation

The digital transformation of an enterprise includes overall digital transformation with respect to corporate strategy, marketing, commodities, business models, management, corporate culture, and business mindsets.

Digital Transformation in Corporate Strategies

Digital technology replicates the real world not only at the physical level, but also at the functional level. There are digital counterparts to almost every entity in the real world, including their operations, and their mutual interactions. From the perspective of the digital transformation of society, digital technology can simulate, reproduce and participate in social activities, as well as progressively integrate physical social space and online virtual space, and gradually bring about the integration and co-evolution of the physical economy and the virtual economy. In terms of organizational behavior, the mechanisms governing information transmission, processing, and control among people, objects, and organizations have all been digitalized, and have resulted in rapid adjustment and updating of the methods whereby an organization undertakes internal and external interactions. From the perspective of human cognition and behavior, both clients and enterprise staff are becoming more used to and relying ever more greatly on digital technology in all aspects of work and life. They do not make a distinction between traditional goods and digital goods.

The digital transformation of corporate strategy seeks to understand and adapt to such changes, adopt measures to actively study and apply digital technologies, improve efficiency and promote innovation, as well as better identify and opportunities to create value during the process of change. For example, the external environment for enterprise digital transformation is increasingly characterized by market subdivision, which also constitutes new market opportunities brought about by digital technologies. With help from digital technology, traditional enterprises can better collect, analyze and predict the personalized needs of more customers. Based on existing superior resources and a deep understanding of their industry and customers, traditional enterprises can source needed talent, suppliers and partnerships from all over the globe, restructure production and innovation, launch richer product lines, and precisely meet demand from client groups (or even individual customers).

Digital transformation of corporate strategy is not just about making data-driven decisions, but rather a progressive process of cultivating digital awareness and work habits in both management executives and ordinary employees, adapting existing processes and organizational structures, adjusting asset portfolios, and supporting new digital operations and business models.

The Digital Transformation of Marketing

According to data from surveys by Kotler Marketing Group in 2016, 81% of companies believe that the key to digital transformation lies in digital marketing, but 68% of companies have not formulated systematic digital marketing strategies, while 58% of companies believe that their digital marketing efforts have not produced expected results. The ways by which traditional companies can better apply digital technology and digital media, build digital brands, enhance user experience, and more frequently and deeply engage with their customers are important components in the digital transformation of marketing.

Building Digital Brands

Digital branding is a form of brand expression through digital media. Compared with traditional media, digital media are richer in content, form, emotional expression, and interactivity. Digital brands expressed through digital media are more easily accepted and especially popular with young people in the digital age. BBC, an established media organization, established BBC Online as its only digital brand in 2011, which would encompass all its digital products and services. Burberry, a luxury brand, began broadcasting live online fashion shows in 2011, and gradually expanded to social media (such as Facebook) and other digital media (such as Apple TV). Through the internet, Burberry overhauled its "head in the clouds" marketing image and became closer to younger digital consumers through live streaming of fashion shows and gradual expansion to social media platforms (such as Facebook) and other forms of digital media (such as Apple TV). In order to better use internet slang and draw closer to young people, Coca-Cola has commissioned a customized set of emojis based on Coca-Cola bottles on Twitter.

Making Appropriate Use of Social Network Marketing

Online social marketing is an effective strategy for building corporate reputations and brands. From a global perspective, online social marketing has become one of the more popular forms of marketing employed by advertisers. According to survey data from the US Retail Alliance and Forrester Consulting, 92% of US retailers engaged in social media marketing in 2016, with the top three social media platforms being Twitter (85%), Facebook (74%), and LinkedIn (72%). According to Weibo's 2016 financial report, advertising revenue in the fourth quarter increased by 55% year-on-year to 1.291 billion yuan. In particular, revenue from brand advertising increased by 149% year-on-year, indicating that companies are placing greater importance on Weibo marketing.

Creativity and Online Interaction Are Key to Social Network Marketing

Digital technologies have provided boundless room for creativity, and good creative ideas are irresistible. They are also the key to grabbing customer attention in an era of excessive information. In 2015, Durex launched a virtual art gallery themed upon "Liquidism," compiled using HTML5. The design of its "gallery" was based on Tatlin's constructivist style and exhibited 12 works from young painters, with Dou Wei's "Lijiang River Water" playing in the background, using art to introduce and promote its range of "play" products. Also, a positive or humorous response to sudden incidents, or answering fan messages, forwarding fan selfies, and participant rewards are also effective forms of online interaction. In 2012, Sephora launched a "15 Days of Beauty Thrills" participative event on Facebook featuring prizes that included Fiat cars, a tour of a makeup school in Paris, and Sephora shopping vouchers, attracting a large number of Facebook users to their products. The number of followers on their Facebook page rose to 3.5 million and was 520,000 posts on Twitter.

Promoting Offline-Online Consistency and Facilitation

New online channels and points of contact created by traditional enterprises based on offline operations will bring about problems of online-offline experience consistency and convenience, including: customer-perceived consistency between online and offline environments (for example, where the design styles of online stores are consistent with brick-and-mortar stores), seamless connectivity between the online and offline parts of the consumption process (for example, whether goods can be collected at a brick-and-mortar store after making an online reservation or online payment, whether membership status and points are applicable at both) consistency between products purchased online and offline (for example, whether the content, functions, and packaging of products purchased online are the same as those purchased at brick-and-mortar stores), and whether post-sales guarantees are consistent (for example, can products ordered online be repaired or returned at brick-and-mortar stores, and whether the same door-to-door services are provided, instead of having to mail it back to the original address). Take the clothing brand Zara as an example. Zara's official website, app, and brick-and-mortar stores are consistent in visual design styles, product classification (women's clothing, men's clothing, children's clothing, discounts, and so on), timing of product seasons, and pricing. Products purchased online can be returned at any brick-and-mortar store. The Starbucks app provides members with services such as locating nearby stores, promotional information, balance top-ups, and personal account information. Users can directly scan the QR code at the login homepage when making in-store payments to save time.

Enhancing User Participation

Good digital marketing encourages people to participate in a company's business activities through the sharing of ideas, the improvement of designs, crowdfunding, the formation of product discussion groups and fan communities. For example, managers of tourist attractions encourage visitors to submit travel photos for social network promotions, and eyewear retailers encourage customers to submit comments and post photos of themselves as models. In 2016, Weiquan Daily C Juice launched the "Spelling Bottle" package. Each of its 7 kinds of juices has 6 packages printed with eye-catching Chinese characters. There are 42 different packaging styles and 42 Chinese characters. When placed in different orders, these juice bottles will form different sentences. For example, 5 bottles with "ni," "hao," "bie," "gan," and "mao" will form *nihao, bie ganmao* ("Hello, don't catch a cold"). Another way of ordering would form *ni ganmao biehao* ("Your cold won't get better"). Other combinations include sentences such as "you lecher, don't hug me," "hug me, I need some warmth," and "take care of yourself." The 42 Chinese characters were carefully selected. About 1/3 of the characters are related to how fruit juice boosts the immune system, while the other 2/3 emphasize caring and concern. Various creative permutations and combinations were forwarded in social media. Weiquan successfully promoted customers from being passive consumers of products to actively participating in product marketing through creative packaging, which increased sales. Monthly sales of daily C juice increased by 40% year-on-year.

The Digital Transformation of Commodities and Production

The Digitalization of Commodities

The digitalization of commodities is the change of the form and function of commodities by digital technology, which can be roughly divided into the following three categories.

The first type of digital transformation of commodities is the digitalization of products themselves, such as the digitalization of products and services in industries such as finance, media, publishing, and education. This form of digital transformation is often accompanied by business model innovations, such as third-party electronic payments, on-demand purchases (such as video-on-demand, purchase of a single song instead of an album, purchase of a service by time period rather than usage), the ad-sponsored model in online publishing, and so on.

The second type of digital transformation of commodities is to use digital technology to add more functions to products. This type of digital transformation is often closely related to market segmentation and differentiated innovation. For example, Nike's Nike+ series of sports shoes record customers' exercise routes, distances, and time through built-in sensors, and are connected to apps, social networks, and customized training programs to meet the various needs of their customers, from science-based exercise to emotional communication.

The third type of digital transformation of commodities is a major innovation in traditional products centered upon digital technology. For example, automobile companies such as Mercedes-Benz and BMW are developing driverless cars, and Rolls-Royce is developing unmanned ocean-going freighters. This form of digital transformation is usually more disruptive and innovative, and has the potential to completely change consumer behavior, habits, or how similar products are used.

In themselves, none of the above three forms of digital transformation are more advantageous or disadvantageous than another. Traditional enterprises may simultaneously pursue one or more types of commodity digital transformation based on industry characteristics and corporate strategies.

The Digitalization of Production

The digital transformation of production in traditional enterprises mainly refers to digitalizing the process of producing products or providing services. For example, the digitalization of BBC content production and the "internetization" of digital content publishing, the use of 3D printing technology by Adidas to produce personalized custom running shoes, and the sustained upgrading and transformation of entire networks by mobile network operators through IP, platformization, SDN (software-defined networks) and other methods and technologies. Traditional manufacturing companies can use digital technology to build models, verify and simulate in entirely virtual environments, and integrate all front-end and back-end links, including production, into a unified data platform, making the production process flexible and intelligent.

Digital Platform Transformation of Business Models

The digital platform is perhaps the most important business model innovation in the digital age. In 2016, the first-, second-, third-, sixth-, and eighth-largest companies by market capitalization in the Forbes Global 2000 were platform companies, namely Apple, Alphabet (parent company of Google), Microsoft, Facebook, and Amazon. The digital platform has disrupted the rules of the game in traditional industries and created one new community market after another. Overnight, originally competing enterprises and consumers with completely different needs have become platform participants who contribute value to the platform. The creation of their own digital platforms is an important way for traditional enterprises to achieve digital transformation of business models and compete with other digital platforms.

Digital Platforms

The digital platform is a bilateral or multilateral market business model supported by online technologies that helps two or more platform participants with potential business relationships to complete transactions. The platform benefits in a variety of ways, and can charge commissions on transactions (for example, Didi charges a fixed percentage), or unilateral service fees (for example, only advertisers are charged for advertisements on the Google search engine while the streaming music service platform Spotify provides paying premium members with ad-free and high-quality streaming music services). Platforms can also provide marketing, investment consulting, and data trading services centered upon platform data. Platform operators can sell their products on the platform (e.g. Amazon, JD.com) or merely provide services (e.g. Google search engine ads, Taobao).

The network effect supported by digital technology is the source of value for digital platforms. Digital technology greatly reduces the physical infrastructure and tangible assets needed for platform operations, and reduces difficulties in development, expansion, maintenance, and upgrades. Digital information, experiences, and digital systems can be transmitted and copied at zero cost, greatly reducing required intellectual capital and relational capital. Digital platforms cover many producers, consumers, and third parties, and their volumes and complexity of relationships within the market far exceed traditional business models. The linear increase in the size of participants and the number of interactions between participants bring exponential increases to the value of the platform. This is the network effect of the platform.

The Significance of Business Model Digital Platform Transformation

Building a digital platform is a strategic business model innovation actively adopted by traditional enterprises in adapting to the digital age. The digital platform business model of traditional enterprises is based on existing resources, deep understanding of their industries and accumulation of capabilities. In the short term, it is an extension of the current competitive advantage of the enterprise. In the long term, the platform itself will become a competitive advantage, where traditional business operations will continue to exist and develop in the digital platform environment.

Building a digital platform business model is an important way for traditional enterprises to compete with other digital platforms. Traditional enterprises attach importance to the cultivation of internal resources, efficiency and business capabilities, and the construction of barriers. Competitors in the industry, suppliers, and channels with bargaining power may be regarded as a company's external negative assets. The platform business model focuses on the economies of scale generated by platform participants and participation. Regardless of whether they are competitors in the same industry or suppliers with bargaining power, all participants engaged in commercial activities on the platform are the assets of the platform, along with data on their platform activities, all of which contribute value to the platform. In other words, the competition between traditional product operations and digital platform operations is a competition between individuals and ecosystems. Traditional enterprises can compete with digital platforms on an equal footing only by adopting the platform business model.

Types of Business Models Based on Digital Platforms

From the perspective of service targets and business scope, traditional enterprise digital platform business models can be roughly divided into four categories.

The first category is simple online business expansion. Enterprises add new functions that support third parties on their own service systems, thereby forming a platform for business expansion. For example, China Merchants Bank's mobile online banking app provides lifestyle services for purchasing movie tickets, meal vouchers, living payment, and clinic registration. China Telecom launched "wing payment" based on its own mobile network and its large user base to enter the mobile payment market.

The second category is to build subdivided ecosystems around their products. Such platforms focus on providing more value to users who use their products. For example, Nike launched Nike+ in 2006, and Nike established Fuel Lab in 2014. Nike also cooperated with TechStars, the second-largest incubator in the United States, to launch the Nike+ Accelerator project, opening the NikeFuel platform to third-party developers, encouraging them to develop innovative sports health applications. Nike+ entices consumers to continuously upload information on their body, exercise, and social media accounts, and mine information such as group sports patterns and forms of marketing that they were open to. After years of development, Nike+ has become a global community of sports enthusiasts, playing a huge role in the success of Nike's wearable sports equipment. Not long after, Adidas and Arthurs also developed distinctive sports communities to provide more services for their users and compete with Nike at the platform level. Such community platforms with significant brand characteristics play a huge role in marketing, product innovation, and increasing "user stickiness."

The third category is based on a company's own superior resources, seizing industrial opportunities to define and cultivate a new ecosystem and seek a first-mover advantage. This type of platform focuses on the growth of the entire emerging business format, and readily leads to a winner-take-all or oligopoly platform market pattern. In 2014, GE announced the launch of Predix, an industrial internet software platform, and opened Predix to all industrial internet application developers two years later. In order to build a better ecosystem, GE partnered with Cisco to launch an industrial-grade router that supports Predix, partnered with Intel to develop an embedded intelligent networking interface reference architecture using Intel processors, partnered with SoftBank, Verizon Telephone Company, and Vodafone to develop connection solutions for the Industrial Internet. After being made fully open, Predix is equivalent to the Industrial Internet version of the Android system, which provides a good platform environment for the development of industrial applications and supports both GE and non-GE devices. Currently, GE and other developers have developed dozens of applications for Predix, while most GE divisions are already using the platform. In the future, GE will also open the data on the Predix platform to third-party developers, hoping to encourage more developers and enterprises to use the applications developed by Predix, expand the Industrial Internet ecosystem, and replicate the success of the Android system in the field of consumer electronics. Similar Industrial Internet open platforms include Siemens' "Mindsphere Open Industry Cloud" and China Aerospace Science and Industry Corporation's "Space Cloud Network" platform. Although all three are still in the early stages of development, they are targeting the same market. Upon maturity, they will soon face off in direct competition.

The fourth category is to expand network effects through platform-to-platform cooperation. This type of cooperation usually occurs between platforms with complementary business operations, providing platform participants with more business opportunities and better services. In 2014, the largest chain retail pharmacy and century-old brand in the United States, Walgreens, and the online medical and health service platform MDLIVE, established in 2009, collaborated in launching a telemedicine service platform that provides seamless services, from medical consultations (from MDLIVE) to medicines (from Walgreens). Walgreens succeeded in its hope of entering the telemedicine market. The

Washington Post now publishes news on the company's website simultaneously on Facebook's "Instant News" platform, using Facebook to expand its readership, improve the reading experience, and increase advertising revenue (all advertising revenue from news content belongs to the media outlet).

The Digital Transformation of Management

Digital technology has promoted the transformation of traditional enterprises from process-driven, centrally controlled organizations to shared platforms and new forms of highly decentralized organizations, which has changed all aspects of business operations and production. The digital transformation of traditional enterprises involves all sorts of issues. Here is a brief introduction from four aspects: strategy, organizational structure, management platform, and talent.

Strengthening the Strategic Position of Digital Transformation

Digital transformation requires strong leadership. The digital transformation of traditional enterprises is a process in which the functions, structures, and operating mechanisms of enterprises are constantly changing. It is a process in which corporate cultures and employees' mindsets and work habits are gradually digitalized, and will inevitably encounter all kinds of resistance. In order to overcome resistance and even conflicts from the organization during the transition process, traditional enterprises need to establish clearly defined digital transformation strategies and goals for each phase from a strategic level, formulate detailed plans, appoint key leaders for digital transformation, and ensure that their vision is clearly communicated from top to bottom to form consensus across the organization, as well as clearly communicate their expectations from digital transformation to those outside the organization.

Adjusting Organizational Structures

Organizational structures serve organizational strategies. Traditional enterprises need to adjust their current organizational structures to better apply digital technology and adapt to the needs of digital transformation.

The more common method is to set up a new department or a new position to oversee the integration of digital-related business operations or functions and be specifically responsible for the digital transformation of the enterprise. Some enterprises may also need to establish new, low-level departments with important functions, such as professional digital analysis departments and network security departments. For example, the BBC established the "Digital Engineering Department" under the "Finance and Operations Department" to be responsible for the development of digital infrastructure for enterprise hardware.

Building Unified Digital Platforms

Unified digital platforms are suitable for the shared platforms of the future and the drive towards decentralized leadership, especially for large enterprises. Enterprises can migrate business and functional systems to the platform, perform data analysis in real time, flexibly optimize business processes, undertake more daily work, greatly improve operational efficiency, liberate more time and intellectual resources for work on strategic priorities, improve the speed of corporate response and accelerate innovation. At the same time, digital platforms can fully unleash the advantages of digital technology in flexibility, elasticity, trial and error, and rapid iteration, and adapt to the pace of work in areas such as business innovation, organizational structure adjustment, work process reform, and digital skills training for staff to help them achieve their digital transformation. For example, the BBC established a unified digital platform during their digital transformation, while supporting content production, content publishing, and internal corporate management of the enterprise, facilitating cross-departmental communication and collaboration.

Cultivating, Recruiting and Retaining Digital Talent

With continual advances in the digitalization of business activities, the problem of insufficient data talent is becoming more and more prominent. There is a lack of talented professionals such as data analysts, data scientists, and human-computer interaction engineers. In addition to intensifying internal training, traditional companies can recruit talent from the outside, adjust their business processes, assessment mechanisms and remuneration policy of the company according to job requirements and staff capabilities, formulate reasonable work objectives, provide suitable working tools and working environments, and make appropriate adjustments to corporate culture. For example, these may include setting up special promotion channels for digital talent, adopting flexible working systems, relaxing or eliminating dress code requirements in the digital department, and so on.

New Problems Brought by Enterprise Digital Transformation

New Issues Such as Privacy and Intellectual Property Protection

While increasing efficiency and promoting innovation, the widespread use of digital technology has brought about issues such as privacy protection, intellectual property violations, network security, and labor security. Laws and regulations often lag behind large-scale problems. The digital transformation of traditional enterprises needs to consider these issues in advance and formulate corresponding strategies. For example, these may include formulating terms and conditions that strictly protect privacy, adopting high-level security strategies and security technologies, formulating merchant credit reviews, rewards and punishments, and user safeguards to protect user interests, and actively cooperating with regulators to avoid regulatory risks.

Decisions Rely Heavily on Data

The data-driven decision-making process may lead to over-reliance on data, leading to managerial decision-making errors. Clayton Christensen, a professor at Harvard Business School and creator of the idea of "disruptive technology," has said that "God didn't create data; Humans create data." He believes that data can only allow people to scratch the surface of the past: from data collection to analysis and interpretation, lots of information is lost at each step. Data cannot allow us to see into the future and are not applicable to the most important things. On the contrary, the experience of corporate managers with regards to products and services and the experiences and fuzzy knowledge of customers, and direct communication with customers (especially important customers), personal experience of products and observation of consumption scenarios, as well as common sense and intuition formed over the years, are still extremely important to major decisions.

Social Responsibility

In the digital age, business activities of an enterprise have become more closely intertwined with personal life. Enterprises are undertaking more social functions and actually monetizing these social functions. In the process of redistributing wealth and social rights, both native digital enterprises and traditional enterprises in transition need to assume greater social responsibility. For example, these include the active management of personal attacks and bullying in the online community, using big data technology to discover and remove counterfeit products, reminding users of the potential dangers of certain websites, building and maintaining public cyberspace, developing and providing accessible digital tools, as well as using their own strengths in technology and data to engage in other social welfare undertakings.

CHAPTER 12

How Governments Go About Digital Transformation

Digital technologies have not only revamped the business arena but have also promoted digitalization in government services and governance. The digitalization of government has continually advanced, from the early days when information technology was used to support government work to extensive IT-based restructuring on a large scale, and then again to the comprehensive digitalization of both frontend and backend government work. In recent years, with developments in mobile technologies and smart technologies, some governments have also begun to actively promote smart mobile services.

The Path Towards the Digitalization of Government

Despite the different strategies adopted by different governments, we may still uncover certain aspects common to their journeys towards digitalization.

M. Huateng et al., *The Chinese Digital Economy*, https://doi.org/10.1007/978-981-33-6005-1_12

The Stages of Government Digitalization

In general, based on their varying levels of digitalization, the digital transformation of government undergoes at least three stages: electronic government (e-government), "one-stop" government, and digital government.

Electronic Government

The process of developing electronic government is simply the IT-based restructuring of government departments. The US was the earliest countries to systematically use information technology to build an "electronic government". In 1993, the US proposed the use of information and internet technologies to more efficiently and economically manage government services, thus launching the development of e-government. In 2002, US President George Bush signed the *Electronic Government Act*, a piece of legislation that further advanced the establishment of e-government. As required by the law, the US established the E-Government Fund as well as the position of Federal Chief Information Officer to manage the development of e-government.

One-Stop Government

Developed countries had a head start in developing e-government. After government administration was "electronized", further reform came to focus on the provision of public services through integrated means. On the one hand, the "fragmented" management of government agencies caused difficulties in intra-departmental and inter-departmental cooperation, as well as collaboration with non-governmental bodies, giving rise to the need for coordinated sharing of information. On the other hand, the public came to demand more personalized, accessible public services. This development trend, mainly characterized by the need for "integration" and "coordination" eventually came to be known as "one-stop government", "whole of government" or "integrated government". In particular, since the 1990s, countries such as Canada, Australia and the UK came to focus on one-stop government, while countries such as Finland, Norway, New Zealand, Scotland, Ireland and Singapore also to adopt the concept of one-stop government when reforming government institutions.

The development of one-stop government in these countries focused on coordinated collaboration between government institutions. Each of these countries believed that one-stop government should transcend the boundaries between different departments to achieve coordinated governance and provide the public with seamless, cross-departmental services. The services provided by one-stop government included "vertical collaboration" between central and regional governments, "horizontal collaboration" within the central government or regional governments of the same level, "adjacent collaboration" between different departments of the same government, as well as "external collaboration" between a government and enterprises or the general public.

Digital Government

With the rapid development of digital technologies, disruptive technologies and products, such as the mobile internet, cloud computing, big data and smartphones, gradually emerged and became widely popularized, while the digital transformation of government continued to advance. In May 2012, the White House issued the first digital government strategy: *Digital Government: Building a 21st Century Platform to Better Serve the American People*, which proposed a roadmap for the digital transformation of the federal government over 12 months. This strategy was an extension of the ongoing IT-based restructuring of the American government, and proposed four overarching principles: an information-centric approach, a shared platform approach, a customer-centric approach, and a platform of security and privacy. As part of the digital government strategy, the American government issued the *Mobile Strategy for Digital Government*, which proposed such goals as developing a basic platform capable of providing mobile services to all government departments, promoting cross-departmental collaboration through mobile technologies, and developing a governance framework for mobile government at the federal level, which timely introduced new digital technologies to government services.

All in all, the transition from e-government to digital government is essentially a shift from increasing efficiency through IT-based applications to using digital technology to address issues faced by the general public and businesses, as well as socioeconomic problems. The OECD's *Recommendation on Digital Government Strategies*, issued in 2014, argued that e-government focused on improving existing government processes, while digital government focused on innovatively designing and supplying public services. In contrast, one-stop government lay somewhere in between: one-stop government represented both an overall optimization of various internal government processes and innovation with regards to the provision of public services. The digital transformation of government was an evolution of IT-based government restructuring. On top of the focus of e-government on work efficiency and costs, digital government has created new demands in aspects such as the content and provision of government services, service innovation, management models, transparency, public participation, organizational structure, and economic growth.

How Digital Government Is Achieved

Stronger Top-Level Design

The top-level design is a method adopted by many countries when they launched the development of e-government. The most common approach was the Enterprise Architecture (EA) method, which refers to creatively integrating an organization's management model, operations process, information resources, information system, and information technologies from a macro perspective, while incorporating the organization's strategic goals and missions into these efforts to guide informatization. American enterprises were the earliest to adopt EA and reap the significant benefits of this approach. The American government quickly came to take note of the benefits of using EA to plan the development of e-government. In the 1990s, the American government began to apply EA theory to federal plans for developing e-government, and successively developed the Federal Enterprise Architecture and the Federal Enterprise Architecture Framework. The application of EA by the US and the success of their efforts to develop e-government spurred similar initiatives by other countries. Currently, more than 9 in 10 countries are using EA to develop e-government.

Optimizing Government Processes

From 1993 to 2000, the Clinton administration announced an initiative to "reinvent the federal government". The team in charge of these reforms produced a total of 384 proposals for reform and 1250 specific action plans. One of the key components of this initiative was to streamline institutions, downsize the bureaucracy and delegate authority to lower-level departments. In 1994, the US Congress passed the *Federal Workforce Restructuring Act*, which provided a clear schedule for downsizing the federal workforce and authorized the federal government to adopt appropriate measures to encourage government employees to voluntarily resign. At the same time, the government relaxed rules and delegated authority to lower-level departments. These efforts yielded substantial results: by the start of 1996, the number of federal employees had been reduced by 240,000 and more than 2000 offices had been made redundant. Nearly 200 federal projects and law enforcement agencies were abolished. In total, these measures reduced federal expenditures by USD 118 billion. From 1995 to end 1996, the federal government abolished 16,000 federal rules that hindered the efficient operations of public services and abolished 640,000 pages worth of internal regulations across various agencies.

Appointing Dedicated Institutions or Officers to Coordinate Cross-Departmental Affairs

Some countries have established dedicated research institutions or ministers to coordinate the development of digital government, in order to manage public affairs involving more than one department, formulate unified plans, implement strategies related to the digitalization of government and coordinate relevant work across government agencies, industries and localities.

The UK established a series of comprehensive institutions directly administered by the Prime Minister's Office or Cabinet Office, which took charge of formulating policies to coordinate cross-departmental work and ensure the uniformity of government policies. These agencies covered areas such as social discrimination and poverty alleviation, women's welfare, crime prevention, anti-narcotics coordination, and services for small businesses. In March 2015, the UK government issued the *Working Together to Safeguard Children* policy. This document defined the responsibilities of various government departments and means for inter-departmental coordination, as well as the specific roles of more than ten sectors, including schools, public health agencies, the police force, and social services agencies, effectively guiding cross-departmental efforts to safeguard children's welfare.

Australia inaugurated the Management Advisory Committee (MAC), a body mainly comprised of officials from government departments and public agencies. The MAC launched specific initiatives centered upon inter-departmental guidelines to promote the implementation of the "whole of government" strategy. Also, each Australian ministry had a cabinet minister with powers that extended to other departments. These cabinet ministers were in charge of strengthening coordination between departments, as well as integrating the policies, projects and provision of public services with regards to various institutions.

The Canadian government established a dedicated panel to be in charge of inter-departmental collaboration. In addition, the country's cabinet has established the post of "minister without portfolio". Though a minister without portfolio does not assume specific responsibilities, he or she may take charge of coordinating the functions of various ministries with regards to a certain policy field. Canada's Youth Employment Strategy, launched in 2003, connects 10 federal departments and agencies to implement employment support projects at both central and regional level to help young people between the ages of 15 and 30 gain knowledge, skills and work experience, allowing them to adapt to the ever-changing demands of the labor market.

Integrating Public Services Through Informatization and Launching Platforms for One-Stop Services

The UK national government retired the various websites maintained by individual departments in 2012. The individual websites run by the 24 departments of the national government were replaced with the gov.uk website. Later on, 358 public agencies and related departments would also migrate to the site. This measure overcame the problems of "departmental segregation" and "information islands" with regards to information resources, allowing for rapid inter-departmental information exchange and a high degree of resource sharing.

Australia integrated services provided by Medicare, the Australian Taxation Office, Centrelink, Australian JobSearch, My Health Record, Child Support, My Aged Care, the Department of Veterans' Affairs and the National Disability Insurance Scheme into a single platform known as myGov, overcoming the boundaries between different functional departments to allow the public to enjoy cross-departmental services through a single portal.

Successively Introducing Related Strategies

The digitalization of government is a long-term, continual process. To this end, government departments should timely issue relevant policies based on the current state of technology and actual needs, in order to promote the further advancement of digital government. For instance, the European Union has long been promoting such efforts.

Systematic IT-based government restructuring in the various EU member nations (successively) began in the 1990s. The EU-level "e-government" strategy was first mentioned in the *eEurope 2002 Action Plan* issued by the European Commission in 2000. The plan put forward 4 requirements with regards to developing e-government: promoting transparency, development and utilization of public-sector information, ensuring ease of public access to necessary public data, promoting online interaction between the public and their government, and enhancing the electronic exchange of information between agencies and the implementation of relevant organizational restructuring.

In 2002, the European Commission issued the *eEurope 2005 Action Plan*, which contained more guidelines with regards to promoting information networks and content development. The plan also contained specific guidelines for six aspects: development of broadband networks, a framework for interoperability, interactive public services, e-procurement, development of public internet access points and cultural/tourism information services.

In 2006, the EU issued the first plan dedicated to the development of e-government—the *i2010 eGovernment Action Plan*, which put forward 5 goals to be achieved by 2010: inclusive public services, increasing government efficiency, accelerating the development of important projects (such as public procurement), strengthening access to public services for enterprises and the public within the scope of the EU, as well as enhancing public participation and democratic decision-making.

In December 2010, the European Commission issued the *European eGovernment Action Plan 2011–2015: Harnessing ICT to promote smart, sustainable & innovative Government*. Improving government effectiveness and promoting the unified development of digital services for the Single Market were the two core goals of the action plan. Based on this plan, the EU proposed dozens of online government services to enhance the efficiency and convenience of government services in areas such as online business registration, tax declaration, social security applications, litigation involving small claims, and registering change in address.

In 2016, the European Commission issued the *eGovernment Action Plan 2016–2020: Accelerating the Digital Transformation of Government*, which proposed to make public administration and public institutions open, efficient and inclusive by 2020, when all enterprises and individuals would enjoy borderless, personalized, user-friendly and end-to-end digital public services. In addition, innovative approaches would be used to design and deliver better services in line with the needs and demands of citizens and businesses, while public administrations would use the opportunities offered by the new digital environment to facilitate their interactions with stakeholders and with each other.

The Digital Transformation of China's Government

The digital transformation of China's government is backed by a strong foundation built over years of government informatization and e-government development. In 1999, the "government online" project was launched. In 2002, the Leading Group for National Informatization put forward guiding opinions on the development of e-government. The development of e-government centered upon informatization officially became national policy. After more than a dozen years, the development of Chinese government departments' internal network and information systems have made huge progress. The types and scale of online public services continue to expand, while the digitalization of public services and social governance continue to advance. In 2016, the Leading Group proposed the "Internet Plus Government Services" national strategy. China has made great achievements in the development of e-government over these many years.

Continued Progress in the Digitalization of Government

Based on figures released by the China Internet Network Information System, as of 2016, China has 53,546 websites under the.gov.cn domain, 164,522 government Weibo accounts, 34,083 government Toutiao accounts and 239 million users of online government services (32.7% of total internet users). The coverage, vibrancy and influence of online government services have risen greatly.

Government departments have used advanced digital technologies to overhaul work models, increase work efficiency, enhance convenience of government services, and encourage greater public participation. For instance, customs checkpoints use biometric information to identify travelers and provide self-service customs clearance services, greatly enhancing efficiency and reducing the burdens of immigration formalities. Taxation authorities have launched electronic systems to manage official tax invoices (known as *fapiao*), revamping traditional paper-based work processes, thus addressing problems with authenticating and timely providing hardcopy invoices, reducing business costs, and greatly reducing the amount of work involved for tax authorities. Another example would be railway departments, which are developing and improving new service systems even while enhancing the speed and capacity of their trains. China Railway launched a customer service website during the 2010 “Spring Festival Rush”, followed by an app in December 2013, allowing users to retrieve information on all passenger and cargo trains in China, purchase tickets through a nationwide ticketing platform, and perform cargo-related transactions. Passengers could also retrieve their tickets from self-service terminals at train stations, while certain routes even allowed passengers to board directly using their ID cards. The launch of these systems has brought great convenience to travelers and eased the burdens on railway stations.

Regional governments are also actively promoting digital transformation. Take Guizhou as an example: the “Guizhou Cloud” platform is the first cloud platform in China to integrate, share, open up and utilize government data. The Guizhou provincial government has mandated that, in the absence of special requirements, provincial-level departments are not to independently purchase IT hardware or software such as servers, network switches, and operating systems, nor independently set up server rooms. All non-sensitive systems should be migrated onto the cloud platform for unified data storage and transparency. In 2016, 481 provincial and municipal-level application systems in Guizhou were migrated onto the cloud platform. Plans are in place to develop four foundational databases on juridical persons (entities), population, spatial geography, and the macro economy, along with a unified provincial government data center, to achieve the integration, co-development, and seamless sharing of data. Based on the "Guizhou Cloud" platform and big data technology, the social governance capabilities of the government have been enhanced in such respects as management of the economy, social governance, market regulation and environmental regulation. The Guizhou government has also built such government platforms as "e-government cloud", "smart tourism cloud", "community cloud" and "public service cloud", enhancing the quality of government services. The government has also developed the "data cage" platform, allowing government work, administrative review and approval procedures, and law enforcement processes to be carried out online, thus digitalizing the exercise of power and enhancing transparency. In addition, in order to achieve the goal of "completing all formalities in the province on one website," Guizhou has built an "online service hall" for provincial, municipal and county-level government services, public services, and business services.

Government departments have actively utilized advanced digital technologies to enhance governance capabilities and promote economic development. For instance, cloud computing and big data are now widely applied to fields such as transport, healthcare and agriculture, enhancing the ability of relevant government authorities with regards to analysis, decision-making, advance warning and rapid action. During the sessions of the NPC and CPPCC in 2017, Zhou Xiaochuan, then governor of the People's Bank of China, indicated that the integration of digital currencies and mobile devices was the most effective way to bring inclusive finance to communities and remote regions. Back in 2014, the PBOC had already begun to study frameworks for digital currency issuance and operations, key digital currency technologies, scenarios for the circulation of digital currencies, potential legal issues, the effect of digital currencies on the financial system, the relationship between government-issued digital currencies and their private sector counterparts, as well as the experiences of other nations in issuing digital currencies. The PBOC believed that the use of digital currencies would better support economic and social development and has worked to issue digital currencies as soon as possible.

Rapid Development of Government Services on Mobile Devices

Mobile government services are one of the most prominent aspects of the digitalization of China's government in recent years. The popularity of smartphones has not only generated huge commercial opportunities, but has also created space for the government to provide better services.

Take the State Council's app, which was launched in February 2016, as an example. The app focuses on government services and has been downloaded more than 20 million times in just ten months after its initial launch. At the same time, more than 146 original articles or products have been read by over 100,000 users after being posted on the Chinese government's WeChat subscription account. The State Council's app offers powerful data enquiry and policy search functions, which are the functions most often accessed by users. For instance, the "at your service" function provides a host of functions, from "five certificates in one" guidelines to "salary, allowances and overtime pay" enquiries, from the use of social security cards to "employment and postgraduate entrance examination advice for graduates," making it the "most comprehensive and practical handbook" to government services. In January 2017, the State Council launched the 2.0 version of its app, with interfaces in both Chinese and English, extending its user base to foreigners. The new app has a "government services" button, which leads users to a page listing various categories, including Ministries, Services, Interactions, China in Numbers, and Publicity. Among these categories, Ministries include 53 government departments and allows users to view their latest policy announcements. The Services are divided into separate sections for citizens, enterprises, foreigners, and social organizations, and incorporates all major government services. For instance, the citizens' section includes information on family planning, education, employment, taxation and social security regulations. Users may even leave messages for the Premier in the "Interactions" and view the various proposed laws and regulations open for public comment. Various documents included by the State Council can be found in the Publicity section. Currently, the team behind the State Council's app is liaising with various ministries in an effort to incorporate a list of 1400-odd functions and 400-odd government services available from various government ministry websites (compiled during the earlier phases of the project) into their app. This would further bring government services to the frontend and provide better one-stop services. The State Council's app has used its interactive functions to organize various activities to encourage public involvement in government services. For instance, the team has received more than 20,000 proposals and suggestions through such feedback collection activities as "streamlining administration and delegating power @ the State Council" which asks questions like "What kind of bizarre certifications have you been asked to provide?" "Which professional qualifications should be cancelled?" "What kinds of unreasonable charges have been collected when you applied for personal identification documents or administrative approval?" On Labor Day in 2016, as a salute to ordinary workers, the app planned and produced the short video "Have you seen the city at four o'clock?" which included such "before-dawn moments" as the setting off of the first subway train, the first youtiao of the day, the printing and delivery of the first batch of newspapers, as well as seven portraits of people working in different industries. The short video was widely circulated online, bridging the distance between the people and the government.

Government services through WeChat are another characteristic innovation in mobile government services. Such services have largely formed a "WeChat official account application system" comprised by government ministries and local governments at various levels, achieving full coverage of such government functions as public security, travel, food and drug safety, Party and government affairs, transport, education, healthcare, life insurance, the justice system and foreign trade. In many fields of government affairs and public service, it has become the norm to deliver public service through WeChat.

During the sessions of the NPC and CPPCC in 2017, QR codes were added to the government work report. Users could immediately retrieve a digital presentation of the government work report by scanning the QR code, where a 2 minutes 50 seconds long H5 animation video would provide the user with a rapid, visually intuitive overview of the major achievements listed in the 2016 *Report on the Work of the Government* on their smartphone. In addition, signages with QR codes were also placed at the ministerial passage, allowing journalists to submit questions to ministers by scanning a QR code. In this way, journalists were able to engage in information exchanges with government departments through smartphones.

"Internet Plus Government Services" Strategy

In order to further promote the quality of public services and governance, the central government issued a series of directives in 2016, indicating that the Chinese government has already made preparations for the next phase of digital transformation, and providing a policy basis, directional guidance and methodological guidelines for digital transformation and the next stage of work to local governments at all levels.

In April 2016, the General Office of the State Council forwarded the *Implementation Plan for Promoting "Internet Plus Government Services" and Conducting Pilot for Benefiting the People with Information Technology*. As a directive providing guidance for the development of digital government in China, the plan calls for optimizing service workflows, innovation in service models, promotion of data sharing, linking "information islands", promoting transparent services, reducing institutional transaction costs, continuing to improve the business environment, strongly promoting public entrepreneurship and innovation, providing the greatest possible conveniences to enterprises and the general public, and remaining committed to the principles of central planning, seeking solutions to problems, coordinated development and open innovation. On September 14, Premier Li Keqiang chaired a State Council executive meeting, during he pointed out that accelerating the implementation of "Internet Plus Government Services" was key to reforms that delegate power, improve regulations and upgrade services, and would benefit efforts to enhance government efficiency and transparency, reduce institutional transaction costs, and transform "people taking trips" into "communication of information" and "enterprises looking for relevant departments" into "departments helping enterprises complete formalities."

With regards to the means of implementation, Premier Li Keqiang pointed out the following. First, service workflows should be optimized and restructured, where relevant procedures should be fully migrated online as far as possible. Second, service platforms should be optimized and restructured, where users could log in to unified platforms with one click. Third, data barriers should be eliminated, allowing all departments, all levels of government, and all systems to be interconnected. Fourth, system and information security capabilities should be enhanced, and important data that involve trade secrets or personal privacy should be more strongly protected. Fifth, all regulations that are not in line with the "Internet Plus Government Services" initiative should be abolished as soon as possible. In November, the General Office of the State Council announced the *Detailed Rules for Implementing Opinions for Comprehensively Promoting Government Affairs Publicity*, further promoting the "disclosure as the norm, non-disclosure as the exception" principle for information disclosure with regards to decision-making, policy execution, public administration, government services and application outcomes. The document also called for greater efforts in such work as policy communication, responding to public concerns and the development of open platforms. In December, the General Office of the State Council issued the *Guidelines for Constructing the Technical System for "Internet Plus Government Services,"* which contained further plans for developing national standards for "Internet Plus Government Services" technologies and service systems.

All in all, the digital revolution, as represented by computing, communications and internet technologies, has given birth to the digital economy. As a new form of socioeconomic development that succeeds the agricultural and industrial economies, the digital economy is undergoing rapid growth and innovation, becoming an increasingly important force driving global economic growth. The development of the digital economy has promoted the transformation and upgrading of traditional industries, cultivated new drivers of development, and bears great significance to improving the people's livelihood and welfare. As pointed out in the 2017 *Report on the Work of the Government*, it is important to push forward with the "Internet Plus" action plan and speed up the development of the digital economy. We must proactively embrace the digital revolution and accelerate digital transformation, in order to benefit both businesses and the people. The continued dividends of digitalization have also caused conflicts between old and new systems to intensify. We must promote the deep integration of the internet and the physical economy through open, inclusive, and forward-looking mindsets, and innovatively address the issues that arise during the course of development.

Postscript

This book is yet another monograph by Tencent Research Institute after the publication of *Sharing Economy*. It provides a systematic treatment of the many aspects of the digital economy and explores the impact of advancements in technology on China's economic development.

Technology is the most dynamic and active factor in an economic system. It determines the ways in which other factors participate in economic production and the outcomes of such participation. At the same time, technology also impacts how products are distributed and consumed, as well as the relationships and interactions among members of society. After mastering the techniques for smelting and forging metals, human society advanced from hunting-and-gathering tribal economies to agricultural civilization. The blast of the steam engine marked the transition from the peasant economy to the industrial era. The past hundred years have seen a significant rise in the pace of scientific and technological progress, resulting in an endless stream of epoch-making inventions such as motors, diodes, computers, biotech, the internet, and smartphones. The economic system is no longer characterized by linear progression, but has instead become a complex entity comprised of convergent structures, such as the energy revolution, bioeconomy, space economy, and mobile internet.

About 20 years ago, the sprouts of digital technology emerged from the subsoil of this complex economic structure. In 1995, Negroponte predicted in his book *Being Digital* that intangible "bits" would replace bulky "atoms" in rebuilding the world. 20 years on, his predictions

M. Huateng et al., *The Chinese Digital Economy*,
https://doi.org/10.1007/978-981-33-6005-1

proved to be true. First came the rapid digitalization of the media industry, followed by the gradual digitalization of various other industries, including culture and entertainment, finance, transportation, health care, education, and manufacturing. On the whole, the pace of digitalization has picked up all over the world.

During the digitalization process, large amounts of data are created in such a way that they can be directly interpreted by machines. The real world is translated to language that machines can understand at a rate of dozens of terabytes per second. Machine learning, computer vision, natural language processing, speech recognition and other technologies have advanced at a speed visible to the naked eye—machines have moved on from passively receiving data to semi-autonomously observing the real world. The streets in Beijing's checkerboard urban layout have become a digital map accessed through smartphones. The aircraft engine is now a motor engine as well as a data engine. Daily transactions are completed by scanning QR codes. The digital economy is truly a "machine civilization", while the era of the digital economy is also the golden age of artificial intelligence.

This era is one of fusion and innovation. The mobile internet, cloud computing, and big data are becoming ever more prevalent throughout human society, while becoming ever more stable and cost efficient. Collectively, they form a new generation of infrastructure. Amidst the wave of digitalization, large-scale personalized customization, multi-party collaborative manufacturing, crowdfunding and crowdsourcing, the sharing economy, creative entrepreneurship and traditional industries have become more integrated. The digital economy is not merely limited to new industries and incremental expansion in economic capacity brought about by cloud computing, big data, and other novel technologies. The digital economy also includes new economic capacity born from integrating these technologies with traditional industries to achieve quality and efficiency.

From the perspective of China's actualities, the development of the digital economy comes at the right time. There are three reasons for this statement. First, annual GDP per capita in China exceeded USD 7,700 in 2016, bringing China into the ranks of middle-income countries. At the same time, China's economic development has come to be characterized by "upgraded consumption" and driven by the service sectors. Second, by the end of 2016, China had more than 731 million netizens, making them the world's largest single market. The sheer size of this market has created several internationally competitive Chinese enterprises. Third, China is still in the "primary stage of the information society", with annual per capita information consumption levels at merely USD300, less than one-tenth in the United States. This means that there is great potential for further developing the digital economy.

In the two years since the implementation of the "Internet Plus" initiative, China's digital economy has made great strides. People are coming to accept the idea of integrated development of digital technology and traditional industries. However, there are still some who see the internet industry as separate from traditional industries and focus on discussions of which is more important. Confusion and anxiety lie behind their opposing views, while the ultimate root of such confusion and anxiety is an erroneous conception of the fundamental nature of integration and innovation through the digital economy. 20 years ago, people worried about the competence of machines. Today, they worry that machines are so competent that they would steal our jobs and disrupt existing industries.

This erroneous conception has led some companies to merely consider present competitive pressures, underestimate their digital technology potential, and ignore the vast markets created by the integration of new technologies and traditional industries. This erroneous conception also shows that there are bright prospects in China for the development of the digital economy in China, albeit with still a long way to go. Digital technology is in itself bringing about major transformation, while artificial intelligence, virtual reality and other such technologies are already on the eve of breaking out. However, the arduous and meticulous efforts needed to bring laboratory breakthroughs to large-scale commercial popularization, and then practical achievements in conjunction with various industries, still requires much cooperation on the part of innovators, regulators and traditional industry players.

In 2011, Mark Anderson wrote in a widely circulated *Wall Street Journal* that "software is eating the world." By that he meant all companies in the future will be software companies. Thereafter, "Internet is eating the world", "Big data is eating the world" and "Cloud computing is eating the world" has become headlines popular among mainstream technology media outlets. Perhaps it won't take much time before the popular media begins to talk about "artificial intelligence eating the world" and "virtual reality eating the world". The world has certainly not been "eaten", but these soothsayers are probably right, provided that we understand "eaten" to mean that all future companies would be internet companies, big data companies or cloud computing companies.

Understanding new technologies, embracing new technologies, and turning new technologies into their own use, all enterprises in the future will be technology companies, and all economies will be digital economies.

To describe the grand blueprint for the digital economy and explore the general laws by which technology promotes economic development, Tencent compiled *The Digital Economy: New Driver for China's Innovation for Growth*. First and foremost, the creation of this book owes its thanks to Mr. Ma Huateng and Mr. Guo Kaitian for their respect for and vigorous promotion of the concept of digital economy. As a representative of China's National People's Congress, Mr. Ma Huateng is very concerned about the role of the internet in promoting the transformation and upgrading of traditional industries. In the past three years, he has put forward suggestions relating to the "Internet Plus" initiative, the sharing economy and the digital economy.

We wish to thank China Industrial Control Systems Cyber Emergency Response Team for its support. Gratitude is also due to the digital economy research and writing team from Tencent Research Institute, who rose to the taxing demands of compiling this book under extremely demanding deadlines.

The digital economy has intruded upon all walks of life and society. When compiling this book, we received strong support from experts and scholars working in different fields. In particular, Ma Chen of Beijing Agricultural Information Technology Research Center assisted in research on digital agriculture, Associate Professor Xu Huan of Peking University's Information Management Department assisted in research on digital literacy, and Dr. Wang Changqing of the China Internet Network Information Center assisted in research on digital infrastructure. Chen Cai, Qing Su De, Jin Hua, and Xu Shan of the China Academy for Information and Communications Technology respectively provided support for research relating to digital transportation, blockchain technology, digital education, and digital healthcare. The Secretariat of the Internet Finance Working Committee of the Internet Society of China provided support for research relating to digital finance Zhou Jian, Chen Jie, Wang Hualei, Zhang Jian, Gao Xiaoyu, Li Bei, Wang Liying, He Bingmei, Ji Qingqing, and Song Ruolu of China Industrial Control Systems Cyber Emergency Response Team also supported our research.

Our gratitude also goes to Ms. Zhu Hong, head of the economics and management department of CITIC Press, Mr. Zhao Hui, Editor-in-Chief, and Ms. Fan Hongyi, Editor, for their great efforts in the publication of this book.

The era of the digital economy is upon us. Tencent Research Institute will continue its research, and looks forward to working with you in exploring the mysteries of the digital economy and promoting healthy and orderly industry development.

Si Xiao
Director
Tencent Research Institute

Bibliography

[1] G20 Digital Economy Development and Cooperation Initiative. [EB/OL] (29 September 2016). http://www.cac.gov.cn/2016-09/29/c_1119648520.htm.

[2] Li Guojie. The digital Economy Leads Innovative Development. *People's Daily*. 16 December 2016.

[3] World Bank. World Development Report 2016: Digital Dividends. Chinese Edition. 2016.

[4] Tencent Research Institute, Institute of Electronic Science and Technology Information of the Ministry of Industry and Information Technology. Digital Economy White Paper. 2017.

[5] Ma Kai. Speech at the Opening Ceremony of the "Deepening the Integrated Development of Manufacturing and the Internet" Seminar for Provincial and Ministerial-Level Cadres // Leading Group for Informatization and Industrialization Integration Management System. Manufacturing and Internet. Beijing: Publishing House of Electronic Industry. 2017.

[6] He Xiaoyin. Trends in the Development of the Digital Economy and China's Strategies. *Modern Economic Research*. 2013(3): 39–40.

[7] Pang Jian, Zhu Xinmin. Foreign Trends and National Strategies in the Development of the Digital Economy. *Science & Technology Progress and Policy*. 2013 (8): 125–126.

[8] Beijing Municipal Institute of Science and Technology Information. The Progress and Characteristics of Agricultural Informatization in the USA. *China Agricultural Information*. 2013 (3): 44–46.

M. Huateng et al., *The Chinese Digital Economy*,
https://doi.org/10.1007/978-981-33-6005-1

[9] Pei Xinning, Liu Xinyang. Education for Twenty-First Century: The Establishment of the EU's Core Literacy Framework. *Global Education Outlook*. 2013, 42 (12): 89–102.

[10] Zhong Zhixian. Towards Lifelong Learning: The Connotations, Evolution and Standards of Information Literacy. *Distance Education in China*. 2013 (8): 21–29.

[11] Ren Youqun, Sui Xiaoxiao, Liu Xinyang. On the European Union Framework for Digital Literacy. *Modern Distance Education Research*. 2014 (5): 3–12.

[12] Li Jin, Feng Xian, Guo Meirong. The State and Policies for Agricultural Informatization in China. *Journal of South China Agricultural University (Social Science Edition)*. 2015 (4): 9–19.

[13] Shi Jing, Zhao Jin. Digital Transformation of Media Literacy in Europe and the USA. *News and Writing*. 2016 (7): 98–100.

[14] Kong Fantao, Zhu Mengshuai, Han Shuqing, et al. A Comparative Study on Agricultural Informatization at Home and Abroad. *World Agriculture*. 2016 (10): 10–18.

[15] Feng Rui. Digital Literacy: The shift from information literacy. *Ren Jian*. 2016, 197(2): 145.

[16] Ruan Gaofeng, Zhang Dongdong. Current State and Lessons from Digital Citizenship Literacy Education in American K-12 Schools. *China Information Technology Education*. 2016(19): 17–21.

[17] Yan Deli. The Advantages of Online Retailing over Physical Stores. *IChina*. 2015, 7.

[18] Deloitte Consulting Ltd. Research Report on Employment and Talent in the Digital Economy. Year 2035: 400 Million Job Opportunities in the Digital Age, 2017.

[19] Miao Yu. Interpreting the Guiding Opinions of the State Council on Deepening the Integrated Development of Manufacturing and the Internet. // Leading Group for Informatization and Industrialization Integration Management System. Manufacturing and Internet. Beijing: Publishing House of Electronic Industry, 2017.

[20] Miao Wei. The Manufacturing Industry Is the Main Battlefield in Revitalizing the Physical Economy [EB/OL] (4 March 2017). http://finance.sina.com.cn/china/2017-03-01/doc-ifyavwcv9291895.shtml.

[21] An Xiaopeng. The Current State and Tasks for Advancing the Integrated Development of the Manufacturing Industry and the Internet (7 July 2016). http://www.cnii.com.cn/gyhxxh/2016-07/07/content_1749541.htm.

[22] Beomsoo Kim. Virtual Field Experiments for a Digital Economy: A New Research Methodology for Exploring an Information Economy. *Decision Support Systems*. 2002, 32(1): 215–231.

[23] BCG. The Connected World: The Digital Manifesto: How Companies and Countries Can Win in the Digital Economy. 2012.
[24] NESTA. Making Sense of the UK Collaborative Economy [BE/OL] (2 February 2014). http://www.nesta.org.uk/publications/making-sense-uk-collaborative-economy.
[25] PWC. The Sharing Economy: How Will It disrupt your business. 2014.
[26] OECD. Digital Economy Outlook 2015 (March 2015). http://www.oecd.org/internet/oecd-digital-economy-outlook-2015-9789264232440-en.htm.
[27] Cohron, M. The Continuing Digital Divide in the United States. *Serials Librarian*. 2015, 69(1): 77–86.
[28] The Information Technology and Innovation Foundation. A Policymaker's Guide to Digital Infrastructure. http://www.infrastructureusa.org/a-policymakers-guide-to-digital-infrastructure/.
[29] Mark Knickrehm, Bruno Berthon, Paul Daugherty. Digital Disruption: The Growth Multiplier. Accenture Strategy. 2016.
[30] Department for Culture, Media & Sport, the Rt Hon Karen Bradley MP. UK Digital Strategy [EB/OL]. https://www.gov.uk/government/publications/uk-digital-strategy. 2016.
[31] World Economic Forum. The Global Information Technology Report 2016: Innovating in the Digital Economy. 2016.
[32] Mckinsey. Digital Globalization: The New Era of Global Flows. 2016.
[33] Richard Samans, Ricardo Meléndez–Ortiz, Harsha V. Singh, Sean Doherty. E15 Report. 2016.
[34] GSMA. Embracing the Digital Revolution: Policies for Building the Digital Economy. 2017.
[35] Cabinet Office. The UK Cyber Security Strategy 2011–2016 Annual Report. 2016.
[36] HM Government. National Cyber Security Strategy 2016–2021. 1 January 2016.
[37] European Digital Progress Report [EB/OL]. https://ec.europa.eu/digital-single-market/en/european-digital-progress-report.
[38] European Commission. E-Government Action Plan [EB/OL]. http://single-market/en/egovernment-action-plan-digitising-european-industry.
[39] Industrial Platforms and Large Scale Pilots [EB/OL]. https://ec.europa.eu/digital-single-market/en/industrial-platforms-and-large-scale-pilots.
[40] Coordination of European, National & Regional Initiatives [EB/OL]. https://ec.europa.eu/digital-single-market/en/cordination-european-national-regional-initiatives.

The manufacturer's authorised representative in the EU is Springer Nature Customer Service Centre GmbH, Europaplatz 3, 69115 Heidelberg, Germany. If you have any concerns regarding our products, please contact ProductSafety@springernature.com

Printed and bound by CPI Group (UK) Ltd, Croydon, CR0 4YY
30/09/2026
02225323-0002